THE BEST
OF FRIENDS

"By giving sensitive support to each other at key moments, these two women both found their way to balancing marriage, motherhood, and creative careers. Their book—a sweet summer read—pays tribute to the advances that feminism brought to a generation of young women and to the enduring value of female friendship." —*Publishers Weekly*

"Filled with details of daily life and concerns about love, work, men, marriage, and motherhood. . . . The strength of their mature friendship . . . is unmistakable. . . . A warm . . . read that, with its insights into the often complicated lives of career women, could be a favorite of women's reading groups." —*Kirkus Reviews*

"As teenage girls are wont to do, James and Mauney first bonded over shared dreams of lives that would take them far from their hometown, lives that would combine challenging careers with travel to exotic locations, where they would court danger and fall in love with men who carried well-worn passports and spoke with foreign accents. Such dreams, of course, are typical of young girls everywhere, yet James and Mauney made good on their promises, though the paths they took were not always smooth and straight. . . . Through thirty years, they would see careers explode and relationships implode, and though they often experienced life's sweetest successes and harshest tragedies separately, emotionally they were always together. With candor, insight, and wisdom, James and Mauney joyfully celebrate the inspiring essence of friendship." —*Booklist*

"Each of these two writers' rich tales could stand alone but spun together offer a unique window into modern women's quest for meaning and calm in an ever more chaotic world."
—Gwendolyn Bounds, author of *Little Chapel on the River:
A Pub, a Town, and the Search for What Matters Most*

"What a great idea for a book—two great friends, two fascinating individual stories, and a memoir that reads like a novel. Sara and Ginger have a friendship that so many modern women can understand, complicated and simple at the same time. Women who in many ways are opposites, yet have a powerful connection that can only be called sisterhood. Everybody needs a friend like steady Sara and everybody needs a friend like adventurous Ginger. This book makes me feel like I have them both as girlfriends."
—Lian Dolan, author of *Satellite Sisters' UnCommon Senses*

"Sara James and Ginger Mauney have created the Bach minuet of memoirs: two distinct contrapuntal voices, two vastly different stories, and yet each plays off of and is woven into the other to form a single, gorgeous melody."
—Deborah Copaken Kogan, author of *Shutterbabe*

"Many wish they could lead a more authentic life, filled with travel and adventure. Yet few have the courage to pursue this dream. How refreshing it is then to follow the footsteps of two gutsy exceptions to the rule!"
—Marina Palmer, author of *Kiss & Tango*

"The more complicated our lives become, the harder it is to maintain those treasured ties. But *Dateline NBC*'s Sara James and her great friend, Ginger Mauney, have mastered the art of staying connected. At twelve, Sara and Ginger were sharing secrets at slumber parties. And now, with marriage, three kids, thirty years, and two continents between them, Sara and Ginger are telling their tale in their new book. It's called *The Best of Friends*."
—NBC's *Today* show

"Sometimes the most unlikely people become best friends. Sara James is a network-news correspondent here in New York City, while Ginger Mauney is a wildlife filmmaker who lives six thousand miles away. They explain their unshakable thirty-year bond in . . . *The Best of Friends: Two Women, Two Continents, and One Enduring Friendship*. . . . A wonderful book."
—CBS's *This Morning*

About the Authors

SARA JAMES is an Emmy Award–winning correspondent and anchor who has reported for *Dateline*, the *Today* show, and *NBC Nightly News*. She lives in New York City and Melbourne, Australia, with her husband and their two daughters.

Filmmaker GINGER MAUNEY has lived and worked in Namibia for sixteen years. Her films have aired on *National Geographic Explorer*, PBS, Channel 4 (UK), and in more than fifty countries worldwide. She lives in Namibia with her husband and their son.

THE BEST
OF FRIENDS

TWO WOMEN, TWO CONTINENTS, AND
ONE ENDURING FRIENDSHIP

Sara James and Ginger Mauney

HARPER

NEW YORK • LONDON • TORONTO • SYDNEY

HARPER

A hardcover edition of this book was published in 2007 by William Morrow, an imprint of HarperCollins Publishers.

THE BEST OF FRIENDS. Copyright © 2007 by Sara James and Ginger Mauney. All rights reserved. Printed in the United States of America. No part of this book may be used or reproduced in any manner whatsoever without written permission except in the case of brief quotations embodied in critical articles and reviews. For information address HarperCollins Publishers, 10 East 53rd Street, New York, NY 10022.

HarperCollins books may be purchased for educational, business, or sales promotional use. For information please write: Special Markets Department, HarperCollins Publishers, 10 East 53rd Street, New York, NY 10022.

FIRST HARPER PAPERBACK PUBLISHED 2008.

Designed by Nicola Ferguson
All photographs courtesy of the authors.

Library of Congress Cataloging-in-Publication Data has been applied for.

ISBN 978-0-06-077949-8

08 09 10 11 12 WBC/RRD 10 9 8 7 6 5 4 3 2 1

For Kimber, Sophie, and Jacqueline
With love

PREFACE

As I pick up the framed photograph from the bookshelf I can't help but smile. One blond, the other brunette, Ginger and I share the giddy grins of friends lucky enough to be posing beside an African waterhole teeming with elephants. The kind of tourist snapshot where you almost imagine scrawled on the back: "Here we are—a long way from Richmond, Virginia!" A moment frozen. A story told. Except the story it tells isn't quite right. We weren't really tourists on safari. And the photo shows only a destination, rather than the journey. Maybe a picture doesn't lie, but it never tells the whole truth.

I examine the photograph more closely, searching for some hint in our sunny expressions to suggest the hidden dramas and heartaches, the dazzling vistas and terrifying free falls, the potentially catastrophic audacity that propelled us to that moment, then churned forward to deposit us here, living lives we could never have predicted. But I see nothing save pals enjoying a glorious, apparently carefree moment. And while our linked arms signal camaraderie, the familiar pose gives no hint of how entwined we were and remain. Lives entirely opposite. Lives uncannily similar. Separated by thousands of miles, yet woven together by time and temperament, by circumstance and serendipity.

Our friendship should have frayed and broken long ago. Africa. America. P.O. Box Okaukuejo, Namibia. Zip code 10021. Wildlife filmmaker. Network reporter. Southern Cross. Northern lights. And yet the bonds held fast. We shared a hometown. A big city. Wanderlust. Ambition. Lipstick. A weakness for men with passports and accents. A longing for home and children. God help us, even a rhinestone tiara. After all, we've known each other since we were twelve years old, back when I went by my nickname Sally instead of Sara, back when Ginger was a knobby-kneed cheerleader.

Back then, we both expected to have everything figured out by our twenties. Instead, our thirties proved pivotal, and we're still figuring things out even now. Along the way, we've hit dead ends. Been flat broke. Found a measure of success. Succeeded in making colossal mistakes. Mourned lives lost, loves shattered. Found happiness in places we never expected to.

Forged in childhood, our friendship has been tempered by experiences so extreme and extraordinary that sometimes it almost sounds like fiction, even to us. And yet, as I close my eyes, the images before me are sharper than any photograph, moments I can never forget interspersed with those I can only imagine, because they happened not to me, but to my friend. Up close, all I see are fragments of memory. The emerald of a Wimbledon lawn. The magenta of a young man's blood. Chocolate flecks in a baboon's eyes. A shower of gold caught in a submarine's beam. A rustle of ivory as a bride threatens to flee. The ebony tracings of a tempest in a baby's brain. And what is the color of a kiss?

But as I open my eyes, years pass in an instant, and suddenly the shards and splinters, chips and fragments, form a pattern. From a distance, shapes appear, a story is told, and I discover that these scraps of memory are pieces of a mosaic, the mosaic of our lives. Only now is it possible to separate the accidental and the incidental. Cause and effect. Fact and fancy. The disposable and the essential. The shape of what is real, the cut of what is true. And while the mosaic may be unfinished, I have learned enough to know nothing much matters without family, without friends, without love. How we got here is an improbable tale, but it is also true. I know because I was there. And so was Ginger. This is our story, laced with the stories of many others we have loved and love. And it begins, as even true stories can begin, once upon a time, not so very long ago.

Sara James
August 2006
New York, New York

THE BEST OF FRIENDS

1

GINGER (1983–1985)

I took a deep breath. Slowly breathing in, concentrating on calming my wired nerves, and trying hard to ignore the churning in my stomach, I let go, breathing out and glancing up. Against a deep blue sky, the sun had finally broken through the clouds, matching the heat and intensity on the court. The smell of fresh-cut grass, grunts, and explosive clapping filled the air. Freckle-faced ball boys and girls, their lean limbs nearly as white as the players' tennis clothes, ran determinedly after each ball. Precise arm movements judged every fault, affirmed every winner. Passion and pageantry, and I simply couldn't believe I was here, courtside Wimbledon, a long, long way from home in Richmond, Virginia.

For years I'd dreamed of running away from home, leaving the azalea bushes, church bells, and slammed doors behind, but at twenty-one years old, I'd never thought I'd get so far so fast. When I was a child, the idea of escaping the ordinary seemed pure fantasy, and I believed more in the magic of miracles to transform my life than in my own tender nascent power. If there was an Oz, and like Dorothy I wished hard enough, I too could escape a predictable existence for a yellow brick road to adventure.

With a deep attachment to the land in Virginia, my family provided love and security, but few role models in running away. For generations they'd lived in farmhouses rooted deeply in the history of the South, with the church being the center of their small community. Outside its white wood-framed structure with the bell hanging high in the steeple, my ancestors put flowers on headstones in family plots where the names varied

little. Inside the same church, my great-grandmother, great-aunts, grandmother, mother, and cousins had all married, most pledging their love to
one of the boys who plowed the fields next door. Growing up, I had tried to
peer behind my older sister Marsha's big brown eyes. I could see she was
dreaming of another life, but as puberty struck, she kept her dreams to
herself. So I moved forward alone, blindly putting my faith and future in
the power of wishful thinking.

At twelve years old, by chance, I found an ally who shared my longing
to break away: Sara James. Though we were from the same suburban side
of the tracks, Sara and I knew each other only in passing. In the hall at
school, Sara on her way to honors English, me on my way to gymnastics
practice. Passing in cars, Sara waving on her way to the Governor's School
for the Gifted, me on my way to cheerleading camp. Sara was taken seriously and I was seen to be about as serious as the last pep rally. Although
she hung out with other straight-A students, Sara didn't share their air of
arrogance. Every school clique wanted her as a member, and she moved
easily from one to another, a part and apart. This openness made Sara ap-
proachable. When I spoke to her, I felt like she was really listening, not
worried about a boyfriend waiting down the hall or a gaggle of friends
from the Honor Society, sneering, wondering why she should be talking
to me.

But at that time in our lives, conversations between Sara and me were
few. Despite the friendly waves, we remained acquaintances, separated by
perceptions: Sara smart, me pretty, and never the two shall meet. But one
night we did, pretty Sara with her auburn hair and intense green eyes and
me smartly daring to expose more of myself than the blond-haired, blue-
eyed façade. At a friend's sleepover party, we shared secrets, whispered in
the dark, confidences from the past that had shaped who we were. Other
secrets were dreams that would inspire us and form the women we would
become. Lying on the floor watching the stars fade, we found words for a
desire to run away in search of a life full of adventure, intrigue, and wonder. We just needed a way out.

And now, nine years later, I'd found mine. On the grass courts of Wimbledon, my boyfriend Kevin Curren was on the verge of the tournament's

biggest upset. Smelling blood, the fans filled the grandstands until they overflowed. Players lined the balcony overlooking court 2—the "graveyard court"—sensing a changing of the guard. The press area bulged with reporters and photographers waiting to document the rise or fall of a champion. Punching volleys, diving for impossible shots, tumbling on the grass, glaring across the net, whispers as sides were changed—all of it was part of an incredible physical and mental contest.

After more than two hours on court, the scores were level in the fourth set. Six games all. Tie break. As Kevin prepared to serve, I ran my hands through my hair for the hundredth time, pushing a strand into the claws of my earring. I'd only had these earrings, a college graduation present from my parents, for a month. I remembered opening the pretty paper and finding a Canon camera box underneath. My smile faded. A camera? Why? I'd never wanted to be the one taking pictures. Then I'd spotted the tiny black velvet box nestled inside and opened it to find a pair of diamond earrings in a beautiful antique setting. They were perfect, plus there were plenty of professional photographers courtside at Wimbledon, with multiple cameras slung around their necks. Instinctively I rubbed the sparkling stones for good luck. Kevin tossed the ball, low, and struck it hard. I looked down, unable to watch, twisting the sapphire ring on my finger, and listened. I heard the ball hit the strings, again and again and again. I heard the players grunt, felt the intake of air from the spectators around me, and then I heard the crowd roar. I looked up in time to see Kevin punching the air with his fist. "Game, set, match, Mr. Curren." He'd done it; he'd beaten Jimmy Connors, the defending champion.

An hour later, after a shower, rubdown, and an intense press conference, Kevin walked into the players' lounge. Slaps on the back and echoes of "Well done, mate," "Great win" greeted him. He shook his head and smiled. When he reached my table, he bent down, brushing his lips across my cheek and whispering, "You must be good luck."

Overnight, after the win over Connors, things changed. Cameras flashed in our faces, a sleazy reporter shadowed me around the courts, and my friend Stacy Margolin, who played on the women's circuit, warned me, "Careful, Ginger, they read lips." Stacy would have known. She'd recently been offered 50,000 British pounds sterling by the tabloid newspaper the *Sun* to "tell all" about her relationship with John McEnroe. She turned them, and the others, down flat.

In the quarterfinals, Kevin beat "Gentleman Tim" Mayotte in a match that was widely heralded as the best in the tournament. There were more reporters, more photographers. As we were leaving the club, a press photographer followed us to the car. The next day, when I opened the newspaper, there was a picture of Kevin and me splashed across the pages of the *Times*. Then Kevin lost in the semifinals to Chris Lewis, an unseeded player from New Zealand, and it was as if we'd disappeared. There was another winner with a different girlfriend to follow, teaching me a quick lesson in the fleeting nature of fame.

But it was a lesson I found easy to forget, because while my trip to Wimbledon—a college graduation present from Kevin—had been my first trip out of the United States, I soon learned it wouldn't be my last. Kevin's success in the UK had thrust us into the limelight and led to a journey around the world. First stop, his native South Africa. An offer to play an exhibition match at the Sun City resort came complete with two first-class airline tickets. We took an overnight flight from London, and just as we cleared customs in Johannesburg, a public relations representative from Southern Sun Hotels which was sponsoring the tournament pulled me aside. "Have you seen today's papers?"

"No."

She hesitated, looked around, and, lowering her voice, told me, "There was an interview with Kevin's father, and well . . . he said you're the reason Kevin lost at Wimbledon. He doesn't think Kevin needs a woman traipsing around the circuit with him."

I shook my head, trying to clear the words and the jet lag away. "You're kidding. There must be some mistake."

"No. Now maybe the reporter got it wrong, but there are many more reporters waiting outside customs for you. I thought you should know."

I was too tired to think his comment through, too determined that it not ruin my first moments in Africa, that I simply tried to laugh it off. "Thanks, I guess."

The sliding doors opened and we stepped into the main lobby of the airport. In the hollow of this huge space, lights flashed brighter, motor drives whirred more loudly, and the shouted questions ran together in a strange combination of English and Afrikaans. Kevin wrapped his arm protectively around my shoulder and we kept walking. After a shower and a press conference by the pool, we quickly settled in, and the headlines over the next few days were different. We laughed at leads like "Anyone for Tennis with Ginger?" "Ginger: The Power Behind Kevin," and then guffawed at the one that read "The Fragile Beauty of Kevin's Ginger."

How could love be bad for anyone? Plus, since Kevin had never reached the finals of Wimbledon before, why shouldn't his parents believe that I was actually good for their son? I could only hope that they too were laughing off the recent run of stories in the press. I'd soon find out, as we planned to meet his family during the exhibition tennis matches at the Sun City resort.

In the middle of rural Africa where the nearest buildings were goat kraals made of sticks and cow dung, Sun City rose like a phoenix, a sprawling, impressive Third World pretender to Las Vegas, full of glitz, glamour, and gambling. For three days I tried to fit into the family and the place, but it didn't work. I was desperate to escape the cutting looks, the monosyllabic answers to my questions, and the incessant sound of slot machines. Kevin pulled me aside. Draping his long arms over my shoulders, he whispered, "Try not to worry. We'll be in the bush soon. I hope you love it as much as I do."

The next day, feeling like I'd only just survived round one in this foreign country, we boarded a small aircraft. As it lifted off, the pressures of the past few days drifted away. I peered below as buildings disappeared; the roads changed from tar to gravel and finally single dirt tracks. I hoped for a glimpse of an elephant or a lion, imagining that the creatures hidden in the bush couldn't be more menacing than those I'd left behind at Sun City. The plane touched down, first one wheel, then the other, kicking up dust and bouncing down the runway before skidding to a stop.

When the doors opened, porters grabbed our bags and a lone white figure stepped forward. "Welcome to Londolozi, Ginger. Don't worry, no one will bother you here." Sporting a French foreign legion cap, a machete, and a mischievous grin, Kevin's friend John Varty wore the role of rebel, filmmaker, and keen conservationist lightly. Ever since we'd landed on African soil, I'd heard about John. Kevin respected his conservation ethics and envied him his freedom, living life in the wild. John, a professed bush recluse, seemed slightly jealous of Kevin's newfound success. Theirs was a man's friendship, all unspoken, backslapping, crackling with energy and competition.

But it was a genuine friendship, with a past, a present, and a future, something far removed from life on the tennis circuit. In the world of professional tennis, week after week, year after year, players face each other across the net. Points are scored any way you can get them, using any weakness—your opponent's feeble backhand, his insipid second serve, or his foundering relationship—to win. Tennis is a physical game, sure, but at the top professional level with big prize money and even more lucrative endorsements on the line, it's far more mental. So little is shared, and no one talks. No one gives up the game.

Week after week, women like me who traveled the circuit—the wives, the girlfriends, the groupies—checked each other out from across hotel lobbies and players' lounges. We also kept score. Who had the biggest diamond, the biggest hair, and whose partner landed the biggest paycheck at the end of the week. Those were the constants. In that world of fast serves and even faster lifestyles, women came and went. The players knew who had the hottest girlfriend or, in the case of some guys, who had the most women. One week it was Allison, next week Julia, after that who knew, who cared. Your real friends—like the real world—were very far away.

"Ginger, hey, Ginger, want a cuppa tea?" John, our host, asked, bringing me back to the bush. We walked onto a large wooden deck fitted into the trees with the riverbed far below. "Oh yeah, great." I accepted a cup of rooibos, or bush tea, and a chunk of what looked like stale bread. I bit into the bread; the power of the crunch turned heads and nearly broke a tooth. Kevin didn't say a word. He dipped his *rusk* into his tea and it melted in his mouth. I stepped away from the small group of game rangers and looked below at the pools that dotted the sand and the birds that fluttered between the reeds. The air was crisp, and the sound of silence infused with laughter echoed across the riverbed.

This was the bush. Peace, quiet, mystery, and an almost tangible magic. I'd seen pictures in *National Geographic* of elephants walking across vast open plains and watched a documentary film on lion behavior in South-West Africa, but those images, though moving, were one- or two-dimensional. Now I could feel the roughness of the earth, smell the richness of the rivers, almost taste life and death. It was fertile and raw, wild and ancient, and I couldn't have been further away from Richmond.

We finished our tea and began a tour around camp. It was clear that John was justly proud of his home. Londolozi was once a family farm, but John, along with his brother Dave and his wife, Shan, transformed it into a five-star experience in ecotourism long before anyone called it that. The Varty family were widely respected and emulated in the conservation world for their practice of reclaiming land, stopping illegal hunting, and providing jobs to members of the impoverished local communities. We stopped outside a chalet where thick duvets and natural fabrics mixed with African art and unabashed luxury. John grinned at me and said, "You can have this room or you can sleep outside the camp, away from everyone, if you want."

Kevin looked amused and I wondered, *Is this a test?*

I laughed, unsure of the right answer, but the thought of no electricity, no toilet, and plenty of animals with big sharp teeth sent a chill down my spine. Power lurking behind the trees wasn't restricted to the pages of a book now; it was palpable.

"I think we'll sleep inside."

It didn't matter. I hardly slept at all. Lion roars, hippo snorts, and owls screeching provided the audio backdrop to a physical yearning to get outside. My eyes picked up the slightest movement; my ears heard every twig snap, every alarm call. I was entranced by the bush, and when I saw a leopard for the first time, I was gone. Diamonds, rubies, emeralds—there was nothing more stunning in the world than her deep green eyes. In them I found the beauty, the tension, and the power of the bush. She was at once enticing and threatening, gorgeous and dangerous. As she disappeared back into the thicket, I felt these natural extremes touch a deep, primal place in my soul. I felt as if I belonged here, and oddly, though it was Kevin who'd introduced me to the bush that he loved, this feeling of belonging wasn't tied to him. It felt unique, mine alone, a feeling that remained with me long after we left Africa.

Whenever possible, Kevin and I returned to the African bush, but our life together revolved around the very unnatural world of the tennis circuit. During the infrequent weeks when I wasn't traveling on the tour with him, I went home to visit my family, but there was rarely an opportunity to see Sara or my other old friends. No sooner had I landed in Richmond than I was back on the phone, using Kevin's calling card to make plans to pick up my prepaid ticket at the airport to join him again. Indoors, outdoors, hard courts or grass, the tournaments melted into one another. Off the courts, life was full of moments I could never have imagined when Sara and I had shared our childhood dreams.

In Tokyo a charming representative from Cartier, complete with gold cuff links and a thick French accent, laid out three watches in front of me on the table. "Please, Ginger, would you select one?" In Montreal, between matches, I wandered the streets of the old quarter alone, returning to the courts in time to watch Kevin play. In Melbourne, alone on the sidelines, I cheered as Kevin reached the finals of another Grand Slam tournament, the Australian Open. Back in South Africa, I was asked to model—all five feet four inches of me, blue eye makeup and pink cheeks, hair teased and the spring wardrobe prepared and presented as a gift. And there was the prospect of another, even better present.

"Gin, what if I gave you a fabulous ring—say, three carats—but then something happened between us. What would you do?" Kevin spoke quietly, not looking at me but gazing out into the distance, across one of the largest, deepest ravines in South Africa.

Below, between the cliffs, a black eagle soared on thermals. His words hung in the air. I shifted closer, resting my head on his shoulder; the breeze blew my hair around his neck. "Don't worry. I'd give you back one and a half carats." A near-perfect ending to another African holiday.

So many times I'd wanted to call home, to giggle with Sara about seeing myself on page one of newspapers, to laugh about nearly plowing down Faye Dunaway on the steps at Wimbledon, or to share the giddy feeling of riding through the streets of London in a Rolls-Royce while trying to act blasé. I also wanted to know what was happening in her life. Was she happy? Was the search for a good story as rewarding as the search for true love? Had she found her ticket out of Richmond? Were we still friends, or would the outside perceptions of our lives once again keep us apart? I wanted to reconnect, but the time was never right. Morning in England meant the middle of the night in the U.S. In most places I was too jet-lagged to even begin to figure out the time difference. Then too much time passed. Months rolled into years and I wondered if my old friends remembered me as part of their present, or just their past. I never called and then I wondered if anyone would answer if I did.

Despite my mother's warnings that I needed to have my own life, my own career, my own friends, I kept traveling, living Kevin's life. Since childhood I'd never needed many people around me, preferring small groups of close friends, but now through choice and time that group had narrowed to one. Kevin. He was all I needed. From Cincinnati to Sydney, London to Los Angeles, I sewed sponsor patches onto his tennis shirts, rang for room service, even polished his trophies. This was his time. Everyone knows the career of a professional athlete is short. We would have the rest of our lives together and my time would come.

But the holidays in Mauritius, the Mercedes sports car, nights out at London clubs, and mornings spent lying close to each other listening to the African bush awaken were all possible because of Kevin's success. He shared them with me on his terms, and then his terms began to change.

"So Wimbledon is coming up?"

"Yeah, I know." That was not the response I was hoping for.

A few days later I asked, "So where will we be staying?"

"What? Where?"

"You know, in England."

"Don't push it, Ginger." I didn't. I washed his clothes, drew the blinds when he was tired, and kept quiet. A few days later he told me sternly,

"Listen, you can come to Wimbledon, but not early. Not for Queens, none of the preliminary tournaments. I'll meet you there later." He didn't explain and I was too afraid to ask.

JULY 7, 1985. It had been two weeks since I'd landed in England and the sun was shining. My Maud Frizon heels clicked rhythmically and a light breeze blew my white linen skirt as I walked down the hill toward the All England Lawn Tennis Club. It had been three years since I first passed through these gates, smelled the fresh-cut grass, felt the energy and the tension. My third Wimbledon, the day of the finals, and I was still there. I remembered nothing of the previous two weeks, couldn't recall whom Kevin had beaten or where the other seeded players had fallen. I only knew that today Kevin was to play for the championship against Boris Becker, an unknown kid from Germany with a big serve and nothing, absolutely nothing, to lose.

I flicked my hair over my shoulder and smiled. And yet, as I climbed the steps to the players' box, I felt tense and it had nothing to do with the atmosphere on court. Only twenty-four years old, I knew that this time I had everything to lose.

2

SARA (1985)

THE POLICE AND fire department scanners clucked quietly, slow and lazy as that steamy summer day. But then, it was still early. It was July 7, 1985, and genteel, conservative Richmond had earned a dubious new distinction: ranking third in the nation for murder. As any reporter knows, on summer weekends tempers soar with the temperature, so I cranked up the scanners and tried not to think of my bikini-clad friends slathering themselves with Hawaiian Tropic at Virginia Beach. My two-piece was a jacket and skirt from Dress Barn and my tan came courtesy of L'eggs panty hose.

I got a sudden shiver in the over-air-conditioned Channel 12 newsroom and rolled another Q-set into the manual Royal typewriter. A stack of white, pink, green, and blue sheets with carbon paper in between, the Q-set allowed me to type a script for myself, the producer, director, and Tele-PrompTer operator all at the same time. At twenty-four years old, I'd recently been promoted to weekend anchor as well as reporter, which meant I had a show to write. But the paper remained ominously blank.

I'd majored in English at the University of Virginia, wallowing in lengthy, delicious novels by writers from Jane Austen to John Irving, and I still struggled to keep my prose succinct. "Heard of the KISS rule, Sara?" a veteran newsman had asked me one day. My eyes widened and I shook my head warily, braced for some lesson in lechery. Instead he'd frowned and pointed at my script. "Keep It Simple, Stupid. Write shorter. Lose those three-syllable words. Picture your viewer cracking open a beer, yelling

'What's for dinner??!!' at the missus. No one really watches TV, Sara, they just have it on all the time. You gotta grab 'em."

Grab 'em. So far our only breaking news was a story about a cheerful hobbyist who built and flew radio-controlled airplanes. If I didn't come up with a better lead than that, not even my doting parents would watch at six.

"Whoa!" exclaimed sports anchor Ben Hamlin. I glanced up. The Wimbledon final was on, and I suddenly realized everybody but me was watching. Some kid from Germany was darting across the court, manhandling his handsome, dark-haired opponent. I did a double take. That had to be Kevin. Kevin Curren. Which could only mean . . .

"Check out that babe," ogled the studio camera operator.

Yep, there she was all right. Chewing on her pearls, looking nervous, but absolutely drop-dead gorgeous.

"You mean Ginger?"

Ben shot me a quizzical look. "You know her, Sara?" Suddenly I realized how improbable it must seem that I would know someone at fairy-tale Wimbledon, especially the girlfriend of a South African player.

"We went to school together," I explained, wondering why I hadn't said, *We're friends.* After all, we had been. But were we still?

It had been at least a year since I'd seen her, and on her last trip to Richmond she seemed so different from the childhood friend I remembered. I'd felt awkward and distant, suddenly clumsy and thirteen instead of twenty-three. It wasn't just the South African vowels that muddied her southern accent. She looked thinner and blonder, and the gold bracelet that dangled like a chain was heavy and new. Kevin was becoming increasingly rich and famous, so who could blame her for enjoying the spoils, not to mention the spillover from his spotlight? Who could blame her for not keeping in touch with old friends who probably seemed provincial and dull? Some friendships you just outgrow. They're moored in time and place and fit about as well as your high school jeans. You're left with little more than a fond memory and a signature in your yearbook. My runaway thoughts suddenly careened into an unpleasant possibility: Had she changed, or was I just jealous?

The sound of applause brought me back to the present. Point, Curren. The camera zoomed in on Ginger, who sighed with relief and tugged a sparkling earlobe. Now the studio cameraman looked from her to me, dubiously. "So where'd you meet? College?"

"Middle school, actually."

"She's from *Richmond*?" His pole-vaulting eyebrows indicated it was impossible that someone that sophisticated could be from our hometown. Or perhaps it was the fact that she glittered with diamonds and my most expensive accessory was a tarnished Timex.

"Believe it or not."

I had a momentary impulse to inform him we'd been selected, back-to-back, as Miss Tucker High School, that I'd passed my rhinestone crown to her. But that was a story I would never confess, and I felt sure Ginger wouldn't either.

Feeling off-balance and suddenly annoyed at myself, I headed for the Associated Press and United Press International wires. The heaving machines churned out paper comet trails of spare, staccato copy filed by correspondents from Nashville to Nome, Manhattan to Moscow. On a quiet weekend like this one, I would "rip and read" to fill out the newscast—simply tear off a relevant story to rewrite or, in the case of an urgent news flash while we were on the air, read it exactly as written. But as I sorted through wire stories that day, I sorted through tangled feelings, too.

After all, what was so surprising about the reaction of my colleagues? Back in high school it hadn't seemed we had much in common, either. Ginger was a popular cheerleader, I was a freckle-faced writer wannabe whose prime source of entertainment was watching the Watergate hearings on TV. I remembered the night we'd met at a birthday sleepover, a night when we gorged on M&M's and confessions. Who had? Who hadn't? With whom? Of course back then what we had or hadn't done was French-kiss, and no one had done less than I. And no one was more fun than Gin, all bright, blue-eyed mischief. I instantly liked her gaiety, spontaneity, and warmth. Later when everyone collapsed into sleeping bags, we'd wound up side by side. As all around us the giggles subsided, we continued our conversation in whispers.

"So how are you going to do it?" she asked.

"Do what?"

"Get out of here. Let me guess. Are you going to write a book?"

I hesitated, and then realized her tone was teasing but not unkind. "I'd like to one day," I confessed. "I'm sure it sounds ridiculous. I don't even know what I'd write about. They say write about your experiences, but nothing interesting has ever happened to me. Maybe if I leave, something might."

"I want to leave, too."

"Why?" The room was warm and smelled of Doritos, and near us another girl snored gently.

Finally Ginger said, "Lots of reasons."

"And what will you do?" I pressed. "Do you have a plan?"

"Not yet. But I will."

It didn't take a crystal ball to predict her way out of town would involve a handsome, wealthy stranger. Then, just as I was about to succumb to sleep at last, Ginger surprised me. She made a confession, too, one that had absolutely nothing to do with youthful, clichéd ambition or even a middle school crush. My eyes opened and I stared into the darkness, listening. And when she was done, I could think of nothing to say except "I'm so sorry, Gin. I had no idea."

Heading back to my newsroom desk with a fistful of wire copy, I wondered why she'd confided in me all those years before. Perhaps it had been the weight of the secret. Maybe it was just sleep deprivation. Regardless, our friendship began that night, because you can't be friends without exchanging confidences. Throughout high school and into college, while we'd often traveled in different circles, we'd never lost that connection. And as anyone knows, as secrets accumulate year after year, old friends become best friends because you trust them. Because they know who you were as well as who you are, but they don't tell.

Or old friends simply drift apart. I realized I had no idea what was happening in Ginger's life beyond what I'd just glimpsed on screen, and that thought prompted me to glance up at the television once more. Kevin took the point and I smiled because I felt I could hear Ginger's laugh as I watched her applaud. Who needed more information? Whether Kevin won or lost, it was obvious her life was perfect and she was blissfully happy. Not only was she traveling the world, but as Kevin's girlfriend, she'd made her debut on network TV—exactly where I wanted to be. She was living her dream while I was just dreaming.

I shook myself, trying to shed the feeling of Inadequate by Comparison. I had no interest in marrying fortune and fame. I wanted to know that whatever I achieved I'd earned on my own, and had felt proud to land a job in my hometown. After all, I hadn't been the only aspiring journalist obsessed with Watergate and enamored of Woodward and Bernstein. Their investigative reporting had toppled a president and helped shape history. And they were cute. By the time I'd graduated from UVA, the market had been flooded with "Woodsteins," and all three Richmond stations had initially turned me down flat. So I'd headed for the local library, checked out the *Broadcasting Yearbook,* and begun cold-calling news directors. Mom and Dad were amused and proud—until the phone bill became so enormous it arrived in two envelopes.

Suddenly realizing that landing a job was a job in itself, I'd pulled out my credit card and headed for Hit or Miss, the best place I knew to buy fashionable clothes on a budget. I carefully selected two new suits—my favorite was a powder blue polyester suit with a white ruffled tuxedo shirt— threw a suitcase into the back of my turquoise 1972 Dodge Colt station wagon, and hit the road. The summer I was twenty-two, I'd logged more than four thousand miles traveling through thirteen states. Having no TV experience proved something of a handicap. From Baltimore to Birmingham, Charlottesville to Charleston, South Bend to West Palm Beach, news directors smiled and said no. In all I visited more than thirty stations, changed two flat tires, and fended off more than one proposition. "What you really need is to come to the Radio and Television News Directors Association convention, Sara," offered one especially helpful executive. "I'll introduce you around. And you can even share my hotel room." So much for the ethics of Woodward and Bernstein. I kept my spirits up by thinking how shocked he'd be when I'd made it to the big leagues.

Instead, the offer that autumn came from a station in Mississippi. Tupelo was the 143rd biggest broadcast market in the country—a long way from number one New York, but a start nonetheless. What's more, I'd not only report but also serve as coanchor of the 9 *Alive News*. Profoundly grateful, I neglected to ask a crucial question. "Next time, before you say yes, you might want to ask about your salary," grinned my new boss.

I didn't care that they only paid me $14,000 a year. In the hall leading to the newsroom was a picture of NBC's Jessica Savitch, gleaming, golden. I wanted to be her. Or at least know her. Little did I suspect how difficult her life actually was. All I knew was that she was paid a fortune to interview the fascinating and the famous and had become a star herself. I wondered what it would be like to have a complete stranger ask for an autograph, and admitted to myself that it sounded appealing. Would it be possible to become a dogged reporter and an anchor, too? Just a few weeks after starting my new job, I was devastated by the news that Savitch and her date had been killed when they took a wrong turn and drove into a canal near a restaurant in New Hope, Pennsylvania. To see such a promising life cut short made me even more determined to reach my goal. Who knew how long any of us had?

While New York seemed impossibly remote from Tupelo's WTVA studio in a glorified shed, which was especially noisy during frequent summer thunderstorms, I loved it. There was the exhilaration of live television, from avoiding gaffes during ad-libs to learning not to grow dependent on the supposedly goofproof TelePrompTer. One night early on, I confidently began the newscast, "Good evening, I'm Sara!" "And I'm Terry *Smith*," continued my coanchor with a bemused shake of his head, and began the lead story. Through my IFB—the interruptible feedback device every anchor wears in one ear so that the show producer can speak directly to them during the broadcast—I heard a snort of laughter, followed by "Sorry to leave your last name off the script. I thought for sure you'd remember it." I had a lot to learn in the field as well, but found everything exciting, whether we were dashing out under a glowering sky, bruised green and purple, chasing tornadoes, or racing after cops, firefighters, politicos, anyone in the know, anyone on the far side of the tape marked "Police Line—Do Not Cross."

Reporting proved an introduction to lives far different from my sheltered suburban upbringing. One of my first stories had been on teenage pregnancy. Mississippi had a reputation for poverty and illiteracy, so children having children wasn't a big surprise. But I was shocked that the pretty blonde with the enormous belly was pregnant with her third child rather than her first, at the ripe old age of sixteen. I still felt like a kid myself and had no desire to be yoked to such seemingly needy little beings, even those decked out in dimples and curls. It was obvious that being a mom was a full-time responsibility and I was nowhere near ready to settle down. I wanted to see the world, swagger a bit, live a little. Virtually none of my friends had even gotten engaged. We'd all gone to college and wanted more, much more. It was the 1980s, and somehow it felt like an obligation as well as an opportunity to storm through doors that had been marked "Men Only" just a few years before.

And a few of those doors seemed to be opening. After eight months in Tupelo, I'd returned to Virginia for my parents' twenty-fifth wedding anniversary and interviewed at the local stations again. When I'd actually gotten a job at Channel 12 my mom promptly burst into tears. I'd moved into an apartment near the station with another high school friend, Scottie Feitig, and started work immediately. Being a hometown girl gave me context and contacts, especially since my father, a professor at the University of Richmond, had also been a member of the state legislature. But I was wary of growing complacent. Richmond was broadcast market 55, and the network shimmered, still far in the distance. Ginger had found her handsome stranger, and love had proved her passport to adventure. I hoped work would be mine.

Just then the scanners fired up, interrupting my reverie. "All units, please respond, report of a shooting at St. James Street . . ." The weekend photographer lunged for the door as the police dispatcher continued, "Victim is a twenty-nine-year-old male. Be advised, perp may still be in the area."

Twenty-nine-year-old Marion Perkins had just become the forty-seventh homicide in Virginia that year. It was time to stop watching television and start working on it.

* * *

THE NIGHT AIR felt wet and warm after the chill of the studio as I headed for my car, glancing at my Timex. In Richmond, it would be July 7 for another twenty-two minutes. In that faraway kingdom called Wimbledon, the sun would be rising soon. Where was Ginger now? I thought about what different paths our lives had taken in the years since we'd both worn that twinkling tiara. I was willing to bet a standard day for her didn't involve anybody getting shot.

I wondered what she would think if I told her about the first time I'd seen a dead body. It had only been a few months before. I'd been on a date with a boyish photographer for a rival station who sported surfer hair and drove a bright red pickup. He was hoisting a forkful of pasta toward his mouth when his pager beeped and he'd raced for the phone, trailing spaghetti. I craned forward, shamelessly eavesdropping, and caught the word "shooting," as well as an address.

"Gotta go, Sara—breaking news," he'd said, grabbing his coat. But when I'd reached for my own jacket, he'd exclaimed, "Don't even think about it!" before bolting for the door. I'd been thinking, all right, thinking I didn't want to miss out, especially since I needed stories for my résumé tape. After a moment's reflection I'd decided he deserved a two-minute head start for inadvertently giving me a tip. A hundred and ten seconds later, I'd called Channel 12 and arranged to meet one of the station photographers at the scene.

Not surprisingly, my date had already gotten there. With a rueful shake of his head, he cracked a sliver of a smile that indicated he'd simmer down in a week or two. After all, we were both young and ambitious.

The boy lying on the pavement had been young and ambitious, too. But he'd lived in a different neighborhood, worked in a different trade. Before that night I'd seen many unsavory things as a reporter, but this was different. There was a certain chaste beauty to the white folds of the sheet that covered him, but the stains were ominous. How many times had he been shot to bleed like that? No one got murdered in the prosperous West End where Ginger and I had grown up. I suspected that the killing had been yet another tied to the drug trade. A fight over turf, over somebody cheated or scorned. But this young man had been so young. It was his feet that gave it away. It was his feet that got me. One sported a fancy white sneaker while the other was inexplicably bare, the toes long and slender. The feet of a boy. Unbidden, the old nursery rhyme played in my brain: *Diddle diddle dumpling, my son John! Went to sleep with his breeches on! One shoe off and one shoe on . . .*

"Cat got your tongue?" a grizzled cop had asked sympathetically.

I'd gargled an answer, unable to spit out a sentence. How could I tell him all I was feeling? That this poor boy's fate was inconceivable to me, and yet we'd grown up in the same city? And did he mind if I vomited? I'd looked down at my pad and pulled out my Bic pen, anything to take my eyes off that foot, those five perfectly formed toes. Anything to escape the vulnerability, the futility of it all.

Head down, I'd struggled to seem professional, tough. "Do you have any details yet, Detective? Who is—I mean, who was he? Who's the next of kin? Who shot him?"

"Not yet, Scoop," he'd answered. Then, looking at me more closely, he'd whacked my shoulder with a beefy paw. "Don't take it so hard. You'll get used to it." I've always liked cops, but it's the kind of work that can turn men to flint. He'd continued, "Besides, Sara, most of them are NKs anyway."

I'd looked up, confused. "What's an NK?"

"They Needed Killing."

AS I TURNED the key in the ignition, I thought of all the things I should have said to that detective. Starting with, *How dare you, he was just a kid. No one deserves to die that way, no matter what he's done.* Something sharp and tough. Something to hold him accountable. But I'd said nothing. He had a badge and experience, and I'd gone tongue-tied and silent, swamped by a wave of sorrow. I'd turned away from the cop, away from the young boy's body, and wiped my stinging eyes. There was no time for emotion, since the station live truck had just rolled up, the engineer hustling to crank the mast, and I would be on air in less than thirty minutes. I'd scribbled a few pertinent sentences on my reporter's notepad, taken a deep breath so my alto voice didn't soar soprano with anxiety, and had been ready at eleven o'clock when the station anchors tossed to me. "Good evening, Gene and Sabrina. There's not a lot of information so far, but what I can tell you is that a young man was shot shortly after ten tonight . . ."

It hadn't mattered that I didn't know much. A young boy was dead. And I was live. At twenty-four I already knew the cardinal lesson of local news: If it bleeds, it leads. On that night, and once again on this one, I wondered what lessons Ginger had learned.

OVER THE NEXT few weeks, my thoughts about my old friend became more insistent. I felt as though I'd misplaced something important. A favorite pair of earrings. A faded pair of jeans. Something that made you feel at home, comfortable. Someone you didn't dress up for, someone who with just one look made you tell it straight.

It wasn't that I was short on company. The pickup-truck-driving photographer had forgiven me for dashing off into the night, and though we were still seeing each other occasionally, it seemed we were both more attracted to our work than to one another. I had plenty of reporter friends who were always up for drinks at the Border Café after work, but just when you got to know someone, they left. That included my newest friend, Linda Pattillo, a reporter for the rival CBS affiliate. I took her out for a farewell dinner.

"Miami. That's practically top ten, LP! Next stop, the network."

"We'll see. First things first."

"LP, professionally I'm excited for you. But you can't do this to me."

"Look at it this way. You get my apartment in the Fan, complete with Lisa, who's a great roommate. I even cleaned my room for you. Besides, you'll be moving on yourself before long," she continued, switching to her mentor voice. In the way in which we categorize our friends, Linda was the big-sister-I-never-had, a life coach before we knew they existed. "Look, here's what you do. You already have plenty of anchor segments, live shots, and breaking news on your résumé reel. What you need is one big story that sets you apart. You'll find it. And in the meantime, come down to Florida for a visit."

"You're not going to disappear like my friend Ginger?" I moaned.

She snorted. "Definitely not. But who says she did? You're a reporter. Find her."

LATER, AS I packed boxes for my move to the city's trendy Fan neighborhood, I thought about how Ginger had accomplished exactly what she'd set out to do when we were twelve. As for me, while I hadn't become a writer, I wrote as a reporter and loved the job. Different as our lives were, did we still share a connection? I didn't know.

What I did know was that I wanted to do more than chase fires and murders. I wanted to be on the front lines of events that changed the world, to tell stories that might change the way people acted, or at least make them stop and think. And yes, I wanted travel and adventure. The kind of life I was sure you led when you worked for the network. But how was I going to beef up my reporting credentials and get there? I realized I just might have an idea. But my first assignment would be to track down my old friend who was Missing in Action.

3

GINGER (1985–1986)

Mom, has Kevin phoned?"

"No, Gin, for the fourth time today, honey, he hasn't." Just then the phone rang. I dashed for it. It wasn't him, and later, when it was, it wasn't what I wanted to hear.

"Should I meet you in Miami?"

"No, my agent's coming in, I'll be too busy."

"I could come to Dallas this week."

"No, Ginger, not this week. I'm too tired."

"How about L.A.? Or Memphis?"

Finally Kevin asked me to meet him in Atlanta. For two weeks I lived on dry toast and water, shrinking down to 102 pounds. I packed his Christmas present, a thick forest green sweater I'd knitted by hand, alongside a sexy new nightgown. He looked at the sweater in embarrassment and didn't touch me. We wandered the shops in an upscale shopping mall, hands accidentally brushing, while guilt forced him to search for my forgotten Christmas present. I didn't want a new Tank watch or a heavy Tiffany bracelet. Christmas had passed, thoughtlessly. We left the mall without packages, without speaking.

Later that night in the hotel room, he sat quietly, looked up at me, and, without preamble, said, "I love you like a sister."

"Like a fucking sister!" I screamed, and threw my jewelry box against the wall, narrowly missing his head. I dove across the room onto the bed, and then I threw myself at him, sobbing, pleading, berating, and begging him to change his mind.

After two hours he'd had enough. "You knew this was coming, and I don't have time for this nonsense. I've got a match tomorrow and need to sleep. Good night."

That was it. After four years that was all I got: one sentence. *I love you like a sister.* Six seemingly harmless words strung together to create a devastating effect. That was how quickly my heart could break; how fast a bubble full of dreams could be shattered, leaving me lost in the wreckage back on earth.

Most of the night I lay on the cold tile floor in the bathroom, afraid that I would vomit. Once I eased back into the room, I crawled into bed. Against the cold, hard sheets, I reached out for Kevin. He took my hand, held it close to his heart. I lay like that for a long time, feeling his heartbeat, listening to the silence, but when I inched closer, he pulled away. Pity. Damn him, he was taking pity on me. What the hell was I thinking? That one moment of intimacy, however false, couldn't rewind time, suck back words and close the distance created in the last few months. Damn him again. I went back to the bathroom and ran a hot shower, drowning out my sobs and trying in vain to take away the chill.

The next morning he watched me pack. Then, in separate taxis, he rode to the courts, to practice, back to his life, uninterrupted, and I went to the airport, searching for a gate to take me anywhere but here.

On the plane, I turned my face to the window, away from the briefcase-carrying, navy-blue-suited businessmen and -women boarding the plane. Tears leaked out of my closed eyes and the flight attendants kindly left me alone, going along with the charade that I was asleep. I had two hours in the clouds to try and make sense of the unfathomable. Every thought shot back as an indictment of me. Why didn't he love me? What had I done wrong? Why wasn't I enough? Why didn't he love me?

I couldn't face the toughest question of all: Who was I now if I wasn't his girlfriend? Why had I chosen to immerse myself so completely in someone else's life, to live his dream, only to find out that I had lost all sense of myself? But no one had forced me into this role. I wasn't trapped in the 1950s. It was 1985. I had choices and a background to support them—a loving family, a college degree, and women in my life who were strong role models. There were so many things I could have done and yet I'd done exactly what I wanted. I'd wanted a life with Kevin. Period. Any other sane choices were overridden by youthful idealism, my naïve belief that if I loved him enough, we would live happily ever after.

I was twenty-five years old, but I hadn't grown up at all. There I was, back in Oz, and now the curtain had been pulled back to reveal the lie. There wasn't an easy way out of town, no simple way of trading one life for another. On the yellow brick road to adventure I'd fallen into a deep, black, gaping hole. The walls were slippery, there was nothing to cling to, no way of climbing out, no happy ending, nothing at all.

The plane took me home, back to Richmond. Cloistered in my parents' house, I hid under the covers, alternately dozing and numbing my mind watching television. Surfing channels, I heard a familiar voice. Sara. It must have been eleven o'clock at night. I rolled over, parted the hair from in front of my face, and saw her sitting up straight, peering into the camera, anchoring the local news. Propping the pillows up behind me, I looked closer, searching for reminders of my childhood friend behind the television screen. Sara's freckles were gone, her hair was tamed but her voice was still the same: warm, intelligent, with just a hint of a southern twang. She glowed, and I knew the camera loved her. But did someone else? I wondered if there was a man behind her smile or if success was the sole cause of her radiance?

My mom must have seen the dull gray glow under my door. She came in quietly and sat down at the end of the bed.

"Gin, honey, why don't you call Sara?"

"Maybe later, Mom."

How could I possibly call Sara? Just look at her, so composed, so pretty, and so professional. In easy banter, she talked to the sports reporter, handed off to the weatherman, and guided us into a commercial break. I could barely answer the phone. While I'd wasted four years of my life following someone else's dream, she'd been focused, steadily achieving her own goals.

When we'd whispered our deepest secrets as kids, Sara shared her dream of writing stories, stories that held such passion that people would stop and listen. And because we were kids and thought all things possible, these stories would change the world. Whether or not Sara's stories were changing opinions, it was clear she was doing something right, because she'd been promoted to weekend anchor. I was sure she'd soon be telling stories in another, bigger city. Clearly she was moving up while I'd moved back with nothing—no money, no job, and no self-esteem.

My parents let me wallow in self-pity for a few weeks before Mom gave me a verbal slap in the face. "Gin, this has got to stop. You must get out, get on with your life. Here's Carolyn's phone number. She's Bessie Mae's niece and she works in placement at a temporary agency. Call her. She'll help."

Two days later I was standing shivering in the frozen-food aisle of the local grocery store handing out samples of the latest concentrated fruit juice. The next day on a crowded street corner in downtown Richmond's historic Shockoe Slip where young, ambitious people gathered, I approached busy executives with free cigarettes. Rushing to the office, rushing to lunch, most of them looked right through me. That was fine. It was the others, the ones who looked at me with pity in their eyes, that hurt.

Then Carolyn called. "Ginger, I have a job for you. It's still just minimum wage, but it's a weeklong job, so that's good?" In true southern fashion, her voice lilted upward with this rhetorical question. I remained silent, forgetting my manners. "Well, okay," she persisted, "you need to be on the 1400 block of the Boulevard on Monday morning at eight. Now don't be late."

Early Monday morning, I opened the door and stepped inside a dark warehouse. A few bare lightbulbs hung from the ceiling. It reeked of mildew and stale cigarette smoke. I tentatively let go of the door and it slowly closed behind me, shutting out all the natural light, all the fresh air, all life. I held my breath. Someone guided me to a clock on the wall and showed me how to punch in. Someone else must have guided me to a table, because I found myself sitting down in front of a large stack of paper with ten gray-haired, stern-faced men and women staring at me. The buzzer sounded and they began. I watched their nicotine-stained fingers shuffling paper like cards, folding flaps, inserting papers, and tossing them aside so quickly that their fingers became a blur.

I turned an envelope over in my hand, examining it as if it were the first time I'd seen one, and then I started, one by one, bending the flap, stuffing the paper inside. Bend and stuff, bend and stuff. I concentrated on the action, afraid that if I allowed any other thoughts in, I might lose my mind. A buzzer sounded and the table was deserted. Cigarette smoke and snide remarks struck me from the corner of the warehouse where the others had gathered. I just sat there thinking of the neat rows of tobacco on my grandfather's farm stretching as far as the horizon, and twisting the gold Krugerrand coin on the bracelet Kevin had given me round and round. Ten minutes later another buzzer sounded. The routine started all over again. Paper cuts, bent envelopes, and another cigarette break. More and more until finally the buzzer rang at 4:30 P.M., the doors opened, and the last light of day crept across the floor.

"LISTEN, HONEY, YOU don't have to go back."

"But I do, Mom. I said I would. I have to."

I crawled out of bed on Tuesday morning to face more of the same. On Wednesday, my dad drove me to work. "Gin, you don't have to do this. I'll give you some money."

"It's okay, Dad, don't worry."

Somehow it didn't seem quite so bad, and I knew why. In just two days the sliver of spirit I had left had been broken. This was it. This was my life now. Dark warehouses and time clocks, humble and humbling. At twenty-five years old, I believed that the best of my life was behind me. I would never love anyone else, and I was unworthy of being loved. For so long I had allowed Kevin's feelings for me to define me, and now I needed to hear him say that this hell was a temporary state. Alone in my bedroom, I picked up the phone and punched in his home phone number, followed by his calling card number. "We're sorry. The card number you have dialed is no longer valid." The last line I had to him had been canceled. I had nothing left.

Back at the warehouse before lunch on Thursday, as I pushed myself away from the table, the foreman stopped me. He had a bitter, twisted mouth. A cruel glint in his eye put me in my place. I stumbled back while he looked down my shirt and the others stared. They knew what was coming next. "Sorry, miss, but you just ain't fast enough. We gonna have to let you go. Go on, get your things and get goin' now."

I don't know how I made it home. There were two tollbooths. I couldn't count my change, couldn't see from the tears that were running down my cheeks in silent torrents. Behind me someone leaned on a car horn. I jerked the steering wheel back, realizing only then that I'd swerved into another lane. I was losing control, of the car and of myself. I'd hated that stupid job, but I hadn't quit. I'd been fired, rejected once again.

I disappeared back into my bed, emerging on Monday morning to read the paper. As if life couldn't get any worse, that Sunday Kevin had won a tennis tournament. The article was brief, little more than the score, but to me it read volumes—the adoring new girlfriend, cheering fans, trophy held high over his head, and, for one week's work, a check for $100,000.

THEN I GOT A call to come back to tennis—a job offer from a sports marketing company in New York City. A call that took me back to my past. Every summer during my college break, I had worked for promoters of a women's tennis tournament held at the University of Richmond. I'd sold tickets, hung banners around the court, stuffed a few envelopes, and made friends with some of the players like Stacy and the women who ran the women's tennis circuit. One summer before my senior year in college, I was asked to organize a series of matches for a new team tennis franchise in Dallas. At twenty years old I suddenly had my own apartment in a massive complex of single, single-minded men and women, a borrowed car, and four professional players on my tennis team. One of them was Kevin. When our professional relationship became personal, I went from working in tennis to living it. Now, at twenty-five, I had an offer to go back in the other direction. In many ways, I just wanted to forget the tennis world. But I needed a job, and to my surprise some old friends were offering me one.

In sweltering July heat, my parents and I loaded a U-Haul and drove to

Manhattan to my new apartment four flights up from the Come Again Erotic Emporium. My mom's startled face reminded me that I'd forgotten to mention this little bit of information. Oh—and the huge, bald-headed manager blocking the door. Kristy Kemm, an old college friend and my new roommate in New York, helped us carry my camelback sofa, brass and iron bed, and wicker table up the steps. Later Kristy offered me her clothes, her friends, a way to find myself in her life. But I didn't want to find "myself"; I wanted to replace Kevin. And since New York was a playground for predatory men, lithe young models, and lost souls like me, there were several contenders, each one worse than the next.

There was the trust-fund-spoiled Ivy League graduate, the self-obsessed Tom Cruise look-alike, and the Latin lover who warned me, before taking me to bed, that I wasn't tough enough to survive in New York. There was the Australian friend of a friend who'd seen me on television during the Australian Open. He was tall, dark, handsome, and totally bored. It was an early night. Twenty pounds heavier and now twenty-six, I must not have lived up to the image he remembered on the tiny television screen. There were others. The cocaine-snorting stockbrokers and hard-drinking lawyers wrapped up in their cases and Hermès ties, the hick baseball player making it big in the Big Apple, and on and on. My list of dates covered every stereotype, including the sugar daddies. With every drink too many, every stupid affair, and every night I crept back into my apartment as the sun rose, I lost more and more self-respect until my bearings were completely gone.

I could never figure out uptown from downtown. I was forever getting on the wrong subway, pointing cabdrivers in the wrong direction. At work, though I'd moved from a tiny cubicle into an office with a real door and a big window overlooking Third Avenue, I didn't hang anything on the walls, had no plants around that needing nurturing, placed no homey pictures on my desk. It was as if my subconscious knew I couldn't make this life permanently mine.

On the twentieth floor of the Philip Morris Building at a meeting of tennis tournament directors from around America, I realized I couldn't navigate here any longer. I had no secure lines, no anchor, nothing stable to cling to. I listened while the chairman followed her agenda, raising points on scheduling, player commitments, and sponsor deals. The other tournament directors spoke with passion about their events, their needs, their sponsors, and I realized I was starting to drift away. None of it was important, not to me, not now. Their voices sounded like Charlie Brown's teacher, all *wa-wa-wa,* and then I heard nothing. The window opened and I was out in the cold, floating down Park Avenue, getting further and further away until I swore I would never come back.

"Ginger, Ginger, are you with us? It's your turn to vote." The others stared at me and I realized with a jolt that I wasn't with them at all. My life had to be about more than whether or not Steffi Graf played in a tennis tournament. For the second time, I knew that to save myself I had to escape. I had to get out of here.

Eventually I started to turn down invitations, testing the unfamiliar ground where a night in didn't feel like a social rejection. I knew I wouldn't find the answer to my life's questions behind the velvet ropes at Nell's. I needed time, space, and a clear head. Kristy came home from work to share cold sesame noodles, Yang-Zi beer, and very bad jokes, new lifelines from an old friend. On Sundays we did the *New York Times* crossword puzzle and lugged our unfit bodies along paths in Central Park. Then I heard from another old friend.

"Gin, hey. It's me, Sara. I got your number from your mom. I know it's been so long, too long."

We hadn't spoken in two years, but once we started talking, it was like turning back time. She still had that infectious laugh and her voice was light and full of fun, describing the net she'd cast in search of a new job, a man who sounded amazing, not some stereotypical cad, plus the most audacious plan to cover a story she hoped might help propel her to the network.

"I'll be in New York soon. Any chance we can get together?"

"Of course, that would be great," I said, feeling a barrage of conflicting emotions. Though I was eager to see her, thrilled that we were in touch again after too long, when I hung up the phone I started to worry about how she would judge my life. In describing my work and friends in New York, I'd skimmed the surface, leaving out the cracks, the heartaches, even the four flights of stairs up to my apartment. I was a far cry from the innocent young girl she'd crowned Miss Tucker. That girl had direction and wasn't afraid to dream big dreams. She was the best part of me for so long, how could I have lost her? I needed to find her, and maybe, just maybe, Sara could help.

4

SARA (1986–1987)

Yᴏᴜ'ʟʟ ʙᴇ ɪɴ town, Gin?"

"Absolutely, Sara, and I'd love to see you. You can meet my roommate Kristy, too. She's a tough-as-nails southern deb. You'll love her."

"And I can't wait for you to meet my friend Judith Fox. I worked for her temporary agency during college. Now she's a friend. We're planning lots of shopping, although she'll case Bergdorf's·and I'm just hoping they don't charge if you window-shop. Is there a Hit or Miss in New York? Where can I find stylish clothes on a budget?"

"Not exactly. Try Saks—they have great sales. I'll be your personal shopper."

"Even better! As you know, I could use the help." And then, just when we were about to hang up, I blurted out the other reason I'd called. "And, Gin—I'm sorry about Kevin. Most of all that I didn't know for so long. I feel like an idiot."

"It's okay. I'm glad we're back in touch."

And so was I. If only the next conversation went as well. I took a deep breath and knocked on the door labeled "News Director."

"Harvey?"

He barely glanced up from reading the *Richmond Times-Dispatch*.

"Mmm-hmm?"

"I have a great idea for a story."

"The drug killings? Already got a series on it for sweeps."

"Not exactly." I could scarcely contain my excitement. He would just love this story, I knew it. He just had to say yes. "Actually, this story is in Nicaragua."

To my consternation, his expression darkened. I cut to the chase. "I want to cover the war between the Sandinistas and the contras."

"Exactly how does that fit into your beat as Chesterfield County reporter?"

"I know it seems a stretch but there's a great local angle."

"A *stretch*?!"

"Some Richmonders are going down to build houses in the countryside and—"

"No."

"—I've been taking Spanish lessons and—"

"*No!*"

I backed out, deflated, to find Mary Katherine waiting nearby. MK was a station photographer and yet another new pal.

"Didn't go so great, huh?"

I shook my head, quiet for a moment, thinking. "I don't think we're dead yet," I offered cautiously before outlining a last-ditch course of action. MK listened. "Think of it as an opportunity," I pressed.

After a short pause she nodded. "All right, I'm in."

I charged back into Harvey's office before MK could change her mind. "What now, Sara?"

"What if MK and I pay our own way?"

Harvey pushed back his chair, fingertips on the desk, eyeing me. He knew better than anyone that I only earned $17,000 a year. But there was always plastic. "And we'll even take vacation time to do it."

At last he nodded. "Just don't lose the camera."

I CELEBRATED THAT night with an interesting new man in my life, a documentary filmmaker who worked for a foreign charity organization. Gin's ex had fame and fortune and traveled to London, Tokyo, Melbourne. The man I fancied was just back from Calcutta. He sported a khaki vest on location, carried a pocket fix-anything tool called a Leatherman, and told me his motto was "Carpe diem."

"So what do you think?"

"I think it sounds like a great story, Sara."

"Thank God you understand. My parents aren't exactly enthusiastic."

"Do you have everything you need?"

"Got any recommendations?"

"You'll need good boots, tropical weather gear, a real first-aid kit. But maybe the most important thing you'll need is permission."

"Excuse me?" I was headed to a land bristling with guns and it sounded like he was suggesting I get a hall pass.

"Every Third World country is a bureaucracy. Especially when the government is Communist, like the Sandinistas. You'll need some paperwork covered in official stamps. In case you get—into trouble."

I shivered in spite of myself. Soldiers in Central America weren't famous for being great humanitarians.

"And if we do get 'into trouble'?"

"Just don't panic. And you'll have those stamps." When he smiled, one side of his face creased, and I wondered if he'd gotten the scar fending off bandits in some exotic hellhole.

I couldn't believe I'd met this guy. It seemed all my high school and college friends were settling down, marrying intelligent, appealing lawyers and doctors and stockbrokers. But I couldn't imagine setting up house, producing an heir or two. Mr. Carpe Diem—CD—seemed like someone I had invented.

Later that night, I found myself daydreaming as I packed, imagining exploring the world with CD. Then I heard my roommate Lisa coming up the stairs. The weekday coanchor and the best reporter at the CBS station, Lisa was beautiful and fun—up for mountain climbing or a scuba trip or hosting a crab-picking party in our backyard. As my friend LP had predicted before moving to Miami, her former roommate had become my friend, too.

"Hey, Boo-boo! How was the new guy?" she asked, handing me a pair of boots for my backpack.

"Too interesting. What's wrong with me, Lis? I have no interest in meeting Mr. Right at the moment. I'm only twenty-five!"

Lisa looked alarmed. My only previous obsession had been getting to the network, just like most other young local reporters we knew. We watched *Today* every morning and the evening news every night, and gabbed endlessly about whether we preferred Tom, Peter, or Dan, Diane or Barbara, Joan or Jane. I worked at an NBC affiliate and had set my sights on the *Today* show.

"Correct me if I'm wrong, Sara, but you've been on one date with this man, right? Who said anything about getting married?"

"It's just that—"

"Just nothing! You barely know him!"

"But, Lisa, he's perfect! He reads good books, he's smart, and he travels the world carrying his home with him like—like a turtle!"

"You have a crush on a turtle."

"Don't mock me. And did I mention? He's cute."

She looked relieved. "Well, now we're getting somewhere. Look, Sara, you're about to do something crazy and go to a war zone. Could you at least concentrate on that?" She gave me a squeeze. "You find it hard to focus sometimes, Boo-boo. I found two more science experiments in the fridge, and have you checked the fern in your room?"

"I know. It's dead. I'm sorry."

"That's okay, but you're going in a lot of different directions. Maybe it's time to slow down a bit." She grinned. "Not to mention perhaps waiting to see if he asks you out again."

I realized I'd better get to Nicaragua quickly before I did or said something ridiculous.

MK AND I checked into the InterContinental Hotel in Managua. Once the people here had been ruled by a U.S.-backed dictator who'd followed the standard banana republic strategy of intimidation, torture, and looting the treasury. After a massive earthquake and subsequent revolution, the Communist-leaning Sandinistas had taken power. Now, in 1986, Nicaragua was very much in the news. President Reagan had thrown U.S. support behind the rival Contras, warning that the Sandinistas—with their Russian and Cuban advisers—could pose a new domino threat and spread Communism north, perhaps all the way to Texas. Surveying the rubble known as downtown, it seemed hard to believe the raggle-taggle regime could carry a canteen as far as the Guatemalan border. But those were Cold War days and regional skirmishes carried international implications. Before heading to a government office to get our passes to the war zone, we met the local NBC crew at the network bureau.

"So where are you from again, Sara?" NBC correspondent David Hazinsky asked. I sat up straight, dropped my voice an octave, and attempted to look as experienced as possible, given I was only twenty-five. "The network affiliate in Richmond, Virginia. We're here to do a story on some locals who plan to drill wells, build houses, help the campesinos—the peasants."

He gave me a look that told me he knew what campesinos were—and a great deal more than that. "Do you guys have a fixer?" Years later I would learn that a fixer was indispensable—a seasoned local who could troubleshoot problems ranging from bureaucratic hassles to accommodations to terrain, but back then all I knew was we didn't have one. "A translator?" I shook my head again. We were relying on those in the humanitarian group and my halting Spanish. "Have you been warned about the roads?"

As MK shot a look at me, he appeared increasingly incredulous. "Both sides have laid mines, so be careful." He paused to let that sink in and I avoided MK's gaze. "Look, if we can help, we will. You can borrow our crew for an afternoon, shoot some promos. But remember, out there you'll be in the middle of a war zone. On your own." I swallowed and must have looked queasy, because his expression lightened. "Look, since you're here, why don't you two catch the concert tonight. Peter, Paul and Mary are in town and President Ortega and his wife will be there."

Which was how it happened that the night before heading to a war zone, MK and I spent the evening in a crowded, sweltering tent in downtown Managua listening to one of the most famous American folk groups from the 1960s. As they broke into "Puff (The Magic Dragon)" we looked at each other. What was so scary about this assignment?

Just as we were about to leave and MK was snapping a final shot to show our friends back at Channel 12, a soldier spied us. With a shout, he hustled over, grabbed her stills camera, and ripped out the film before gesturing angrily that we leave that moment, or else. We had our answer.

That night, lying on one of the lumpy twin beds, I couldn't sleep. What had I roped us into? Friends Don't Let Friends Get Killed.

MK wasn't sleeping either. "So what are you thinking?" she asked.

I was thinking how stuffy the room was. I was thinking how much my stomach hurt. I was thinking of the way Mom's face had crumpled when she'd realized she couldn't change my mind about coming, how she'd bitten her lip and how even my ever-the-optimist dad looked grave. I was thinking about how I could still taste the first mango I'd ever eaten, off a street cart that afternoon, about how much fun we'd been having and how beautiful the people had seemed before a soldier stole a roll of film, and before I'd absorbed the words "land mines" and "war zone." How those words reverberated in my brain, one muffled explosion after another, because I suddenly knew I was just a kid and not nearly as smart as I thought I was.

What I said was, "I think we'll be okay."

AS IT TURNED out, trouble found us a few hours into the trip. We'd hooked up with an American who worked with an international human rights group. He had serviceable Spanish, access to a vehicle, and some knowledge of the backwater we were entering, and agreed to give us a lift to the house-building Richmonders, who would bring us back to Managua.

We drove slowly, scanning for land mines. The road was rutted, and every time we struck an especially deep dip I winced, squeezing my eyes shut, half waiting for a rush of air and an explosion. Then I realized that if we hit a mine, I'd never know until afterward, if I found out at all. The jungle was cloying, dark green disappearing to black, impenetrable, unknowable. Which was how it happened that we didn't see the gunmen until they'd surrounded the car, shouting for us to halt in machine-gun-rapid Spanish.

Were they Sandinistas or Contras? I couldn't tell, and didn't know which was worse. Whoever they were, they were young and scrawny, alternately angry and nervous. Clearly gringos didn't blunder their way every day. My mouth tasted like copper. I realized I was biting my cheek. I was also sweating through the khaki shirt I'd bought for two bucks at the A&N store back in Richmond.

"Mom is going to kill me," I thought, but some words must have leaked out.

"What did you say?" MK hissed back.

"I'm sorry I got us into this mess."

"Let's just get out."

As the gunmen fanned out, a couple of them searched the back of the vehicle, picked up a few of our canteens, then pointed at me. My *¿Dónde esta el baño?* Spanish was hopelessly inadequate. "What are they saying?" I asked our American guide.

"They think we're U.S. military. Or CIA."

"What! Can't they tell we're journalists?" I huffed. "Just look at our camera gear and notepads!"

"How about look at what you're wearing! Where did you buy that khaki crap, and those army-issue canteens? Are you trying to get us killed?"

My mouth went dry as my stomach lurched. I made a mental note in this do-it-yourself foreign correspondent training class. Never, ever shop at the Army & Navy store.

The gunmen huddled in conference. I tried not to imagine the options. Kill us? Come up with some imaginative torture? Hold us for ransom? I closed my eyes, then opened them again to escape the image of being buried in the middle of nowhere, disappearing without a trace.

I sought to recover my composure. "Look, show them these." I shoved forward the permission documents we'd gotten from the Sandinistas. There was a risk, of course. What if these soldiers were Contras? But as they flipped through the papers, paying close attention to all those pretty embossed patterns, I suddenly realized with a start *why* the stamps were so important. Some of those soldiers couldn't read. I made a mental note. Rule number two for foreign correspondents—stamps, stamps, and more stamps.

After a few moments that seemed to last forever, they must have decided we really were journalists after all. Or maybe they just figured that live, dumb gringos were less trouble than dead ones. With a disgusted wave, they let us go, then melted into the jungle as quickly as they'd appeared.

I had survived my first trip to a war zone. It wouldn't be my last.

"SO WHAT HAPPENED when you finally got into the countryside, Sara?"

"I think the Richmonders found their building project incredibly difficult. It didn't help that we were told to sleep with our boots by the tent flap in case the fighting got too close."

"It must seem like a million miles from here."

I looked around at the fancy decor and fancier people in the tony Manhattan watering hole and nodded.

"Well, thank goodness you're okay. Let's drink to that." Ginger clinked my glass. "And here's to success in your hunt for a new position in a bigger city."

"I dunno. I wonder if I'll ever get to the network."

"Don't say that. If you want to, you will."

"Did I tell you I was crazy enough to send a tape to LP's agent? Some underling there sent it back. Basically: Keep up the good work, but what's with your hair? Like I had time for a blow-dry just after I shampooed in the stream."

"You're only twenty-five, Sara. There's plenty of time."

And I thought, *For both of us.* But I said nothing.

Ginger looked as beautiful as ever, but there was a weariness I didn't remember and she didn't explain. In losing Kevin, Ginger had lost a way of life as well as the man she loved. Gone were the days of traveling first-class, of Tiffany baubles and Gucci loafers. She didn't complain about the tiny apartment, her twin bed with its Barbie-sized dresser in a curtained-off corner of the living room. And I instantly adored her roommate, Kristy. But this wasn't the life Ginger had expected. The life any of us had expected for her. "Do you ever hear from Kevin?"

"A while ago I got a box with his return address—in a woman's handwriting. Some things of mine he thought I'd miss."

"Ouch."

"It gets better. I called a friend of Kevin's about it. Know what she told me? 'Ginger, in a breakup, you have to pick sides, and we've chosen Kevin's.' "

"How unfair!"

Then suddenly Ginger giggled, a sound I remembered well. "But you know what, Sara? Some people like me better without him!" Her laughter was infectious.

"Well, I do, too. And I'm just glad we're back in touch."

"Me too. But forget work. I want to hear more about your new guy."

I paused. I had a strange fear that Mr. Carpe Diem might vanish if I talked about him. Besides, I felt rusty confiding in Ginger. Over the past few years we had lived our lives so differently. Funnily enough, I felt far more comfortable seeing her in New York than I had on that previous occasion, back home in Richmond. We both had careers, and while tennis and television might be worlds apart, the fact that each of us was single, poor, and self-sufficient gave us connections we hadn't shared when her only job was to be Kevin's gorgeous girlfriend. Still, the man I cared for was nothing like Kevin and I wasn't sure what she'd think of my choice. But Ginger had always been easy to talk to, so I took the plunge.

"Well, he carries everything with him—boots, tent, Leatherman— probably his heart. But somehow I'm sure he's the one. And I actually think he feels that way, too."

"How long have you known each other?"

I hesitated. "Actually, just a few months. Not even, really, because he's always traveling."

Ginger was tactfully silent. Back in high school she would have told me exactly what she thought. But that night we were both finding our way. Although her knitted brows urged caution, all she said was, "I can't wait to meet him."

"And I can't wait to meet your new guy."

"Well, you won't have to wait, because here he comes now." The man who bent to kiss her was well groomed, well dressed, and well heeled. Gin had told me his dad owned several Upper East Side skyscrapers. But I took an instant dislike to Tall, Rich, and Handsome. Gin's smile glittered but there was a brittle quality to her laughter that alarmed me. I knew she was on the rebound but I didn't think this man was good for her. He seemed about as deep as a vodka martini. I tried to keep pace with the evening, with the rolling party, but felt clumsy and awkward, the small-town girl who would never be hip enough for New York.

"So what did you think of him?" Gin asked the next morning.

Now it was my turn to hedge. I hardly knew the guy. For that matter, I was just getting to know Ginger again. When in doubt, speak the truth. Or as much of it as you can. "He's certainly handsome."

ON THE FLIGHT back to Richmond, I pondered our friendship. It had been a long, long time. While we were back in touch, we weren't back to where we'd been back then. There were things we didn't ask, didn't tell, murky depths still off limits.

I had a new man in my life. I had new friends like Lisa and Linda, with whom I had a career in common. Would I keep up with this old friend? Would she keep up with me? We shared a past, but would our friendship share a future? I hoped so. But we lived in different cities and seemed to be heading in different directions. It was just too early to tell.

5

GINGER (1987–1989)

DAMN THIS AIR conditioner." Outside it was 98 degrees and 100 percent humidity. Inside I hit the steering wheel, fought with the air conditioner, and cranked up the music. The sound of Steve Winwood singing "Higher Love," the unofficial anthem of the summer of '87, and the sight of sweaty, muscled construction workers lining the interstate almost made me forget that my legs were stuck to the rental car's vinyl seats. My skin glowed, a euphemism distinct to the South, as in "Ladies never sweat, no sir, we glow." Only problem was, I was glowing so brilliantly that I couldn't see where I was going. I took off my Ray-Bans to wipe away the moisture, and when I put them back on I looked up and there was Sara, larger than life, smiling down on me from a billboard. "Welcome to Charlotte—Home of Channel 3 News."

The sports marketing firm I worked for in New York had scheduled amateur tennis tournaments in three different cities that weekend. I needed to work one, and the choice was mine. I could have been poolside in Miami Beach or gazing across the Golden Gate Bridge in San Francisco while making the draw for the tournament, but I'd chosen the heat, the noise, and the charm of Charlotte, one of the country's fastest-growing cities, where Sara's presence was larger than life, both on billboards and as coanchor of the evening news. Those were her public roles. I needed Sara in her role as steadfast friend, a friend I could trust to keep my secrets.

I was twenty-six years old, which meant that Sara and I had been friends for fourteen years. Back when we'd met at Tuckahoe Middle School, we'd shared a table in the cafeteria during lunch, compared class schedules and homeroom teachers, but we'd never spoken about life below the surface. Not until one night at a friend's sleepover party. We were two of ten young girls sprawled on a thin carpet, lying between empty pizza boxes and M&M's. A trace of Charlie perfume hung in the air, and most of the girls, wearing Lanz flannel nightgowns with pink roses all in a row, were lost in the world of deep sleep and dreams. What did we dream of at twelve years old? Boys or Barbies? Mud pies or makeup? Taking tentative steps into our teens, our world ricocheted from Truth or Dare to trigonometry, spin the bottle to sock hops. What did we know of life, real life with all its shadows and textures? And if you did know some of the pain and drama found in its darker places, whom could you tell? Whom could you trust to keep a secret?

Sara and I were still awake, lying close together, whispering quietly. Tentatively I let my secret creep out. I told Sara about my sister Tish.

Tish had only been four years old when she had her first seizure. Without warning, she'd fallen to the ground and begun to shake. She moaned, deeply, a sound completely at odds with her beautiful, delicate face. Her arms and legs became rigid and her small body shook convulsively. She wet her pants and then she was quiet. Twenty minutes later she woke up and wanted to play.

For years Mom and Dad took her from doctor to doctor, searching for a specialist, a drug, a magician, anything that could make things right. Tests showed little hope. Tish had brain damage. Simple, irreversible brain damage. No one knew why. It was nothing she had asked for. It was nothing she had done. Faced with a diagnosis that turned the future into a void, Tish's life would unfold in unimaginable ways. As she grew older, her behavior became more erratic, her seizures continued, and her list of medications grew. That was her pain.

My secret was that I was afraid of being her. We were only eighteen months apart in age. With our fine blond hair and skinny legs, everyone thought we were twins, but I was older. Old enough to know that screaming at your mother in public isn't polite behavior, old enough to know that touching a hot stove can burn you, but not old enough to accept that my sister wasn't capable, mentally capable, of grasping these simple concepts. Whenever she was ill—which was often—or behaved badly—which was more often—I could only think: *She could have been me; I could have been her.*

In 1972, when I shared my secret with Sara, no one I knew spoke of illnesses or any other troubles at home. In the years of limbo between *Leave It to Beaver* and *Dallas,* problems and pain, if they existed, crept out in whispers in the kitchen and never in front of children. Watching *The Brady Bunch* was as close as we ever got to being inside a broken home. Whatever happened to the Partridge Family's father remained an unspoken mystery. Of course television, like real life, portrayed some people who were less than perfect, and like life, it did so coldly. Usually the poor soul was a chubby boy, his white shirt untucked, his pants too short, weaving through the hall at school carrying a stack of books. With his glasses slipping down his nose, he couldn't see where he was going until the big, handsome football player intentionally bumped into him. "Where you going, retard?" A gaggle of popular students laughed, "Yeah, retard." In a world of perfect people, he was obviously going nowhere. I heard all this in the halls of my own school. I never laughed, but I also never came to the defense of that sad, confused boy. Often I wished that I was strong enough to scream out about the injustice, to challenge these people to be kind, or if that was too hard, to at least do no harm. Mainly I wished I were somewhere else, far, far away. So I kept quiet, kept my secret. No one knew that I was afraid that one day I'd wake up and God would have realized he'd made a horrible mistake. I should have been the one who was sick, not Tish. No one knew of my fear until that night.

After I finished talking, I was still, staring at the ceiling, waiting for Sara to react. A new fear temporarily replaced the old: maybe she'd be repulsed, pull away, thinking I wasn't who she thought I was after all. Not the bouncing cheerleader with the perfect life, but me with the imperfect family and the sad secret. But she reached out and touched my arm.

"Oh, Gin. I am so sorry. I had no idea."

We talked a long time that night. Later, at school, when we met on an empty sidewalk or in the frenzy of the lunchroom when no one could hear themselves, much less us, she'd ask me about Tish and I'd always say, "Fine, everything's fine." But she knew. At twelve years old, we shared a secret, a bond. The beginnings of a friendship.

How did I know I could trust Sara to keep my secret, not to see it as a weakness or somehow hold it against me? Was it as simple as being in the right place at the right time? On that night, had the pressure of carrying that secret simply boiled to the point where release was inevitable, and Sara just happened to be close by? I didn't think so. When you've carried a secret for years and believe that revealing it will expose you in a naked, awful way, telling someone has to be more than a random draw of proximity or timing. That night, when nine other girls, girls just like me, would have listened, how had I known I could trust Sara? Was it instinct, intuition, dumb luck? Or did I sense a kinship in Sara that she too knew the gift and the pressures of being randomly blessed? I'm not sure, but whatever it was, it was reliable, and so was Sara. Years later, I still trusted her.

Fast-forward fourteen years and I had another secret to share with her, nothing as devastating as the first, but one I hoped would change my life. After a quick shower at the tennis club, I was refreshed and excited as I drove off to meet her.

As I walked up to the deck at the Mexican restaurant, I heard Sara laughing while the waiter fawned over her. Clearly he too had seen the billboard. Though we'd talked on the phone often, I'd only seen Sara once in the months since we met for dinner in New York, and that was on her wedding day. She'd looked positively radiant in her ivory dress and flowing veil, with her sisters by her side. The groom was handsome, a smile etched into his chiseled features. No one mentioned that they'd gotten engaged after knowing each other only seven months and gotten married a few months later. It didn't seem to matter. They were smart, levelheaded, and obviously in love. Why wait? Why not get married?

Along with the rest of the guests, I marveled at the fact that they'd actually met in Richmond. To me Richmond still meant a tight circle of family and old school friends, never venturing too far from the city's West End and the protective cocoon of the white middle-class stereotype. Exciting strangers showed up in someone else's home movie. But for Sara, CD had suddenly appeared, flying in from the West, camera slung over his shoulder, ready to share her life and her dreams. Clinging to the wall and studiously avoiding anyone who might ask, "Ginger, when are you getting married?" I watched as Sara and her new husband mingled with guests and talked about their future—the places they would go, the films they would make together, each place more remote, each story more intoxicating. Sara wouldn't have to worry about him taking his heart with him when he traveled, soon she'd be going, too. But their first stop was Charlotte, a new job for her in a bigger market with more money and that huge billboard.

"Hey, I saw you today."

Sara laughed as she got up to hug me. "Where?"

"On I-85."

"Oh no. Was the smile a little bright?"

"I'm not sure. I was blinded by your suit!"

"Okay, okay. Maybe the red is a bit vivid. But enough about my wardrobe. How are you?"

The pitcher of margaritas arrived just in time. I took a big gulp and blurted out, "I'm going back to Africa."

"You mean on safari?"

"No, I miss the bush. I crave it, and I have got to get out of New York, so I've written to an old friend of Kevin's, this guy John Varty who makes wildlife films, and asked him for a job. I can do research. I can type."

"Are you sure about the job description? And what's he look like?" she asked with eyebrows arched.

"Okay, okay. Enough about men. I mean it. Maybe he needs help, maybe not. I haven't heard back from him yet, and I haven't told a soul about this—not my family and no one at work knows either. It's our secret."

"I think this is one secret we may have to break."

The next night over pasta and red wine Sara introduced me to her friends Julie and Jim Bruton. I quickly realized that Sara was connecting the spark that had flashed through her mind the evening before, the reason she had refused to take a vow of secrecy. Julie's parents were famous wildlife filmmakers and she'd spent much of her life in the field with them, including a few years in Etosha National Park, a game reserve in South-West Africa, a protectorate of South Africa that was fighting for its independence. Years before, I'd sat on my parents' den floor, riveted to the television, soaking in every moment of the Jen and Des Bartlett documentary film *The Lions of Etosha.*

"Gin, while we were riding bikes and making mud pies in Richmond, you won't believe what Julie was up to." Julie just laughed and modestly began to share stories from her childhood—following snow geese down the central flyway from the Arctic to the Gulf of Mexico, photographing koalas in their native Australia, and growing up in Kenya, where she nearly ended up as dinner for a friend's supposedly tame lion.

"That was a little scary." Only Julie could have made these stories seem ordinary, just your typical childhood.

Later, over coffee back at Sara and her husband's perfect home, where handmade curtains framed a view onto old oak trees in the garden and their wedding photographs rested on the piano, Julie's stories became more magical. She spoke of a land where sand dunes were the color of blood and stood tall as skyscrapers. Where elephants slid down them just for fun. A place where lions feasted on whales washed ashore by an ice-cold current and where beetles stood on their heads to drink fog water. All of this was happening in a remote park in South-West Africa called the Skeleton Coast, and her parents were there filming it.

If those impossible things could happen, then anything was possible. For the first time in a long time, I felt a sense of hope begin to stir. It was as if I'd been shown a door to an enchanting new world. By introducing me to Julie, Sara had pushed it wide open. At the end of the evening Julie smiled warmly at her friend and then turned to me, saying, "When you go to Africa, you must meet my parents."

When I returned to New York, I opened the mailbox and the magic continued. There it was, a letter from John. He could use some help on a film about bird migration and he needed me right away.

While I reassured my family that I'd only be gone for a year, my mom and sisters still questioned my sanity and worried about my safety when I quit a good job to embark upon an uncertain adventure in the wilds of Africa. The one person who understood my desire to test my limits was my father. For nearly thirty years he had been tied to a job that provided a steady paycheck and sound health insurance, elements of security his wife and four daughters needed, but little stimulation and few opportunities for himself. He had given up his choices so that my sisters and I would be free to make ours.

"Gin, go. Have fun, but remember, you can always come home."

I felt the safety net spread beneath me, and I was off.

I spent two thousand dollars, half my life savings, on a ticket to Johannesburg. I had a six-month contract with John and was back in the bush.

"GINGER, WAKE UP." John tapped on my door. "Come on, we're rolling."

"What?" It was December of 1988, but here in the southern hemisphere, that meant it was summer. But switching to opposite seasons wasn't the only source of my confusion.

"Come on, it's nearly sunset."

My days were still turned around. I was jet-lagged, up before sunrise and trying to catch up on sleep during the day, tossing and turning at night.

"I'll be right there."

The Land Rover started. He threw it into gear. He wasn't kidding.

I shimmied into my jeans, grabbed a sweater, and ran outside.

"Sorry."

A glance passed between John and Elmon Mhlongo, his trusted friend and tracker. I didn't need to be a mind reader to understand it. After nearly a decade of working together, John and Elmon communicated silently, in code, yet the look that flashed between them was clear—they didn't need a green, stupid American or anyone else around. I was trying to fit in, trying to learn about lenses, apertures, and f-stops, but there was still so much more I needed to know, not only about filming and reading minds but also about reading the bush.

While driving along the bank of a dry riverbed, John suddenly slammed on the brakes.

He whistled, pointed to his right, and Elmon jumped down from the Land Rover.

"What is it?"

"Mozambicans. Refugees."

This time, instead of seeing leopard tracks in the sand when I looked down, I saw footprints. At least eight pairs spread out in a tangle of different directions. Eight people who'd heard us and scattered, long before John had seen the embers of their campfire. Elmon slipped away, following one set of tracks. He moved quietly, gently, and then spoke softly in Shangaan, a language understood across regional borders. A woman emerged from behind a tree. Tied to her back were a few clothes, a chipped enamel mug, and a few loose pots and pans. When she turned around, I saw a baby clinging to her breast, eyes wide open but quiet, as if sensing danger.

"Ginger, you wait here with her. We'll go find the others."

There was an unnatural quiet, the birds were hushed, no cicadas called. In the silence, the woman stared at me and I looked away first, embarrassed by an abundance of blessings, often taken for granted, like choice, freedom, security. Her life was reduced to the most basic element— survival. To be this far away from her homeland, she'd been walking for at least five days. Five days across land ruled by elephants, lions, and soldiers. At night did she dare make a fire to cut through the darkness? Did she allow herself to dream about a new life uninterrupted by gunfire? Slowly but steadily she was putting distance between herself and her war-ravaged country. That is, until now. If caught, refugees were supposed to be returned to Mozambique. But everyone knew that as soon as they were taken back, they'd regroup and try to leave again. When you have nothing left to lose, what is there to fear? Not leopards, not the heat, and certainly not me.

She looked up, making eye contact with someone behind me. Without a second glance, she repositioned her baby, lifted her head proudly, and walked silently past me, leaving behind her blanket and all that was left of her world.

For a few minutes I heard footfalls on the sand, then nothing. The sun had slipped behind the trees before the quiet was broken by the sound of laughter, strange too in the bush, especially tonight. John and Elmon had returned with six of her fellow refugees. There was backslapping and tears as Elmon explained that no one would force them to go back to Mozambique. Instead John would drive them to Gazankulu, one of ten homelands in South Africa, recognized only by the South African government, where borders didn't matter. There they would find members of their tribe and hopefully their future.

We picked up the abandoned blanket and threw it in the back of the Land Rover. For the next half hour it was quiet as we drove through the bush. A few of the refugees closed their eyes, daring to relax for the first time in a long time. Most of them stared into the distance, their eyes hooded, perhaps haunted by what or whom they had left behind.

It was dark when we reached Gazankulu. The air was cold and the smell of raw earth engulfed us as we slowed to a stop. The engine shut down and sounds of life—men laughing, babies crying, the blaring of music from an old transistor radio—hit us. In the local store, a single naked lightbulb hung over shelves of cooking oil, washing powder, and corn meal. This was home. "Thank you, thank you" was spoken in a jumble of languages, through a mixture of laughter and tears, as everyone climbed out of the back of the Land Rover. I passed the woman's blanket to another refugee and looked around for her and her child. They weren't there yet, but I was certain they would make it.

She'd risked everything for a chance to start over, a chance to live a life without fear of rebels burning her village in the night or having to plow a field of corn laced with land mines. My risks were completely insignificant. There was no comparison, yet seeing her made me resolute. I too would make it here. No matter what complications abounded in the bush.

Almost daily in the weeks that followed, John and I climbed into his old Land Rover and went in search of one of Londolozi's famous leopards. One afternoon we found her draped over a branch of a marula tree, one paw resting on the remains of an impala, last night's dinner. She barely lifted her head as we approached. For the past seven years, John had filmed her life—from mating, to raising and losing cubs, to hunting. And John knew a lot about hunting. He was an advocate of man's primal need to hunt, to conquer, and move on, and his prey was women. Luckily for me, he didn't have his conquests stuffed and mounted; they either accepted the fact that he was off in pursuit of his next prize or they could leave.

But I wasn't ready to go just yet. I had finally found something to love.

"Look at this shot." Shelly Wells, the film editor, sent film flying as she rewound the spool on the editing machine.

"Here, Ginger. See how the cameraman locked the camera in place? He gave me an editing point. Once the bird flies away—there—that last wobble of the branch—I can use that. But look at this. This leopard never walks out of frame. She just keeps going and going. Where the hell is she going? Where can I cut that shot? I can't. It doesn't work." I sat with Shelly for hours at a time, cutting shots in my mind, drafting stories from reams of film, absorbing all she generously shared with me about how to tell a story with images. I knew I could do this, that I could be a wildlife filmmaker. Would it make me complete? Would it fill the gap left by Kevin, the one widened by my life in New York and aggravated by my dalliance with John? Who knew, but at least I had direction and it wasn't linked to a man.

For once, my timing was perfect. After six months of often tough but valuable lessons at Londolozi and a series of letters I exchanged with Sara and her friend Julie, I was on my way to spend a month with Julie's parents, the filmmakers Jen and Des Bartlett. I packed a few clothes, a notebook, and my going-away present from John, a battered but sharp Nikon FE2, my first camera, in my suitcase. Once again I'd made a promise to do anything to help, anything to learn, but I had no idea what that would mean for the Bartletts until I arrived in the Skeleton Coast Park in South-West Africa.

Whether we were in their tiny wooden shack at the beach buffeted by strong Atlantic winds or putting up tents in the middle of a dry riverbed, we were isolated, alone, and together round the clock. The Bartletts weren't just sharing their work; they were sharing their lives. From before sunrise to long past sunset, I was underfoot. Yet they taught me how to change a tire in the sand, how to pull focus to follow the flight of a bird, and how to turn a bucket of water into a luxurious bath. Setting up his cameras to capture another spectacular sunset, Des explained the art of "painting with light," his inspired version of cinematography. Later we cooked chicken in a solar-powered oven and counted satellites drifting between the stars at night. Before climbing into our tents, we listened to the evening news on the BBC World Service, and in the morning we read the news imprinted in the sand.

Bundled in down jackets against the cold fog air, I often found Jen standing at the base of the dunes, lost in thought. This was where she taught me to read "the desert's morning paper," tracks in the sand that told the story of the night before. The wide track of a lizard showed that while we were asleep it had scurried over the dunes to nibble on the branches of a nara bush. Sometime later, a white lady spider had emerged from her burrow in the sand to grab a four-legged meal, leaving behind her pinprick-sized footprints and a thin drag mark. As the sun rose, we had heard a jackal's plaintive cry nearby, followed by a howl rising up over the dunes. Now we saw the jackal's paw prints layered over the other tracks. In the desert, the morning news was of life and survival, as raw and as powerful as anything Sara might have reported on television the night before.

In thirty fleeting days, the Bartletts shared their passion for the bush, their incredible knowledge, and then their wealth of contacts. "When you get to town, contact Mary Seely. She runs Gobabeb, a research station in the Namib Desert. Tell her we suggested you visit. Maybe you'll find a story there. Could turn out to be your first film."

A few days later I walked out of a trailer into the mist across the gravel plains at Gobabeb. Fog clung to the ground, obscuring the research station's huge white water tower and shrouding the dunes in a blanket of mist. I looked down and spotted a tiny gerbil-like creature scurrying across the plains toward me. Behind her strode a tall man, with dark hair, darker skin, wearing the shortest shorts and the dirtiest jacket I'd ever seen. When he got closer, I saw that his big brown eyes were flecked with green and rimmed with extraordinarily long lashes.

"Hey, where do you belong?" I reached down to pick up the meerkat, putting her inside my coat for warmth. She soon wrapped herself around my neck.

"I wouldn't—"

"Shit. She bit me!"

"That's what you get when you try and tame a wild animal."

"What? I—"

"Don't worry. You didn't do it. Some other idiot got to her first. Forget about it, just come with me before you bleed to death."

While he swabbed my nose with ointment, we swapped stories. "So that's it, just another crazy American in search of a story." I finished describing my life to date in a few short paragraphs.

"Lucky we met. I just came back this morning to grab a few supplies, then I'm headed back upriver."

"For how long?"

"About three years."

"What?"

He laughed at my startled expression and opened another beer. His fourth.

"Yeah, just me and a troop of baboons, living the high life. They run away from me, while I console myself with hot beer."

"But why?"

"There's no refrigerator."

"No, not the beer. Why are you alone with a troop of baboons?"

"I just finished vet school, and I have absolutely no desire to treat tiny Chihuahuas or their neurotic owners. Baboons are much more interesting."

Turned out that his name was Conrad Brain but everyone called him Nad. Just twenty-five years old, three years my junior, and fresh out of veterinary school, he was starting a Ph.D. project studying a small troop of baboons, primates like you and me, living in the desert.

"These guys live right on the edge. First of all, it is hot as hell—50 degrees in the shade at times. What's that for you, around 110 degrees? Then they have very little water to drink, sometimes no water at all. How can they live here? It's nuts, or maybe I'm nuts, but I'm going to try and figure out how they manage to survive." That was it, his future in a paragraph.

In an instant I realized that it might possibly be mine. This was the story I was looking for, another ticket out of town.

"Need any help?"

Conrad looked pleased and skeptical. "Okay, why not. Let's give it a month."

This was one of the countless times I'd longed for a phone. A pen would have to do. I couldn't wait to write to Sara.

6

SARA (1990–1991)

I WAS PANTING AS I rounded the corner toward our brick bungalow, the steamy Charlotte air making four miles seem like forty, wondering if one run could erase the five pounds I always wanted to shed—especially when my husband was about to return from a trip. As I reached the front door, I discovered a thin blue international envelope tucked inside the batch of bills poking through the mail slot. I ripped it open and read where I stood. Then I kicked off my shoes, sat down on the pink wing chair in sweaty clothes, and read it again. My friend with the Gucci loafers had moved to a canyon with a total stranger and a bunch of monkeys.

My protective instincts kicked into overdrive. Couldn't Ginger see that once again she'd linked her destiny to a man? Who was this "Nad" playing Me Tarzan, You Jane? I felt both alarmingly underinformed and somehow responsible. After all, I'd introduced Gin to the woman who had the parents who barely knew the man who was now the only living human within thirty miles of my friend. It might be her life and I might live far away, but I felt entitled to worry. Was he trustworthy? Was he kind? Would he treat her well?

I tried to calm down. Julie was one of my best friends, and her parents, Jen and Des Bartlett, were people of great integrity in addition to being legendary filmmakers. If they liked Tarzan, he couldn't be an ax murderer. Still, after everything Gin had been through, he'd damn well better be a Boy Scout. Besides, what a gamble. From the letter it sounded as if Ginger expected to find a film and transform her future, all in four weeks or less.

Talk about a tall order. Was she daring or desperate? The handwriting was as neat and steady as ever—no loopy, lurching scrawl like that of a couple of lunatics who occasionally wrote me at the television station. And Ginger sounded excited, even happy. But why the hell couldn't she have a phone like everyone else so I could call her, get a sense of how she really was? I'd been the biggest supporter of Gin's career change, but I feared she was in a free fall, this potential film the third parachute she'd attempted to open in as many months.

SEVERAL HOURS LATER at the station, I thought about Ginger's gamble in a different light. The truth was, it sounded fun. Free-spirited and gutsy, brimming with adventure. The kind of life most people fantasize about without ever getting up from the sofa. In fact, uncomfortably close to the future I'd once imagined for myself with CD. Instead, he still traveled the globe making films while I read the news at six and eleven. At the ripe old age of twenty-nine, I was growing restless and bored.

"Simon says face left. Simon says cross your arms. Uncross your arms. *Got you, Sara!*"

"Excuse me?" My colleagues chuckled.

"You must be daydreaming. I didn't say 'Simon says'!"

"Sorry." I quickly recrossed my arms, brought my right shoulder forward, lifted my chin, and flashed a blazing smile as the photographer resumed snapping. We were two hours into the shoot for the latest WBTV Channel 3 "On Your Side" billboard and my smile wasn't the only thing cracking. The makeup felt like spackle and there wasn't a freckle in sight. My turquoise jacket was clipped in the back with clothespins for a smoother fit, and the stylist had back-combed my hair until it looked like it had been inflated with a bicycle pump. The only things larger than my hair were my earrings. Thank God no one saw us up close.

MY COANCHOR, Bob Inman, smiled indulgently at the group gathered by the back door. The most respected newsman in town, Bob somehow also found time to write lyrical novels, and his first book, *Home Fires Burn-ing,* had been turned into a television movie. By 11:35 P.M. he was ready to head home to his adored wife, Paulette, and their two girls.

"Where to this time?" Bob asked.

"We're going to the Artists' Café to hear Margaret," I replied. My friend Margaret Kennedy was an engineer at WBTV as well as a gifted musician. "But I can't stay long—CD's coming home tomorrow and I've gotta get ready."

"Where's he been?" asked Baron Murphy, a station photographer.

"Africa."

Baron shook his head. "Doesn't all that traveling drive you nuts?"

I hesitated. "Not really. It keeps things fresh, makes for great home-comings."

He rolled his eyes. "You in-love types make me sick."

BUT LITTLE COULD he suspect that in spite of my cheery response, I al-ready had a knot in my stomach from wondering how this homecoming would play out.

I'd set the table with our wedding china but the sauce on my half-eaten chicken had congealed, the candles in their crystal candlesticks had gut-tered to stubs, and just as it had during that billboard photo shoot, my smile felt forced and frozen. "So, overall, the trip went well?"

"Yes, it did."

Suddenly fed up with trying to spark a conversation, I blurted out, "I just feel like there's so much you're not saying. I mean, you've been gone so long. Didn't you miss me?" Playfully, I reached a hand across the table.

"I'm just tired, okay? Long flight." He pushed back his chair. "I think I need a hot bath, then a good night's sleep."

I stayed up late with a bottle of wine and our wedding album for com-pany. There we were in the limo. What giddy grins. And there, dancing. Both of us laughing as he stepped all over my toes. I came across a picture of Gin watching, her expression a cipher. Had she worried as Mom did that I'd Married in Haste? Or was she thinking, *Lucky you, you found your guy, why wouldn't you Seize the Day?* She'd never told me. And I'd never asked. I'd been twenty-six and certain about everything. I'd only just landed a job as weeknight coanchor at the CBS affiliate in Charlotte, North Carolina, a large, successful station in market 32. It had been a major step up, and CD had quit his job to come join me.

At first, moving up had brought nothing but excitement and perks. The station paid for my frothy new hairstyle, then sent me to Dallas to join a fashion consultant on a clothes-buying spree. I especially loved a new turquoise dress with enormous shoulder pads I hoped made my waist look small. At the news desk, Bob, sports anchor Paul Cameron, and weathercaster Mike McKay were bright, talented, and welcoming. I relished the anchoring and reporting. From the excesses of Jim and Tammy Bakker at the crumbling religious empire PTL, to profiling a woman with multiple personalities whose saga was portrayed in the movie *The Three Faces of Eve,* to covering hurricanes, work was exciting and engrossing.

So were our new friends, people like Julie and her husband, Jim. When they weren't trekking with their travel company, Old World Safaris, CD and I would meet them for breakfast. Sporting a Polo shirt and African kikoi, Jim would pour the French-press coffee and Julie would serve one of her signature vegetarian dishes. Sometimes Margaret would join us as well as another new pal, Fiona Ritchie, a gifted raconteur whose Celtic music show on National Public Radio, *The Thistle & Shamrock,* had a growing national following.

But our marriage was another story. Before producing documentaries CD had been a local television reporter, but because I was in such a prominent position as coanchor, his own on-air options proved limited. He'd started his own business and seemed to relish the freedom and autonomy, traveling the globe for a variety of creative projects, including one film we bankrolled ourselves. But as any freelancer knows, it's hard, lonely, and often thankless work. I flinched whenever a stranger called him "Mr. James." After three years in Charlotte, he seemed frustrated. I felt guilty. It was a miserable, toxic mix.

I slammed the wedding album shut. How had we spiraled from smiling newlyweds to discontented husband and wife? Was it that we hadn't

really known each other? Or was it that we hadn't entirely known ourselves? Sometimes I wondered if each of us in part craved what the other
had. While the prestige and platform that came with being in front of the
camera were certainly seductive, at twenty-nine years old, I found myself
hankering for the freedom, the travel, and the soulfulness of the life he led.
Like Ginger, he'd taken one of author William Least Heat Moon's "blue
highways," while I'd stuck to the interstate. Which explained how I'd
wound up with my face on a billboard, just another brunette with a big
smile and a red suit. Like the Channel 3 billboard, our marriage looked a
lot better from a distance.

THE NEXT MORNING I awoke groggy and CD was already up. His cool
expression made my stomach hurt.

"How can you live like this?" he asked quietly.

"Like what?"

He pointed to a mug of tea from the day before that I'd left on an end
table. Suddenly I remembered the clothes in a heap on the bedroom floor,
the half-opened mail strewn across the dining room table. My mess and
clutter could drive anyone crazy.

"I'm sorry," I said.

But he was already out the door.

SOMETIMES WHEN YOU least expect it, life changes overnight. That's
what happened for thousands of people at 2 A.M. on August 2, 1990, when
Iraq invaded Kuwait. Thousands of miles away, I was one of them.

"Sara, the 1454th Transportation Company from Concord has been
called up as part of Operation Desert Shield." News director Bill Foy looked
grave. "If you're interested, we could send you to Saudi Arabia with them.
Of course we don't know when—or if—the U.S. will decide to strike. And
Saddam could launch a Scud missile anytime, even use chemical weapons.
You don't have to go. This is volunteer only."

My friend Linda Pattillo, now a network correspondent for ABC News, would also be covering the conflict. I couldn't wait to tell her.

"I'd love to go," I told Bill.

While my husband was supportive, Mom was far less enthusiastic. My sister Elizabeth had gotten married a few years before to John Gallagher, a handsome, wry history major she'd met at Indiana University. John's childhood passion for flying had prompted him to join the U.S. Marines, where he became a captain and a Harrier pilot. Everyone in the family already worried about the dangers John would face. But my parents also knew this was the kind of story I'd always wanted to cover. Besides, this time when I headed to a war zone, I wouldn't have to take vacation time. I wouldn't have to pay for my ticket. I'd even get a paycheck. I wanted to prove to myself that I'd learned a thing or two since the mistakes I'd made in Nicaragua. And I was hardly the first person to escape trouble at home by running away to war.

NORTH CAROLINA BRISTLES with crack troops at military bases from Fort Bragg. But these men and women were engineers and teachers, real estate agents and factory workers. After all, they'd joined the National Guard, not the regular army, and normally drilled just one weekend a month, plus two weeks a year. Their last major deployment had been clearing away wreckage left by Hurricane Hugo. Now they'd be stationed in the Gulf until someone back in Washington decided it was time to come home.

"Never in my wildest imagination did I ever think I'd be in Saudi Arabia at fifty-one years old," one man told me. "It's payback time. Gotta get over and ride the camel." From misty-eyed grandpas to bright-eyed college kids, most of the 165 soldiers in the unit were men, but 8 were women, some moms. Overnight they'd gone from tucking a baby in bed to tucking a clip in an M-16, from racing after toddlers to racing toward army trucks, because their role would be to support the infantry in an invasion. After a farewell kiss, each soldier grabbed a forty-pound pack and boarded a waiting Pan Am jet, one of the civilian aircraft ferrying troops to the Mideast.

When we arrived in Saudi Arabia, I was shocked to see this desert up close. Ginger had written of a magical kingdom where soaring dunes twinkled with garnet dust, an oasis where flamingos frolicked and even sober elephants cavorted. This sandy wasteland was vast, scrubby, and gray, scabbed with oil derricks. Highways tracked like varicose veins across the empty expanse. Forget *Lawrence of Arabia*. I didn't see a single camel. While the predators in Ginger's world were jackals, hyenas, and spitting cobras, here we feared Saddam's crack troops, the Revolutionary Guard. His forces were out there, just across the border, watching, waiting. How strong was he? we wondered. How strong were we?

At night we ignored the frosty stars and scanned for satellites. They were comforting beacons, since we knew the U.S. government used them to monitor Iraqi ground troops. "What happens if he launches a Scud missile?" I asked one soldier.

"They might try to knock us out," he acknowledged, "but we're trained for that, too."

I shivered, hoping the troops would chalk it up to the evening desert chill. At least I wasn't alone, but with Steve Ohnesorge, who was field-producing, and our photographer, Tom Atkins, not to mention the soldiers themselves. I looked around and realized I wasn't the only one nervous. "Tom," I whispered, pointing to a G.I. whose clenched jaw and tense expression said it all. By instinct we'd discovered the favored trick of journalists in danger zones the world over. Whenever you're scared, try to look at fear through a long lens. It's the best way to keep it at bay.

WE LIVED WITH the troops and I liked bunking in the women's tent. It smelled of talcum powder, suntan lotion, and chocolate. Late each night I shook out my sleeping bag before tumbling in, checking for scorpions, a small worry compared with the uncertainty and anxiety all around us.

Each morning I'd rise before the sun creaked over the horizon, splash water on my face, scour my teeth with toothpaste and bottled water.

Seeing how far I could spit in the sand was immensely satisfying—the kind of uncouth behavior frowned upon if you're female and born south of the Mason-Dixon. Conditions were primitive. A shower was limited to three minutes or less. The latrines came equipped with screened windows for ventilation, so a trip to the loo was not exactly a private affair. Still, it beat conditions in the field. One day the convoy I'd been riding in had squealed to a sudden, unscheduled stop. The sergeant jumped out, hand already at his belt buckle. "No need to panic, Sara, but turn your head," he advised. "Just gonna wet the wheel." I immediately decided to drink as little as possible, willing to risk heatstroke rather than pee in front of an audience.

While sometimes the raw humor was a jolt to my southern sensibilities, I loved the rough-and-ready camaraderie, and proximity bred laughter and confidences. We chuckled about the favorite spot for a tryst—the huge cement pipes that surrounded the compound to protect us from some suicide bomber driving a truck loaded with explosives. Suffice it to say those tunnels were often noisy at night, and the sound of such uncensored passion filled me with an unsettling mix of loathing and longing. How could they be so carefree? And why was I settling for so much less?

I concentrated on thinking about the soldiers' lives instead. One morning, after dining on western omelets drenched in Tabasco at the mess, Steve, Tom, and I spied a cluster of soldiers huddled around a radio. We hustled over, notepads in hand, Tom's camera already rolling, wondering what ominous news report had them looking so serious. As we got closer we heard a voice on the radio say, "First down, and the ball's at the twenty." A soldier grinned, "Tuesday morning—Monday Night Football."

But reminders of the real mission were never far behind, like the accessory worn at all times, even with shorts and a T-shirt on a training run—a gas mask. "What bothers me most, I think, is to know he has chemical gas, being as close as we are to Kuwait," one soldier admitted. Off camera later another added, "If he does strike, we'll never have time to grab those suits. And they say he has biological weapons, too." He shuddered. We all knew Saddam Hussein had used them on his own people, so why would he hesitate to turn them on us?

While everyone in the unit expressed pride in the transportation company and in serving their country, there were nagging doubts, a few reservations. "This is all about oil," more than one told me off camera. "That's the real reason we're here."

Some women pointed out drily that they were risking their lives to protect a country where women weren't even allowed to drive. "We get a lot of stares, maybe they think we can't perform as well under these conditions," a female truck driver observed. But for some dads and especially moms, the greatest frustration was realizing that a second job they'd taken to support their families had instead taken them thousands of miles away from those they loved.

"I have children and I think it's harder for a mother because when my daughters fall down and get hurt, they call for me, not my husband," another woman worried.

As for soldier Tracy Smith, she simply held out her arm and tapped her wrist. "I'm not gonna adjust my watch. It's gonna stay on North Carolina time and I'm just gonna add eight to it and I guess I'll know what time it is here. I'll look at it and say, 'Mama's asleep, and it's about time for Jess to get up for her midnight feed.' "

As I fell into my sleeping bag on my final night in Saudi Arabia, I thought for the first time in a long time about being a mom. I liked children, but still couldn't imagine having my own. I wondered if that would change. After all, I was nearly thirty—hardly a kid anymore. I hadn't dared to tell any of these women about the nightmare I'd had only a few months before.

I'd dreamed that I'd had a baby but I'd lost her and simply couldn't remember where I'd left her. I'd been frantic, terrified for her safety, but also keenly aware of how absurd it was to misplace a baby. And then I'd remembered that I'd put her on the roof of the car, which seemed even worse. Who puts a baby on a car? And was she still there? I'd reached up to check, desperate to find the child, and woken up, panting, heart thumping, never to know if she'd been there or not. The dream had been so potent and terrifying that I'd had to remind myself I didn't have a child at all.

Lying in the tent, I pondered what that dream meant. Was I terrified to have a child, afraid I was too selfish and irresponsible to be a mother?

Or was my deeper fear that I'd never have a child at all? These women had no doubts, only anguish at an unexpected and lengthy separation. And when they showed me pictures of daughters and sons, children dark-haired and fair, faces fringed in bangs or curls, I found myself picturing the scenes back home: a skinned knee bandaged by Dad, a grimy, tear-streaked face wiped by Grandma, a temper tantrum at bathtime or bed-time or for no reason at all, save the reason that someone small was missing Mom, wondering when she'd be back, and perhaps wondering if she'd return at all.

BACK AT CHANNEL 3, those "Soldiers' Stories" seemed to write them-selves and I dared to wonder if I might finally have enough material to send to the network. The only person I knew from Charlotte who'd moved on was the sports anchor at the competition, Hannah Storm, who'd been picked up by CNN. She looked glamorous and competent and I felt sure she hadn't needed nearly as much help as I did.

I needed a new résumé reel, and when CD took time from his travels to craft one for me, my heart lifted. He must still care. Meantime, my friend Linda had offered to put me in touch with her agent.

"But I already sent him a tape, LP."

"That was back in Richmond. Now you have more experience, plus you met him at my wedding, remember?"

It was impossible to forget Stuart Witt. He worked for the N.S. Bien-stock agency in New York and was smart and caustic—a marathon-running, fur-hating vegetarian and former marine. Which was why I shouldn't have been surprised by his blunt assessment of my work.

"*Sara!* Did you rob King Midas's tomb or what?? What is with those earrings?"

"You think they're a little big, Stu?"

"Big?! They're the size of *hubcaps!*" Finally he calmed down. "But I like the story where you're in the middle of the hurricane and the series about the soldiers. That won an Emmy, right? And the magazine profile on you is good, 'cause it mentions that Nicaragua stuff."

"Well, thanks—"

"I'm not done. Just get me some new anchoring. *And don't wear any jewelry. None.* I don't trust you. And I'll see what I can do."

I got off the phone worrying about uniforms. Soldiers wore khaki and camo. Local anchors wore cardinal red. What was the style for network reporters? I'd never been good at fashion, and Ginger was nearly seven thousand miles away. I'd just have to figure it out.

A few weeks later I was just back from a run when CD waved me in with a big smile. "Sara," he whispered, handing over the phone, "it's Don Browne."

Don Browne! Gin had sent me a *Vanity Fair* profile about him. Was it possible the executive vice president of NBC was calling me at home?

"Yes?"

"So I had to talk to someone who was crazy enough about this business to pay their own way to a war zone. Did you really cover Nicaragua as a reporter from Richmond?"

I'd read that Browne had been NBC's Miami bureau chief during the conflict, the person responsible for deploying network correspondents and crews not only in southern Florida but in Central and South America, too.

I laughed, suddenly at ease, because I liked this man immediately. "I guess it does sound nuts."

"Well, I like that kind of crazy. How'd you like to come to New York for an interview?"

When I hung up, breathless, CD was beaming at me, and I felt better than I'd felt in months.

"Congratulations, Sara," he said with a kiss. Oh my God, there was hope for us, I just knew it. If we could just get out of this town.

BUT THEN GULF WAR I started, and everything else was on hold. I sent Browne a note. "Bags packed. Stop. Arabic dictionary in hand. Stop. Are you sure you don't need another reporter in Kuwait?"

He called, chuckling. "Sit tight, Sara. We're spending a lot of money on this war. But if I can't get you in the front door, there may be a window."

But there wasn't time to contemplate cryptic network hints. In between anchoring newscasts I constantly scanned the wires, checking every report slugged "Harrier Down." Mouth chalky, I'd ring my sister Elizabeth, who would cut the chitchat short with a terse "It's okay. It wasn't John."

"How'd you know why I was calling?" I asked the first time.

"The wives. We know first."

I comforted myself that at least while John was away Elizabeth had moved in with our youngest sister, Susan. Elizabeth was working on her doctorate in voice while Susan pursued her master's in music. Both studied at the University of North Carolina in Greensboro, just a few hours from Charlotte, and the three of us got together as often as we could.

And then there was Linda. LP had promised her photographer husband, David Murray, and her parents that she'd stay safe. Which explains how she wound up being the only female television reporter with the front-line troops, storming into Kuwait with the Second Marine Division. Then again, what could you expect from the daughter of a marine? But at last the war was over, and LP was giving an exclusive interview to Barbara Walters, and John was on the boat steaming home.

It was months later when I got another call from Stu.

"Sara, I got good news and bad news. Which do you want first?"

"I'm an optimist."

"Good! Are you sitting down? You are going to the network."

I collapsed into a chair. "Stu! That's incredible!" I could scarcely believe I was going to live my dream of getting to be a network reporter. Catching my expression, my husband grinned, too.

Then I sat up straight. "But wait—what's the bad news?"

"Well, the job's in the middle of the night. And—it's in Charlotte."

"What?" I wailed. I'd counted on moving to a different city, one with more opportunities for my husband. "But there isn't even a bureau here!"

"True, but there's News Channel." NBC News Channel had only recently begun operations. An affiliate feed service, it collected relevant videotape and editorial information from each NBC station which could then be dispersed to one and all. Stu continued, "You'll interview with News Channel president Bob Horner, and if he likes you, you'll be an anchor.

A network anchor, Sara. Of course, you'll be up all night, have to live like a fuckin' bat. And it's a start-up, so you'll work your ass off. But play your cards right and you'll get to New York."

A network anchor. In Charlotte. My star was rising. But at the realization that this latest career move wouldn't mean moving to a new city, the smile on my husband's face faded to black.

"THANKS, MARTIN. THAT'S Martin Fletcher, reporting live from Jerusalem. And that wraps it up for us for this half hour. Thanks for watching *NBC Nightside*." I did the obligatory anchor paper shuffle as we cut to a commercial break.

"Jerusalem. I'd love to go there," I said to my coanchor, Antonio Mora. "Do you think one day we'll get to report from overseas?"

Antonio considered. "Perhaps. Personally I'd prefer to host my own show, interview key newsmakers," he replied. "I've already spent a lot of time overseas."

I nodded, remembering that Antonio's family had fled Cuba when Castro came to power, and he'd lived for a time in Venezuela before moving permanently to the United States. "Fair enough. Meantime, there's some breaking news. The Krispy Kreme donuts just arrived—and they're hot. Which kind do you want?"

Sharing a grueling shift meant I'd not only learned about Antonio's family history, but that he possessed a wicked sweet tooth.

"Great! I'll take chocolate frosted."

It wasn't easy to stay up all night. But it was harder to go home. Between leaving for the office at 9 P.M. and hitting the sack at eleven in the morning, not to mention CD's travel, we saw less of each other than ever. When we did, he seemed increasingly remote. One especially bad day, I drove to the Harris Teeter grocery store and called Linda from a pay phone in the parking lot.

"You two need a vacation," she decreed.

"Actually, we're leaving for Namibia soon," I replied, telling her about an upcoming trip to see Ginger, as well as Julie, Jim, and baby Tarl, who'd be visiting Julie's parents. But Linda had switched to her drill sergeant voice. "But, Sara, use the time away to really talk to each other. You have got to face—whatever this is."

I struggled to compose myself, suddenly keenly aware that a woman was waving at me, heading my way. She wanted an autograph. I remembered that once, I'd longed for such a moment. Today I dreaded such an encounter, afraid my face would give my pain away. I signaled for her to wait a minute.

"Ginger made it through a bad breakup, too," Linda continued, "and look how happy she is now. I bet she'll have some advice."

I hung up the phone and took a deep breath to compose myself as the woman with her pen and pad swooped in.

"It's nice to meet you, Sara Jane." I smiled as I scrawled my name. In the South, my last name sometimes became part of my first. Then she gave me a sharper look. "But I do have to say, you sure look different from that billboard."

I jangled my keys, headed for my Mazda. I couldn't get to Africa and Ginger quickly enough.

7

GINGER (1991–1992)

How far can negative energy travel? Can it be packed alongside suit-cases, board a plane in Charlotte, and be flown halfway around the world? Given time and a stiff drink, it should dissipate over the Atlantic. The very idea of a holiday should transform it. But what if it doesn't? What if jet lag only makes it worse? Does negativity then have the capacity to land in one of the most remote places in Africa and wreak havoc? Shake canyon walls, drive snakes from their burrows, knock food onto the sand? Will it con-sume life in the desert, or will the wind, the heat, the sheer scale of the desert give it perspective and swallow it whole?

Just two years before, in 1990, South-West Africa had gained its indepen-dence from South Africa and was now recognized as Namibia. That had been the same year I'd moved to the Kuiseb River Canyon with Nad and a motley troop of baboons. Nad and I had come to expect the baboons to fight to the death, to literally bite each other in the back in order to maintain their strict ranking structure, keeping one another firmly in their place. But our survival depended on taking a different approach. Since there were just two of us, living more than one hundred miles away from the nearest city, we needed to keep the peace. The baboons' world might disintegrate into anar-chy, but we couldn't allow that to happen in ours. We tried not to let heavy unspoken feelings invade the riverbed. But lift the lid on sadness, on pain, and it blows through the desert like the east wind, turning dreams into dust. This is what happened when Sara and her husband arrived.

I didn't wear a watch, didn't have a calendar, but for months I'd been counting down the days until their visit, waiting anxiously for June. I knew their trip would be quick. They had to divide their time in Namibia between visiting Julie and her family four hundred miles to the north in the Skeleton Coast Park and us, but I would have traded many things for just one day. For the first time in over a year I would see a real human friend, one who knew how far I'd come from a high school stage to a vast desert arena. She knew the curves, the potholes, and the roadblocks that had marked my journey from a young girl with big dreams to a woman whose dreams were now incomprehensible to most. Though my family and friends were oddly, tactfully silent, I knew they worried about my decision to live such an isolated, uncertain life, one without immediate comforts and where the future seemed to be rooted in vague hopes. I needed Sara to feel the soft sand, to see the glow of sunset on the dunes, and to hear the story behind the baboons' gentle murmurs so that she would understand the allure and my choice. Then at least one person would realize I wasn't completely mad.

The night before they arrived, Nad and I had watched the baboons climb up their sleeping cliff, before driving twenty miles back to the research station in the dark. Back at the station, we shared a few beers with other researchers in from the field, refueled the Land Rover, and then we waited, and waited. Sunrise, midmorning, noon had passed, midday followed, and still nothing.

It was late afternoon, the time when light plays on the dunes, creating long, graceful shadows, and the air is cool enough to breathe again, when Sara and CD's rented vehicle drove through the gates. Immediately we bundled them into the Land Rover and drove from the research station upriver to find the baboons. We drank warm beer and held on to each other as the Land Rover bounced down the dirt track. At first I was so excited to see them that I didn't notice the friction in the air. I simply put it down to fatigue. It's an arduous thirty-hour trip from the U.S. to Namibia, changing planes, changing time zones, and changing perspectives as cities melt away, replaced by wide-open spaces, the perfect backdrop for losing or finding yourself. Though I knew Sara craved a more natural life, she was working the night shift, surviving on fast food, and willing herself to ignore the fact that she hadn't seen the sun or her husband by the light of day in a long time.

"So this is it. We're home," I told them as we turned a bend in the dry riverbed and met the baboons as they were climbing down a sheer cliff face. For the past two years home had been anywhere this ragtag troop of baboons was, within their range of only twenty miles. No living room, no kitchen, no toilet. Open-air ceilings and walls of wind. Just space. To the uninitiated it varied little, just one long stretch of sand bordered by gray canyon walls to the north and endless deep red dunes to the south. But we knew this riverbed intimately, every bend, every seep of water, every tree that sustained the baboons when the river ran dry. We knew where each of our favorite little baboons had been born. We also knew where many of the others had died. Every night we threw our sleeping bags down on the sand below the troop's preferred sleeping cliff. And tonight, for the first time, I'd have a chance to finally share this amazing place with someone else I loved. I could be forgiven for not seeing the cracks yet.

"We'll set up camp here tonight," said Nad as he eased the Land Rover up and over an embankment of silt. He stopped in the sand opposite a seep of water cut into a sheer rock face seventy-five feet up from the ground. For the past week the baboons had been drinking here, one by one, from the highest- to the lowest-ranking member. Nad climbed out from behind the wheel, opened the back of the vehicle, and began our nightly routine.

"Here, grab this table, and Sara, the box of wine goes on the bonnet. Sorry, the hood."

"He's catching on to American, isn't he, Gin?" Sara grinned.

Table opened, gas cooker placed beside the tire, and wine in place, Nad grabbed a shovel, looked around, and said sheepishly, "I'm heading for the hills," an expression understood in any language.

Sara, CD, and I stretched out on the sand, sipping our drinks and enjoying the quiet. "This box wine isn't—" Sara stopped midsentence and we all turned to see Nad tearing out from behind the trees.

"Shit," he laughed.

"What, what is it?"

"A fucking six-foot cobra. Right where, well, you know. Shit."

If it was possible, Sara turned even paler.

"Nad, be quiet. Please. Sara hates snakes."

I turned to Sara. "He's making this up."

"No, I almost sat on the damn thing. And, well, don't look but I left my underwear back there."

Now it was Nad's turn to change color.

"Don't worry, Sara. One look at that little white bottom and I'm sure the snake was scared away."

Later that evening after accidentally dumping our pasta dinner in the sand, Sara whispered, "Did you hear that?"

The eerie laughter of hyenas bounced off the canyon walls, creating a bizarre harmony with the sound of our crackling fire. Their whooping and cackling grew louder as the hyenas edged closer, and I told Sara how I'd grown leery of them. "I met a guy who was sleeping with his head outside a tent and a hyena bit his ear off. And once, when we were sleeping, they dragged a blanket off of us. We found it on the cliff the next morning."

"Gin, stop. Now you're trying to scare me."

This time Nad spoke gently, in his seldom-used "I'm a doctor, you can trust me" voice. "No, no, Sara, don't worry. Hyenas are just curious. Normally they just sniff around camp and move on. You have nothing to worry about."

That night while the rest of us were sprawled in the sand, Sara slept alone in the back of the Land Rover. The next morning she was strangely apologetic. As if, instead of making a sane decision, she'd shown some horrible weakness and earned another demerit in a marriage that was increasingly keeping score. I could suddenly see that it wasn't jet lag or fatigue stifling Sara's bright nature. Her confidence was shattered, a painful symptom caused by a relationship rupturing, one I remembered all too well from my breakup with Kevin.

"Come on, Sara. The guys can pack up camp. Let's go find the baboons." We took our chipped enamel mugs, steaming with coffee, and walked quietly up the riverbed. The sun touched the lip of the canyon, warming the sand and turning the treetops an iridescent green. "Shh," I whispered. We stood still and listened to the contented sounds of *mm-mm* coming from a grove of acacia trees.

"Found them. Now let me introduce you." As we adjusted our eyes, images, black blurs of movement, took shape, revealing individuals behind the branches and leaves.

"There's Grin. He's the alpha male," I said, pointing to a huge baboon sitting under the tree, shifting through the sand for pods and then putting them behind his sharp canine teeth to break them open with his molars.

"And that one with the white hair on her shoulder, that's Patch.

"Over there, the one nursing her little baby is Bo. She's also Cleo and Smudge's mom.

"Oh, and don't look now but that ugly one, climbing down the tree, that's Constance." I'd written to Sara about my loathing for Constance. How I hated her so much that Nad and I had debated killing her. We had good reason. Constance was a kidnapper. She wasn't alone. Amy also snatched babies from the arms of their mothers. Neither Constance nor Amy had ever had a baby of their own survive more than a week. With high rank and what must have been a pathological desire for a baby, they started kidnapping the babies of lower-ranking females. They groomed the kidnapped babies, allowed them to nurse, but they never had milk and every kidnapping ended tragically. Within three days each kidnapped baby had died. We knew of seven cases where natural mothers had watched their babies die in the arms of one of these two baboons. It was heartbreaking, and a clear sign that in their struggle to survive in the desert, the desert was winning, causing the troop to self-destruct. These devastating facts made this horrible behavior important to Nad's study and our embryonic film project.

Even so, if Constance was the kidnapper, we packed up our cameras and left the riverbed. As long as we were around, Constance would remain on her guard and the natural mother would never have a chance of reclaiming her baby. Sadly, it didn't seem to matter. The mothers might reach out and touch their infants, but they never held them while they were alive again. We would disappear for days, but always return to find drag marks in the sand, wretched signs of death.

As if on cue, Constance looked up at us and barked, a warning call. "I wish she'd shut up."

The others looked up, saw us, and then ignored Constance. After two years the baboons accepted me completely, and so, despite Constance, they accepted anyone who was with me, including Sara.

"Gin, what a gift. Thank you." Sara knew through my letters that we hadn't just strolled up the riverbed one day, shaken hands, and made friends with the baboons. It had taken four long months of hard work and frustration. Slowly, with our presence alone, giving them nothing as a bribe, we waited for them to accept us. At first they didn't even accept our Land Rover, scurrying over the canyon walls at the sound of the engine. We spent days in the river without ever seeing them, just following their tracks in the sand, searching for clues that would provide some insight into their lives. Finally they accepted the car, but only if we stayed inside it. After a few days Nad tentatively got out of the Land Rover and began walking behind them. At first he had to stay at least twenty-five feet away or they would flee. Then the gap became fifteen feet. A few days later, another milestone, Nad could get to within ten feet of the baboons.

Then one day Cleo, the sweetest little girl baboon, turned and walked toward us. Her mother, Bo, barked, the others screamed, but Cleo just kept walking. With a twinkle in her eye, she circled the Land Rover where I was sitting and ran back past Nad to her family. How brave! And how very lucky for us that the next day Cleo's mates, Smudge and Pandora, followed her to greet us. With Cleo's acceptance, I could now get out of the sweltering-hot Land Rover, too, and within two weeks we were walking with the troop. Without the inquisitive nature of the young baboons, I doubt this ever would have happened. Emboldened, they broke down other barriers. Pandora flirted wildly with Nad. Using his slender, thickly padded fingers, Bamuthi groomed my hair. Smudge pulled thorns out of our sandals, and then Cleo crossed another critical boundary of understanding and survival.

One afternoon after we'd been with the baboons for about a year, we were resting on a cliff with the troop. Slowly, as the day cooled, the baboons climbed down from the solid shade of the canyon to start their search for food in the riverbed. One by one, they walked by us. Cleo scurried down the canyon past me, but when she reached the bottom of the cliff she froze directly in front of Nad. She looked down at his feet, then up into his eyes, and barked. To make sure he got the message before she scampered away, she looked down, up, and barked again. We knew the call, a bark rarely used and only when a baboon had seen a dangerous snake.

Nad got up slowly, took two long strides, and put five feet between himself and the black spitting cobra hidden in the rocks below where he was sitting. Cleo, sweet girl. The fact that she trusted us to understand her language still amazes me. No wonder she remained my favorite baboon. Without her so many wonderful moments, flashes of insight and discoveries about the troop and ourselves, would never have been possible. We would never have known their story, nor would we have been able to share it with friends.

"I can hardly believe it. They are real," whispered Sara, her eyes riveted to the action in the trees.

"Look behind you." Sara turned, moving slowly so as not to startle the baboons. Standing just three feet away from her and gazing up in awe was Smudge.

"Looks like you have an admirer."

As delighted as she was, a look of sadness swept over her face.

"If only it were my husband." Then the truth finally spilled out.

"Gin, the harder I try, the worse it seems. During the week my life is upside down: when I come home, he's heading out. On weekends I switch my hours completely to spend time with him—like if I pretend everything is normal, it will be, right? But it isn't. I think it's me. I'm not right, at least not right for him."

"Why didn't you tell me?" I asked, thinking, *Why wasn't I there?* Isn't that what friends are for—to be there when you need them, when you are in crisis? Friends don't disappear into a remote desert thousands of miles away when they are needed most. Since my circle of friends has always been small and extremely tight, I usually have a strong sense of when I'm needed. I don't have to be told. Why this time, of all times, did my instincts fail me, and, worse, let Sara down?

"I couldn't. I suppose I thought it would make the problems too real.

Every time I thought about writing, I convinced myself that by the time you got the letter everything would be fine, so why worry you. I talked to Linda, and she thought a vacation might help, but if anything I think it's just made me see the fault lines more clearly."

Thank God Sara had Linda, a friend I didn't know but loved just the same for being there. Though I wished I'd been close enough for Sara to reach, the fact that she confided in me made me feel part of a greater circle of friends who would bind together to protect Sara no matter what.

Up until two days before, I'd thought Sara had the perfect marriage— strong, supportive, and equal. On paper, it looked like it should work: both of them were smart, talented, ambitious, and in love enough to say "I do." I'd never been married, but I'd learned a lot from those years when I'd polished someone else's trophies.

"You know, if I learned one thing from Kevin, it's that the scales often favor the partner who cares the least. I felt like the more I tried to reach him, the further he pulled away. In the end, he walked away with his dignity while I tipped right over and landed flat on my face."

"You're suggesting perhaps I shouldn't try so hard?"

"Maybe, but I also know that's a lot easier said than done. And I really do believe it will be okay." The words sounded trite, yet I believed them. Relationships naturally ebb and flow, love changes, but Sara and CD had made a commitment, one they both took seriously. And just as Sara had decided not to write to me, believing that things would improve, I decided not to say anything more. When their relationship healed, I didn't want our friendship wounded by anything I might have said. I pulled her close and started walking. "Come on, let's get back to camp."

On their last night with us, we returned to the research station. Searching through half-empty cupboards, Sara and I scrounged up the ingredients to make an orange poppy seed cake. That evening we lit candles and sang "Happy Birthday" to CD. I looked at them together, against the black emptiness of the desert, an all-too-fitting backdrop for this stage in their relationship.

The next morning, as they drove away, Nad asked me, "Why can't they just be happy?"

"They will be. Sometimes getting there is just plain hard."

"It doesn't have to be."

"You're right, but don't forget, not everyone was lucky enough to grow up in a cave."

"A sad truth."

We laughed at our inside joke, which reflected Nad's ability to see life on a scale most of us could never imagine. As a child, he'd spent weekends and holidays helping his father, Bob Brain, excavate early human and animal remains at Swartkrans Cave in South Africa. Digging down into the earth and back into time, they'd uncovered secrets from the past, discovering clues as to when man mastered fire, and who retreated to the safety of the cave, the hunter or the hunted. For Nad, two million years ago was like yesterday, and today would survive as a blink of the geological eye. Our lives were short, fleeting, and, in the scheme of things, not that important, so lighten up, have some fun, don't take it all so seriously.

Nad took my hand, saying, "Maybe on their next trip we'll go to the caves."

"I'd love that, but right now I just want to get back to the baboons."

8

SARA (1992)

SOMETIMES WHEN YOU least expect it a dream comes truc. What a cotton-candy phrase. But what no one tells you is that the dream comes with a contract, one you don't remember signing, full of "whereas's" and "in return said party will refrain from's" and other snaky phrases and ambiguous language you only notice when you can't remember why the dream was so important anyway. Or when it's been superseded by the next dream, or the one after that. When you've learned that a dream, like a home renovation, costs 50 percent more than the original estimate and that you never pay in cash.

It was Columbus Day, 1992, and the morning after the first round of presidential debates between Republican President George H. W. Bush, Democrat Bill Clinton, and a folksy billionaire from Texas who'd thrown everyone for a loop. Back then, the freckled face looking back at me in the mirror looked alert and fresh even in fluorescent lighting—even at 4:46 A.M.—a perk of being barely in my thirties. I did a quick time conversion: it was nearly noon in Namibia, and Ginger and Nad would be taking a break from shooting, sitting on those rugged, snake-infested cliffs watching the baboons. Not that Gin would know the exact time. As I'd discovered, in the African bush a day wasn't measured in hours, but in ancient segments: daybreak, sunrise, morning, noon, afternoon. Then came the golden hour— that fleeting wash of honeyed light so crucial for photography—followed by sunset, twilight, night. Minutes were necessary foot soldiers creeping from now to then, but invisible as molecules.

I looked back at the clock. Just five months after visiting Ginger in Namibia, I was about as far from her world as it was possible to be. And not just by a distance of more than six thousand miles. While Gin lived and toiled under the searing sun today, I sat in a small windowless room in Rockefeller Plaza. While she wore a sarong to work, I was decked out in a red dress, hose, and heels. While she never wore makeup, someone was applying mine. And while she didn't even have a tent, much less a bathroom, I was having my hair blow-dried even as I typed away on a computer. Ginger had become the queen of do-it-yourself, while suddenly I was the one pampered like a duchess.

But there was one thing we shared. We'd both discovered something we loved. And while Ginger had found her calling in a remote desert, I'd found mine in a skyscraper so large it had its own zip code. After months of feeling anguished and uncertain about my marriage, work had come to the rescue, and I'd discovered with a start that I was happy. But what a milquetoast word for such a fierce, untamed emotion. I hadn't known happiness in so long I was wary of its appetite. What did you have to feed this beast? Your firstborn? All I knew was that I would pay almost any price to hold on to this astonishing, unfamiliar sense of elation, to prevent it from loping out of my life as unexpectedly as it had arrived.

"There!" A voice broke my trance. Anna Febres, the hairdresser, fired a last salvo of hairspray, admired her handiwork. "Girl, were we ready to get our hands on you! No offense, Sara, but you oughta fire whoever does your hair and makeup in Charlotte."

"She's right," offered Bobbie Armstrong, the makeup artist. "That blush—"

I cleared my throat. "Actually . . . I do my own."

"So that explains it!" Anna marveled. "Well, this is the network, *chiquita,* and you gotta look good to sit on the sofa with Katie. And you'll meet Stone Phillips, too. He's filling for our man Bryant."

My stomach flop-flipped. Margaret Larsen was on vacation, and there I was, in New York, about to serve as her replacement on the *Today* show news desk.

Jeff Zucker poked his head around the door. In three-inch pumps I could almost look him in the eye, but the *Today* show's executive producer had a swagger that matched his keen gaze and carnivorous grin. His competitive appetite was already legendary and it was easy to see why he dated a string of beautiful women. "How ya doing, Jamesey? They treatin' you okay?"

"It's unbelievable!"

"Ah, come on. It's just like *Nightside,* right? Except for the millions of people watching. Hey, don't tense up. I watched you on the overnight, you can handle it. That's why you're here now." He sidled over, massaged my shoulders like a prizefighter's coach, gave me a smack on the back, and headed back out the door. He might call me Jamesey, but his nickname was "Doogie Howser TV"—a reference to the hit TV show about a doctor who was just a kid. Zucker was just twenty-six—the youngest EP ever to run a morning news show—and *Today* was number one. Bryant Gumbel and Katie Couric, two of the best anchors in the industry, not only worked with Zucker but respected his judgment. If he believed in me, perhaps I could make it in this town after all.

Even though the broadcast didn't start for another fifteen minutes—an eternity in television—the "on air" light was already flashing as I pushed through the scene dock and waded through the arctic studio air toward the news desk. I wanted to have time to meet the crew, get hooked up. I ran into a blizzard of introductions and instructions.

"Hi, Sara, I'm Jimmy. Can you drop this IFB cable down your dress?"

"Sara, I'm Mark, I'll be the floor director. Let's go over the cues for a countdown to tape, okay?" The smiling dark-haired man promptly bent one arm at the elbow and made a fist. "Here's the signal for thirty seconds"—he then swished his arms into a cross in front of his chest, hands fisted—"this is fifteen"—then, holding both hands up, fingers extended, began folding his fingers down one by one—"the standard count from ten down to one, and of course the hard wrap. Got it? Same as *Nightside?*"

"What do you take to drink?" I turned my head as someone else said, "I'm Lou."

"Sara, can you just look straight ahead so I can set the camera? I'm Ropes, by the way."

Suddenly I jumped as a voice in my ear said, "Sara? It's Alex in audio, can you hear me?"

"Yes, I can, Alex."

"And this is Bucky," another voice drawled. "I'll be directing the show, so ignore everyone but me, right?" Another chuckle.

"Sara, have you decided what you want to drink?" Lou again. Or was it Mark? I was fast losing my composure and trying not to show it.

"I'll have tea, thanks."

"Sara, here's your copy." Thankfully, this time the person speaking was someone I'd already met. Jim Dick was the senior producer in charge of the news cut-ins on the *Today* show. He handed me a sheaf of lead-ins to taped pieces and voice-overs that I'd already read and edited, most of them stories about who'd scored points in the previous night's debate. What a change from the overnight show in Charlotte, where Antonio and I were all but alone in the studio.

Just then Stone sauntered in, gave a friendly wave. "Hi, Sara. Welcome to New York."

A few minutes later, just before airtime, Katie zoomed in, flashed a big smile. "Hey, Sara! I hear you're another Virginia gal! We'll chat later."

I mumbled an attempt at hello. It wasn't just the sheer number of people that overwhelmed me but their competence. How exhilarating to work in this league. It had taken me nine years to get here, but it had been worth every minute. Now if I could just avoid being sent back down to the minors.

"Two minutes to air, folks, two minutes to air," said Mark.

Even though Stone was also a fill-in, he and Katie seemed to chat easily as they drank coffee and read through their scripts. But for me, the faint flutter of butterflies had turned into great swooping owl wings beating against my chest. To be here. To be here with them.

I tried not to think about all the times I'd watched this show from the newsrooms in Tupelo, Richmond, and Charlotte. I tried not to think of all the fill-in anchors I'd critiqued while drinking my morning coffee over the years—too smiley, too stiff, no good at ad-libs, too flippant, or—the worst failing of all—didn't seem to know what they were talking about. But what would people think of me? How impossible it seemed that I would be here, in this chair, about to read the news.

"Hey, Sara." In the now quiet studio this calm, steady voice was audible to no one but me. I looked up, nodded slowly to the camera. "Take it easy, Jamesey, breathe. You're gonna be fine. You can do this. Now just have fun, okay?!" Jeff Zucker made it sound like a requirement and a prediction. I took a deep breath and grinned. And later, when Katie said, "Let's get caught up on the news. And for that we welcome Sara James of the NBC news program *Nightside,*" I didn't bobble my "Thanks, Katie" as I turned to face the camera. "The political heavyweights jumped into the ring in St. Louis last night in the first round of their presidential debate bout. George Bush, Bill Clinton, and Ross Perot failed to land any knockout blows." To my surprise, the nerves settled and I was having fun.

When I got back to my office, the phone started ringing.

"Way to go, Boo-boo!" cheered Lisa in Richmond. "I'm toasting you with my coffee mug."

My sisters Elizabeth and Susan both called, as well as Linda and, of course, my parents, Mom on the kitchen phone, Dad on the extension in his study. "We're very proud of you."

The next day CD accompanied me to the set, snapped a few photos, shook a few hands. His smile was back. He had some leads regarding producer positions in New York. Things were looking up.

Nevertheless, I still had a year left on my contract with *Nightside* in Charlotte. While this fill-in opportunity certainly seemed like an unofficial audition, the week wasn't over yet. No one had said anything about what might happen next. I closed my eyes and said a little prayer. Please, please let me finally get to the network—in New York.

9

GINGER (1992)

Good morning, sweet Cleo." The sun was just on the horizon, but already Cleo was down from her sleeping cliff, ready to start the day. I watched her run off and thought about Sara, living in the city that never sleeps. Sinatra was right. If she could make it there, she could make it anywhere, and finally she was getting her chance. I pictured the two of us diving off a bustling sidewalk into a corner café to celebrate this huge move in her career, and to toast her marriage also being on the same positive track. The picture faded as I climbed out of my sleeping bag and filled the silence with the hissing of the gas cooker. As the water boiled, I acknowledged that I still worried about Sara, a divine right of friendship, but I was sure that in time she would strike the right balance between working at the network and making her relationship work.

Meantime, I was also finally starting to figure my life out. I was dirt-poor, dirty, and deliriously happy. Maybe a bit crazy, too. Few people I knew would willingly live out of the back of a Land Rover, far from civilization, in a place of such extremes. Here, the east winds blew hot enough and strong enough to kill you, hyenas were a menace, and the threat of contracting tick bite fever clung with the little creatures to every blade of grass. Fewer people still would do this for free at the age of thirty-one, when even the formerly footloose often succumb to words like "pay raise," "health care plan," "401(k)'s," and "stock options." Crazy, maybe, but I loved it, loved the baboons and the fact that they accepted me, and I loved being behind the camera, finally making my own film.

The Bartletts, Julie's parents and Sara's friends, had loaned us a 16 mm camera, a few lenses, and a slim, yet costly amount of film stock. They trusted us to figure out the rest. Their generosity was overwhelming, and knowing the financial risk they were taking, it was also daunting. When our first set of exposed film came back for viewing, I laughed only to keep from crying. Nad turned to me and said caustically, "Interesting. Where'd you find a headless warthog?" My head would be the next to go if my camerawork didn't improve quickly.

When Sara had visited, she'd watched the rushes and offered help, urging me to follow my instincts, to get in close for those intimate, emotional shots that would tell the story. Taking direction from anyone, even a friend, had never been my strong point, and I felt myself becoming defensive. Sara's role was in front of the camera. How could she possibly appreciate how difficult it was to lug equipment up and down sand dunes while chasing four-legged creatures? Did she understand that when sweat pours down your forehead, it's hard to maintain focus? Couldn't she sense my fear that my talents were as limited as our film stock? But when I quieted that negative voice, I knew she was right. I was also sure that she understood my fears and knew the only way I'd overcome them was by making a good film. If I just shut up, I could learn from her experience and make the story better. After all, the story was all we had to hold on to.

Baby baboons were dying, females were kidnapping other infants, and males, with no offspring to protect, had begun fighting to the death. The baboons were primates like us, yet they were somehow surviving weeks, even months without drinking water. But that struggle was taking a psychic toll on their tiny society. Life in the riverbed was one big soap opera, but tragically, it was real. Survival of the fittest in a place that was unfit to live in. I had chosen this life, once again isolated, once again with one man for company, and this troop of desperate souls had chosen me. Hard as it was, this was exactly where I wanted to be, living as part of a troop.

In New York, acceptance was based on who you knew, what you looked like, or what you could do for someone else. In the Kuiseb, the baboons' acceptance was honest. It felt ancient, natural and pure, and it gave me what

no man had ever given me. It made me feel worthy. And it came as an incredible surprise to know that Nad accepted me in the same way.

During Sara's visit to the desert, the two of us had coasted down a steep
dune, coming to a soft stop at the bottom. Out of breath and lying in the
sand, she'd asked, "So what about you and Nad. What's happening?" After
spending just a few days with us, she knew he was funny, kind, and smart.
What she didn't know was that he washed my hair with precious water,
held the flashlight for me at night so that I wouldn't step on scorpions when
I needed to pee, or that he was as demanding of me as he was of himself.
"We're friends. Good friends," I told her, hoping that if that's how I labeled
our relationship, she wouldn't ask any more questions that I didn't know
how to answer. "Friend" wasn't exactly the right word, but I wasn't sure
what was.

Growing up in a house full of women, I didn't understand men and
was doubtful that a strictly platonic friendship with a man was possible. My
girlfriends would tell me a thousand times over, "Yes, I have tons of male
friends," but that hadn't been my experience and maybe that's why I shied
away from making friends with men, creating a cycle that became my loss.

That hadn't been true with Nad. We became friends quickly, and I'd
resolved to keep it that way. Each night we rested our heads on pillows
placed against different tires, hoping this setup would keep us safe from
hyenas, jackals, and each other. Then one night, through the thick mist of
sleep, I'd heard Nad talking.

"Stop it. Come on. Now look what you've done. I told you guys to get
lost."

I lifted my head and saw him standing up pointing to the remains of a
chewed indicator light on the Land Rover. Two hyenas with round bellies
and big brown eyes stood in front of him. Nad had a whip in his hand and
was wearing a tiny pair of red underpants. I tried hard not to laugh.

"What is it?"

"Nothing, don't worry. Go back to sleep."

Not only did I feel safe, I felt full of affection. The next night I asked if
I could rest my pillow by his tire. My resolve had lasted about a month. Nad

might have been the only man within an hour's drive, but it was more than that. He made me laugh, he made me think, he made me forget some of the pains of the past, and like a good friend, he also made me feel free to be myself.

It was a relationship that was easy and relaxed and Nad wasn't asking for a definition. At night, over hot beer, we laughed about SP's exploits during the one week of each month when all the males wanted her, when she went from being the lowest-ranking baboon to the baboon with the most power, the power to conceive a baby. We bet on who would become the new alpha male and then we would lie quietly, waiting for a shooting star to blaze across the sky before falling asleep. By 1992, nearly three years into Nad's study, our relationship, the research, and the filming were going well. And then, in the pursuit of science, we nearly ruined it all.

Nad's doctoral research wouldn't be complete unless he could answer a fundamental physiological question: How could these baboons survive in the desert without drinking water when every medical fact agreed that they should be frying inside? We'd collected a lot of information. The dry slog of documenting what they ate, when they ate it, how much moisture it contained, when they rested, how long they rested, data bits and bites that added pieces to a complex puzzle of survival. Now, to understand how the baboons regulated their body temperature, Nad needed to dart several with a sedative and then surgically insert a temperature-sensitive telemeter. The telemeter would send out core body temperature readings during the day and Nad could compare these with what was happening when they were drinking as opposed to when they weren't; or when they were running as opposed to standing still; more data to paint a richer picture.

Forktail was to be the first. Like me, he was low-ranking and accepted it, which meant that removing him for the surgery, and to sleep off the effects of the drug, wouldn't change the dynamics in the troop. Turned out, it changed everything.

For three weeks Nad shadowed Forktail with a long steel blowpipe. Finally his opportunity came. I heard the whack of the dart hitting skin, followed immediately by Forktail screaming. Baring his teeth in submission, the dart dangling from his backside, he ran past me, straight toward the safety of the sleeping cliffs. The other baboons converged in the middle of the riverbed and I ran to meet Nad there.

Together we watched in silence as Forktail lay down alone on a sheer cliff and fell asleep. We gathered Nad's surgical instruments and the telemeter, but before we could reach Forktail, another baboon got to him— Gable, a male who had known Forktail his entire life. He stood over his sleeping troopmate, his mantle hairs on edge, and then pushed Forktail, just like a rock, over the edge of the canyon. We heard Forktail's skull crack when he hit the ground.

"No!" I screamed. Mine wasn't the only voice echoing off the canyon walls. Gable barked, those hideous *wahoo-wahoo* barks, as if boasting. Then there was silence as every female baboon in the troop ran to Forktail. They surrounded him, mumbling soft sounds of reassurance when he moaned. Each of them had a special relationship with him. He protected them; had mated with some of them, had fathered others. Yet not a single baboon touched him. Then, one by one, they moved away.

"We can't let him die alone," I whispered, remembering the hyenas that had kept us awake the night before.

"That won't happen." When we reached the base of the canyon, Nad gently touched Forktail's head. He felt the bones shift. His skull was shattered. I ran my fingers through his coarse hair while Nad rubbed Forktail's leg, trying to raise a vein, and then he shot an overdose of morphine into his system to ease the pain, permanently. It was all he could do. The moaning stopped. Forktail was dead.

Nad was shell-shocked. He'd planned this operation for months, trying to eliminate every potential threat, every obstacle, anything that could put a baboon in danger. We never imagined that the canyon itself would get in the way.

"That's what you get when you trust humans," Nad said, choking on his words. But it wasn't "humans" they trusted, they trusted us. Just us. When Forktail died, Nad and I held each other for a long time, our tears mixing with our guilt. Now, as much as my heart ached, and as much I feared it would complicate things, I knew I loved this man.

It was after dark when we packed up and headed for Swakopmund. This time there would be no dinner out, no celebratory phone calls home. We sat on hard twin beds in a tiny pension and debated whether we should continue our work with the baboons. We blamed ourselves for this ultimate betrayal of trust, for killing Forktail. We cried, we had a fitful, sleepless night, and then we got ready for the long drive back to the desert.

When we reached the research station, there was a package for us from Sara. Inside was a selection of delicacies—coffee, pistachios, chocolate—and a note, signed "With love," from Sara and her husband. I took this as a sign that they were pulling their marriage together. If they could do that, then surely Nad and I would be able to pull ourselves together and go back to work. The next day we drove slowly back upriver to where the next drama was unfolding.

10

SARA (1992–1993)

OUT ON THE rink, skaters twirled, silent as snowflakes, and I smiled as I threaded through knots of tourists gawking at the signature glittery giant spruce and pushed through the revolving door into Rockefeller Plaza. If only there were a white Christmas, everything would be perfect, because as 1992 drew to a close it seemed like opportunities were piled like presents under the tree.

After a lunch with NBC News vice president Elena Nachmanoff at the Rainbow Room on the sixty-fifth floor of Rockefeller Plaza—during which I was so nervous I could barely touch my salmon and asparagus with hollandaise, much less enjoy the view—Elena asked with a smile, "How would you like to move to New York to be an NBC News correspondent?" I stared at her just to make sure I was really hearing these words, words I'd dreamed of hearing for more than a decade. I wanted to jump up and down, to scream so loudly they'd hear me all the way back in Richmond. But instead I blurted out, "I would *love* to!"

Two months later it was still so fresh and new, I was experimenting with how to record the tagline at the end of every *Nightly News* spot, "Sara James, NBC News, New York." Emphasize the first syllable of Sara? Hit "NBC News" harder? Regardless, I liked the sound of what felt like a new last name, and I got a charge each time I heard Bryant and Katie introduce me on the *Today* show. I enjoyed Bryant's dry wit and easy banter. Meantime, over a cup of coffee with Katie, I learned we had more in common than both being Virginians and graduating from UVA. In the way that friendships can intersect and lead one to the next, I discovered that Katie's husband, Jay Monahan, was old friends with Lewis Powell, the fiancé of my dear friend and Richmond roommate, Lisa. Katie soon became a friend, offering savvy tips on *Today* and life at the network.

As much as I was reveling in my life in New York, my network dream was to go overseas. But so far my highest-profile *Nightly News* story had been to cover the Macy's Thanksgiving Day Parade. Which explained why I was standing outside the door marked "Foreign Editor." Finally I knocked.

"Mr. Miller?"

The tall, distinguished gray-haired man looked up over his copy of the *New York Times*.

"Mmm?"

"I'm Sara James." He looked vaguely perplexed, suggesting more biographical detail might be in order. "The new correspondent in New York. Look, I know you don't know me well but I wanted to let you know that I've been following the famine in Somalia and the U.S. humanitarian mission."

His eyebrows rose a fraction.

"I know I'm not technically a foreign correspondent and that I'm new, but I also know that it's nearly Christmas. So if you have correspondents who want to come home for the holidays and you need replacements, I would love to go." There. It was done. I'd raised my hand.

Which apparently had gotten me exactly nowhere. David Miller nodded, mumbled something noncommittal, and I backed out of the door. He couldn't fire me for volunteering, could he?

The next day a desk assistant tracked me down. "Sara? Have you had your shots?"

"I beg your pardon?"

"Hepatitis B, yellow fever, tetanus. They can do them upstairs on seven in medical. Oh, and you'll need malaria tablets." Who ever heard of malaria in New York? My bewilderment was obvious.

"Didn't they tell you? You're going to Somalia. And you'll need a tent and sleeping bag. I hear conditions are pretty basic. You leave tomorrow."

I knew CD, a veteran of trouble spots, would be pleased for me, but I dreaded calling Dad and especially Mom. I kept it breezy and brief, but this time Mom almost seemed resigned to my call and tried to keep her worry on a short leash. "Will you be home for Christmas? Beth and John will be here, and Susan, too."

I hesitated, suddenly picturing the tree in the corner opposite Mom's Steinway, and my throat tightened. "I don't think so, Mom. I'll try to call."

"Well, be careful," she said. And Dad added, "I'm sure you'll come back with lots of stories in addition to the ones we see on the air."

I caught an American Airlines overnight flight to London, adjusting the overhead light so as not to disturb my snoring seat companion as I read article after article about the famine. Rubbing my eyes as we landed in Heathrow, I changed planes for Nairobi. While this was my second trip to Africa in less than a year, Somalia was nothing like Namibia. Ginger had introduced me to a vivid land of improbable animals and extraordinary people. Though beautiful, her world could be dangerous—hyenas, spitting cobras, puff adders, malaria—but those dangers were from the natural world. This was another Africa entirely, in which poverty and weapons had turned kind people into strangers capable of doing despicable things to one another and themselves.

This feudal country perched on the Horn of Africa, so vital to American interests during the Cold War, had suddenly become as obsolete as Checkpoint Charlie. But when the big boys pulled up stakes they'd left plenty of guns behind, which the locals were using to settle ancient and recent grudges. The U.S.-backed dictator had been overthrown just a year before, after which rival warlords Ali Mahdi and Mohamed Farrah Aidid turned their weapons on one other. The fierce fighting disrupted planting, which led to a massive famine and the starvation of hundreds of thousands of people. Their wretched plight had brought in the international relief agencies, but virtually all of the food shipments had been hijacked and immediately sold for more weapons. The humanitarian disaster had grown so immense that President George H. W. Bush had just deployed 28,000 U.S. troops in what was being called Operation Restore Hope, an effort to ensure that food got to the starving. Though harrowing, it was just the kind of assignment I'd dreamed of.

I boarded a charter in Nairobi for the final leg of my journey. After a short flight across East African savanna, we landed in Mogadishu, where an unsmiling Somali with a sign that said "James" met me. I wasn't complaining about the welcome. Just a few days before, NBC anchorman Tom Brokaw and his team had landed on a remote tarmac only to be nabbed by a band of brigands. They'd managed to persuade the gunmen to take them to the police station, where Tom ultimately managed to extricate them using his patented blend of wit and charm.

I threw my backpack in the car and tried not to look conspicuous. Since credit cards were worthless in Somalia, I was carrying more cash than I ever had in my life—ten thousand dollars in small bills. I'd padded every curve I had, added a few nature hadn't given me, and draped myself in an enormous khaki shirt and loose slacks. It was 100 degrees outside and I looked like the Michelin Man.

Mogadishu was like some wretched postscript to civilization. The landscape had been bled of color, lacerated and cratered by bombs and bullets, a vast expanse of cascading rubble pierced by the occasional stump of a building, a city like a row of broken teeth. As we bounced over the mortared road, a truckload of U.S. soldiers rattled by, the look in their eyes suspicious. A year before the events that inspired the book and movie *Black Hawk Down,* I suspect they'd already seen enough to fear this humanitarian mission could turn into a suicide mission. But I wasn't nearly that smart. I was young, ambitious, and anxious to prove myself. I was too concerned about whether I would get on the air to worry about what might happen to me on the ground.

Indeed, when I arrived at what was known as the Sahafi Hotel, headquarters for NBC and several other news organizations, I had to pick my way across a lobby littered with exhausted reporters catnapping on the cement floor. Living conditions were austere, but it wasn't the squalor that I noticed. Suddenly faces that I knew only from TV were all around me. Not only did I see Brokaw, sporting an NBC News baseball cap and an easy grin, but I spied Martin Fletcher from Tel Aviv chatting with Jim Maceda from Moscow, who'd obviously been here a while, since his sunburn was peeling. And that must be Keith Miller, from London. While I

felt a sudden flush of happiness to find myself there, now part of the reporting team I'd admired from afar for so long, I was also worried. With the
first string in town, how would a cub like me get assigned a story? *Nightly
News* was a thirty-minute broadcast—more like twenty-two minutes of actual news after anchor lead-ins, teases, and commercials—and there were
other stories besides Somalia.

As I continued to scan the room anxiously, I noticed a tall dark-haired
guy wearing glasses and an intelligent expression. Clearly a producer. Better yet, he looked about my age. I introduced myself and learned his name
was Justin Balding and he was from London. He was happy to offer advice
over a late lunch of canned tuna and beer. "The water here is full of para-
sites, so close your eyes when you take a shower. That's if you get one. The
water's only on for fifteen minutes a day and we never know which fifteen.
And eat only fruit you peel yourself, like bananas or oranges. Otherwise
stick to tinned." Then Justin proceeded to fill me in on the identities of
several people I didn't recognize, including one man with a curious nickname, "the Wanker."

"What's a wanker?" I asked.

Justin gave me a dubious look, and one corner of his mouth tightened as
if he were holding back a grin. "Why don't you ask him? But see the gray-
haired chap next to him? That's London photographer Ken Ludlow—we
all just call him 'Father'—and his soundman, John Hall. They're joining a
convoy that's leaving tomorrow morning for the town of Baidoa. Maybe
you can team up with them."

Fortunately, arranging that proved easier than I'd imagined. The har-
ried London bureau chief saddled with the thankless job of deciding who
stayed in Moga and who headed deeper into the country clearly had more
important things to worry about and nodded yes. I was free to spend the
rest of the evening enjoying myself, reveling in the casual camaraderie of
that traveling fraternity, not to mention the attention that comes with being
new, young, and female in a predominantly male environment. What's
more, these men seemed universally good-looking and witty, and their stories, even if embellished, were genuine war stories. I kept mum about my
experiences in Saudi Arabia and especially Nicaragua, not quite believing

that naïve young girl had been me. Instead I settled back to listen to the lighthearted banter perfected by those old enough to know better who nevertheless intentionally put themselves in harm's way. I caught a surreptitious look at the ring finger on my left hand and was glad I was married. I could see how it would be all too easy to get into trouble.

The next morning Ken, John, and I grabbed our gear to join the convoy of trucks that would deliver wheat to Baidoa, the town hardest hit by the famine. I suspected the only reason they'd agreed to be saddled with me was that in television, a camera crew and a reporter are each equally worthless without the other. I hoped to convince them they'd made a good decision in joining forces.

"I bet you guys have seen it all," I said.

John pulled up his sleeve to reveal a jagged scar from what looked like a bullet. "Iran-Iraq War. Nearly lost the arm."

"Bugger me, not the war wound already, John, we've got hours yet." Ken grinned, then took a second look at the gunmen by the trucks and turned serious. "Besides, we've got our own guards this go-round, right?" He gestured toward the sullen, red-eyed Somalis who'd been hired to accompany us, since Baidoa was anything but secure. One gave a malevolent look, then shifted his aging AK-47 from one arm to the other so that it appeared to be aimed directly at us, and spat.

"Could you kindly point that thing over there?" John suggested, then turned to me. "They're chewing *qat,* Sara, a local drug, and they're stoned. Chances are our greatest danger here is getting shot in the back when we hit a bump." I felt alarm flow like a quick, sharp poison to prick my fingertips. Instinctively my toes curled in their dusty boots, another reflex when I'm nervous. But fear is a funny thing. We humans are pack animals, and if the collective herd isn't overly alarmed, individual anxiety quickly diminishes. Clearly Ken and John were a seasoned crew who'd survived far worse. I shook off the feeling and started to climb into the nearest jeep. Suddenly the soundman yanked my arm, shaking his head. "Not that one, love, it's third in line," said John, steering me toward another vehicle in the caravan.

"You're joking, right? Are you superstitious or something?"

His look told me this was an even more serious error than not knowing what a wanker was, if such a thing was possible. "We're traveling to Baidoa ahead of the marines, remember, so no one's cleared the road. You never want to be first in a convoy, Sara, in case of land mines."

"But that wasn't the first truck, it was—"

"And you don't want to be third since an enemy spots the first vehicle, aims at the second, and then—" He made a motion as if firing off a round. I glanced quickly at Ken to see if this was some sort of trick designed to haze a rookie, but he concurred with a curt nod. I threw my backpack on the second truck. On such a clear, sunny day it was impossible to imagine being blown to smithereens.

If you talk to soldiers or the journalists who cover them, chances are they'll tell you that if they die in combat, so be it. Such a death can be heroic, noble. But there are far too many ways to die in war zones that are pointless and even stupid. A miscalculation, being in the wrong place at the wrong time, a snafu. No one wants to die like that. And the worst of it is, you rarely see those situations coming.

A few hours later, as we were waved to a halt at a checkpoint, I felt my toes curl again. We'd been stopped by a no-name ragtag gang, well armed, poorly disciplined, and young. A bad combination. One soldier casually aimed his rocket-propelled grenade launcher at us, leering. I stared at his red vacant eyes and found myself wondering how many people he had killed. And then I wondered if he liked it. What did he think of the carnage, the sound of people screaming? Did he get a jolt, a buzz, from the blast of a weapon? Did it make him feel superior? He seemed ominously bored, spoiling for something, and behind us our paid guards tapped their weapons, a sort of return growl, although we were no match for this much muscle. But the first truck in our convoy had already made it through, so this should be simple.

Just below us the driver carried on a rapid conversation with the leader of this gang. John and Ken made a point of looking away from the scene, a template of studied calm I found difficult to mirror. How many times had they been in a similar spot? I was suddenly keenly aware of my collar, how it dug into my neck, how the sweat beads which daisy-chained along my hairline had begun to drip like a leaky faucet, how I wanted to wipe them away but didn't want to lift my hand. Would one hand lifted at the wrong time alter this equation? That thought was enough to make me close my eyes, only to open them again immediately. I focused on trying to make myself invisible. A heat wraith. A mirage. A nonentity. Down below us the brief conversation had apparently reached a successful conclusion because the driver engaged the clutch and we lurched forward. But the soldier with the RPG didn't seem to agree and kept his weapon trained on us. Finally, with a lingering look of loathing, he lowered it, his expression indicating he'd have liked to, but we weren't really worth the trouble.

As the truck picked up speed, the breeze on my damp neck made me shiver involuntarily. Or perhaps what made me shiver was that toy soldier. Because the soldier armed with an RPG couldn't have been more than ten years old. When children are soldiers, it's far too easy for adults to die. And as I could already tell, it was far too easy to die in Somalia.

BAIDOA HAD NO functioning hotel, but my new team was accommodating. "This will do," said Ken, claiming a small roofless hut where the three of us laid out our sleeping bags side by side. "We'll just tell everyone back in New York that you slept with both of us," he added mischievously.

"Great—two days in Somalia and already my reputation is ruined." I laughed.

Night had fallen, bringing with it a limp, shallow breeze. I could glimpse the stars overhead through the mosquito netting we'd strung over us. Before I knew it, it was morning and I woke to the noisy rattle of the generator. Time to get going.

It was in Baidoa that I saw the face of famine and it was a dreadful sight, especially since this disaster wasn't the result of poor rains or failed crops but the pox of war. Their faces still return in my dreams, impossibly thin men and women waiting for hours under a relentless sun. Sometimes the hungry would fall where they stood in line. I remember how the smell of gruel slopped into those bowls made me queasy, how the sight of a grown man desperately gnawing a child's biscuit made it nearly impossible to eat.

But hardest to witness were the little boys and girls, their bodies like a child's stick drawing, all angles and lines, topped by terrible skulls with enormous eyes and chapped, bleeding lips. And then there were the babies, tiny bloated souls too famished to cry. As we made our way through the feeding camp, I saw one infant who clearly hadn't made it, although his mother clutched him, refusing to give up hope. When the baby I assumed was dead gave a plaintive mew, I jumped.

The aid workers at a feeding center run by Irish Concern were exhausted and beleaguered. One strapping man choked back tears as he pulled a torn sheet over a woman he'd just fed but who had died anyway. And as if hunger weren't enough, the doctors and nurses also knew to expect typhoid, TB, and cholera, the coven famine brings in its wake. And yet as I stood there under that scorching sun, overwhelmed by the scope and scale of a catastrophe unlike any I had ever witnessed, I suddenly knew that as dangerous as Somalia might be and as devastating as this was to witness, I was glad I had come. This was an assignment worth the risk. Naïve as it might sound, I believed that if perhaps those at home saw the extent of the starvation, the misery might be brought to an end.

Ken tugged on my arm, derailing the train of my thoughts. "Make sure you get a doctor for Bryant and Katie," he advised.

I was mystified. "What do you mean, get them a doctor?"

"He means a live guest," John interpreted.

"You need to think like a producer, since we don't have one," Ken continued. "The show will want someone here in the field that the hosts can interview in a cross-talk." It would be one of the many prudent tips Ken and John gave me. I quickly rounded up a doctor and another aid worker, then rang New York on the satellite phone back at our base to set things up.

By then it was afternoon, which meant with the time difference it was nearly time for my own *Today* show live shot. I pulled out a lipstick and brushed my ponytail before clapping on an NBC News baseball cap. Thank God Brokaw had decided to wear a hat, since that meant the rest of us could. As I finished my report and removed my mike, I could hear Jeff Zucker in my ear from New York. "Good job, Jamesey. Keep it up."

I stepped away from the hot lights and instantly bumped into a reporter I didn't know, a young guy with a big smile and a hearty handshake. "I'm David Bloom," he said, "from Miami." It was easy to tell that, like my old friend Linda, he too would soon be at the network. It wasn't so much that he was boyishly handsome, but that he quivered with restless energy, ambition, and charisma, all leavened by a wide, friendly smile which said, *You'll like me. Everybody does.* And of course everybody did. Later that night he beckoned me over, pulling out his wallet. What secret did he wish to share?

"See her?" he said, pressing a photo into my hand. "That's Melanie." His expression was so pleased and proud that for a moment I couldn't speak, could only twist my wedding band. Would my husband speak that way about me? Would I speak that way of him?

"She's beautiful," I replied.

"Isn't she?" he agreed, then gave a wistful sigh. "I can't believe she loves me. I miss her."

Although the night was warm, I wrapped my arms around myself as I rejoined the circle of colleagues, a circle that had suddenly doubled in size with word that the marines would be arriving the next day. How I wished that instead I were joining a far smaller African circle, sitting by a crackling fire with Ginger and Nad. I missed her friendship and steady counsel and had instantly been captivated by Nad's intelligence and self-deprecatory humor. His assessment of humans—just a complicated, confused, and often very foolish animal—also had a way of putting problems in perspective. To think I was there on the same continent and yet wouldn't get to see them. Ginger had sent several letters, but once again I hadn't written back. I'd wanted to, had thought of it many times, but each time I sat down I wasn't quite sure what to say about my marriage. Afraid to write of my fears, in the end I'd written nothing at all.

But then, as I looked around me, my spirits lifted. While I recognized that these gregarious men and women weren't actually friends—not yet, anyway—I felt sure many could be soon. Given the intensity of life on the road, the way everyone worked, ate, even slept side by side, it wouldn't take long. And while some might find such relentless proximity claustrophobic, even incestuous, I loved the roly-poly tangle of it. I'd found a tribe. A tribe that almost felt like a family.

Still, I also knew that I must venture away from the security of this pack if I wanted to discover this place as a reporter, and try to understand it. Which is why I cannot think about Somalia without thinking about a woman called Muslima.

We met her in the center of town on a bright sunny day, one of several dozen people being helped by an aid agency, given sacks of grain to plant in her village. Muslima was young and winsome, even if sorrow threatened to extinguish the laughter from her eyes. She touched the red scarf on her head with a delicate hand. "My widow's mourning," she told us matter-of-factly, explaining that her husband had died in the famine, leaving her to try to raise their little boy on her own. But her responsibilities didn't end there. She also had to care for her brother. And her brother was blind.

In spite of her burdens, on that day Muslima sparkled with energy, spirit, and excitement. The aid agency was paying for Muslima and the others to get a ride back to their village. As her fifty-pound sack was hoisted onto the truck, Muslima's gaze was sharp and proprietary, as if the burlap bag were loaded with emeralds. This is a great opportunity, she explained through a translator, proof that the evil days are at an end, the famine vanquished. She wasn't alone. As we clambered aboard the truck with her small family, virtually everyone was laughing, joking, in a good mood.

Then, less than an hour into the trip, the rickety truck suddenly ground to a halt. It took several confusing minutes to figure out the situation. Finally our translator explained that the drivers insisted they didn't have enough fuel to drive all the way to the village. Although everyone felt certain the drivers had actually sold most of the gas and pocketed the proceeds, what could anyone do now? The villagers were forced off the truck and ordered to walk the final twenty miles home and their precious sacks of grain unceremoniously dumped onto the dirt track. I looked at Muslima. The look of expectation on her pretty face had guttered and blown out. She stood there, abandoned and betrayed, a woman whose plight symbolized that of so many Somalis. In this heartbreaking land, food and fuel weren't the only commodities stolen. Hope had been hijacked, too.

"Muslima, what will you do?" I asked as we scrambled to get a few final shots before the truck lumbered off and we, too, were left stranded.

"What can I do? I must go home," she replied.

"But how?"

In answer she retrieved the heavy sack from the path and carefully balanced it on her head. Her little son carried the family's other possessions—a pot, a blanket, a spoon. Next he picked up a long pole and gently placed one end in his blind uncle's rough hand before picking up the other to lead him. And that was the last we ever saw of them—Muslima, head high, leading her son, who in turn led his uncle, as the family disappeared around a bend in the winding dirt track toward home.

Did they make it? I think so. I hope so. Did they plant their crop, reap their harvest? I am less certain. The story of Muslima was the story of Somalia, the story of so many troubled lands. It was a bleak tale with a beginning and middle but no end.

In late December, John and Ken and I hitched a ride on a Black Hawk back to Mogadishu, feeling incredibly safe in that mighty, forbidding machine. I spent Christmas Eve with the marines. As I listened to them belt out "Hark! the Herald Angels Sing," then scale the treacherous slope of "Silent Night" under a giant spangled sky, I imagined their families back home. I pictured them baking Christmas cookies and wrapping presents, the house scented with pine and cinnamon but the presence of someone absent even more powerful. I felt I could see their reflections in the eyes of those marines as they gathered around their makeshift tree, a pole draped in camouflage netting and festooned with pictures of little girls with ponytails, boys in braces and baseball caps, sweethearts in V-neck sweaters. And it was impossible to watch that scene without thinking of my own home, the tree we hadn't bought, the ornaments we hadn't hung, a marriage which had once blazed bright as a Christmas star now sparking on, then off, like a worn-out strand of lights. I shook myself. How frivolous to worry about whether my relationship would survive when so many here were fighting to survive at all.

* * *

BEFORE I KNEW it, it was New Year's, 1993, and I was back in New York, where I logged on to my computer to discover a string of congratulatory messages, including a warm note from Bryant about the story on Muslima. I let out a deep breath. Not only was my work going well but CD had landed a job as a producer. We celebrated by buying a three-story Victorian in the suburbs, wedding cake white, with a mint green yard for the dog. It seemed both of us had everything we wanted.

And yet. The house echoed with silence even when both of us were home. I got vertigo stepping onto the front sidewalk. I would look up at that looming structure, which suddenly seemed crooked, flawed in some invisible yet fundamental way that no amount of remodeling could fix. And once inside, in the chill front hall, I would pause and brace myself for the plunge through the outer wave of ominous quiet, knowing that I should ask questions, yet that I didn't want to. Perhaps tomorrow he would be the man I remembered instead of a polite, reserved stranger. I told myself I loved him too much to lose him, but of course I had nothing of his worth keeping anymore, and in such willful self-deception, all I was losing was myself.

I'd been assigned to London for a month of bureau duty that summer— an opportunity to fill in for one of the foreign correspondents who was taking a vacation. By then the silence had become a vibrating presence, building like a great cumulus wall, impossible to ignore. And as I packed my suitcase, layering plastic dry-cleaning wrappers between each fold so the clothes wouldn't wrinkle, it felt like something inside me broke and the first drops began to fall. When the alarm went off at 4 A.M., I was shocked to see how horribly puffy and miserable I looked. I doused my face in cold water, pressed a compress against my eyes, and then caked on under-eye concealer because I was filling in on *Today* before leaving that night. After the show, I stopped by my office and heard the phone ringing before I unlocked the door.

"What's wrong with you? You looked awful." My agent was apoplectic.

"I'm a little under the weather. Was it obvious?"

"Obvious!? Get over here. *Now*. And tell me what's going on."

In the spare, cool skyscraper which houses N. S. Bienstock, I made my way back to Stu's office, where I closed the door and gave a Cliff Notes version of my personal life. He listened patiently, and his response was sympathetic but firm.

"Listen, I know this is rough. Marriage is tricky. You'll figure everything out when you come home. Meantime, you have a great job, a job you've wanted your whole life. And if you pull another stunt like you did today, you are going to blow it. There are too many people who want to be network correspondents, who want to fill in on *Today,* who want your life. Now get on that plane, get over to London, and do a hell of a job."

Once again I boarded an American Airlines flight that left JFK at 11 P.M. Once again I left the overhead light on and burrowed into my seat, opening a book and angling my body toward the aisle to liberate myself from any obligation to socialize. Surely there must be something I could do. And surely there would be time enough to do it when I came home.

11

GINGER (1992–1993)

No!" I screamed. "Oh God, please no." Nad hit the brakes and the Land Rover skidded to a stop. I saw the scene in pieces—the tattered pants, the leather belt, the shriveled skin. This couldn't be happening. In Mozambique or Angola, perhaps, and certainly in Somalia, where Sara was covering the war, for those were places of meaningless death. Not here. Sara had volunteered for such assignments. I hadn't. She'd seen death and knew that, almost in spite of herself, she could handle it. I wanted none of it. Yet it seemed that our world here had gone crazy, that the natural cycle of life in the Kuiseb River had spun out of control. There, lying in the sand, was the latest proof. Half of a man.

"What on earth is going on?" I was thirty-two years old, far too young to be losing my mind.

"Oh, Ginger. I don't know." Nad looked at me sadly, afraid that this would push me deeper into the abyss of depression. "You stay here. I'll go have a look."

I slumped down on the seat and sobbed.

In the next two days the pieces fell into place, creating a sad, senseless answer. Though his sun-wrinkled corpse looked as if he were seventy, this man was no older than I. He had tried to walk from his village on the escarpment to the coastal town of Walvis Bay. On the advice of his elders, he'd chosen a path through the Kuiseb River where both shade and water should have been found. He'd found neither.

He had died alone under desperate conditions. An infernal east wind had howled across the desert for a week. It was like opening the doors of a furnace, the air desiccating, the baking heat trapped by the walls of the canyon. The river was dry, yet he was eight miles away from a village with a hand-pump well. Two empty water bottles were found among his few possessions. The rest, including the other half of his body, had been dragged away by hyenas.

Nad and I had been away for four days, but that was long enough for this drama to play out in the riverbed—one man alone against nature. If we had been there, he would have stumbled toward us, we would have run to him with a water bottle and watched as he drained it and another. We would have saved him. But we weren't there, and now his death was on my conscience. There would be others.

After three years of sharing the ephemeral Kuiseb River with the baboons, we knew the cycle of life well. Each year huge storm clouds would build far to the east, in the 14,000-square-kilometer catchment area. The clouds would grow bigger and bigger, consuming each other like cannibals until one mass dominated the sky. These were the lion tamers, cracking lightning, whipping thunder, and stirring emotion. Only after three days of watching them grow and change did we start to listen closely for signs that the rains had forced the river to flow.

The first sound that the fury of these clouds had unleashed a flood was the rattling of seedpods. As the waters swept down from the highlands across the sand, they gathered speed and pieces of fallen debris in their path. Pods, tree trunks, and animal bones were pushed by headwaters in a cacophony of sound. We raced the headwaters out, running back to tease them, then racing ahead again. We swam, we laughed, we celebrated. It was the best game of the year. But this past year the rainy season had been brief, rainfall light, and river flow meager. The river had flowed for just four days. Where pools would normally have recharged seeps, it was dry. The cycle wasn't complete. A man was dead, the baboons were running out of water, and yet it would be months before rain clouds appeared on the horizon, months before there would be another chance of a flood.

Just as their ancestors had done for more than one hundred years, the baboons adapted to life in the desert. They ate moist foods, they rested, they avoided moving too far in the heat of the day, and then they began to die. So far the troop had lost just one member, a tiny baby we had yet to name for fear of becoming too attached to it.

"I can't stand this, Nad, I really can't."

"Can't stand what? What are you talking about?"

"It is too early. There is no water and I am not going to watch them die. Not all of them, not Cleo, I can't do it."

I knew he hated the thought of them suffering, too, but his advice to "just think about something else" didn't work. The fear of watching the baboons waste away consumed me. Day and night, I couldn't escape it. The horror of their dying haunted my dreams.

One night we slept on the roof of the Land Rover to avoid a wave of ticks crawling on the ground below. I tossed as much as I dared and gazed up at the sky for a long time before falling asleep.

Ginger, listen to me. I rolled over, eyes tightly closed, and listened. I knew I was dreaming, but the voice was so honest and reassuring I wanted to believe it was real.

You don't have to worry about us. We will be fine.

The voice belonged to Bo, the smallest, toughest female baboon, mother of Cleo and Smudge. I felt her beside me, touching me gently on the shoulder, saying, *Soon we'll get water.* Then she was gone. The dream was over but the impact remained. I woke up feeling rested and absurdly confident. The baboons would be all right. Somehow I knew they would make it.

Two days later, in the late afternoon, the sky darkened prematurely and we followed the baboons up to the top of the canyon. I wasn't sure what was happening, only that it was far too early for them to sleep. They mumbled excitedly as lightning flashed in the eastern sky. A tower of clouds was unleashing a mighty streak of rain, falling in sheets over one tiny speck of this vast desert. For a half hour we watched, mesmerized by the promise. Then, as suddenly as the storm arrived, it disappeared.

The next morning, long before sunrise, we heard rocks falling and excited murmurs as the baboons scampered down from their sleeping cliff. We skipped coffee, grabbed cameras, a handful of nuts, and set off after them. Following their tracks, we crawled over rocks, rounded trees laden with pods, passed one tiny seep, and covered about eight miles quickly. "Where could they possibly be going?" was the persistent question. We turned a corner against the north side of the canyon, a place we had never been before, and climbed. Nad lifted me up over boulders. I shimmied through crevices and we found them, drinking from a huge rain puddle. The dream had come true, saved by a freak thunderstorm. I thought this pool would be big enough, deep enough to sustain them until the floods came. It turned out that Bo and I were almost right.

Over the next six weeks the pool grew smaller. Evaporation was taking its toll, while Grin, the dominant male, took his. He always drank first. Some days he sat by the pool for hours, allowing females to groom him, and the little ones to dart in and steal a quick drink. Only when Grin left the water's edge did the rest of the baboons drink in order of rank, males first, followed by females. After a few weeks the pool was so small that SP, the lowest-ranking female, gave up even trying. She was forced to satisfy her need for moisture by stripping bark from nearby trees.

Years later I can still hear the gnawing of tooth on wood, the sound of desperation. With the troop spread out in a grove of acacia trees, the baboons used their teeth to cut through the bark, ripping, biting, all in the struggle for a tiny drop of water. It took hours of repeated motion, tearing through the bark, stuffing strips of wood into their mouths, and squeezing, like wads of tobacco in a baseball player's mouth, before spitting out a solid mass of wood. It was just enough moisture to survive another day.

By the middle of November 1992, the baboons had gone thirty days without drinking water. Thirty days under the blaring sun, thirty days of stripping bark. Then sixty days. After ninety days, they moved less than ten feet during the day, and ate at night to avoid the sun. Then Patch disappeared. She had survived ninety-five days without drinking water. When she died, the troop lost its highest-ranking female and Jesse, her first baby to ever survive, lost her mother.

We had been living with the baboons for three years, filming their lives for half of that time, but now when I loaded film into magazines my hands shook at the thought of what might be captured. What was unfolding was almost too difficult to bear, much less film.

When SP's baby died after being kidnapped by Amy, we drank flat, hot champagne. Such was the horror of this baby's short life that we celebrated her death. Within the first hour of its life, Amy had lifted the infant from SP's arms and carried it away. Amy tenderly groomed the baby; she allowed it to suckle but she didn't have milk, and soon the baby didn't even have enough strength to cry. SP maintained a silent vigil at Amy's side, watching the color drain from her infant's face. A day later, she watched her baby die in Amy's arms.

Pandora, a baby when we first arrived, was now biting her own mother in the back, challenging her for a higher rank, for the chance to jump ahead in line to drink, to survive. Friends didn't help friends in this animal world. Coalitions were made for momentary gain and then abandoned. In a battle against Mother Nature, each individual, myself included, was alone.

Our paradise was lost and I was so depressed I could hardly get out of bed. Nad combed my matted hair, wiped the tears from my eyes, and said over and over again, "This is their history. They will survive this." They might have survived previous droughts, but by early 1993 there wasn't a cloud in sight.

Back in 1989 when we'd started our project, Nad and I had vowed not to change the baboons' world—to habituate them only by our presence. We wouldn't give them food or water; we'd keep things utterly natural. We'd been so naïve. Now they were dying. In the back of our Land Rover, we had twenty gallons of water, the power to change this, to save them. And we didn't. In the pursuit of science, of truth and a good story, what had we become? Were we monsters? I hated Nad because he wasn't as weak as I was. He clung to the belief that we were right not to alter the natural order, and because I needed to believe, I clung to him. He held firm, observing behavior, making notes, gathering data, staying rooted in what was controllable. I couldn't. I questioned everything. Did I love him or did I just need him in this place? I questioned my morality, but most of all, I questioned my sanity.

We drove back and forth from the riverbed to the research station twenty miles away, spending days at the station looking for mail and listening to the radio, hoping for news from Sara and of rains inland. Neither came. Nad sat in a dark office surrounded by research papers and academic books, using a pencil stub to write his thesis. I hardly left our tiny trailer. I couldn't sleep, couldn't focus. I wasn't sure if I felt worse when I was with the baboons or away from them.

A week later we returned to a scene of utter disaster. Nad found Grey's dead body. Her broken finger that had been her signature in the sand stuck out from the decaying bones. Later we found Bo's body in the middle of the riverbed, as if she had fallen over in her tracks while trying to keep up with the others. I wondered if Cleo and Smudge had stayed with her, tried to lift her, willing her to walk with them. Did Oke, her four-month-old infant, cry to be nursed? When did the three of them decide that to survive themselves they would have to abandon her? If we had been there, we might have been able to save Bo and Grey. But would we have made that choice? I don't know. I only know that with Pandora we tried.

It was late that same night and we'd just laid out our sleeping bags when a tiny figure rounded the canyon wall. It was Pandora. She stumbled like a drunk and sat down beside us. Her eyes were swollen shut and she was so thin we could count her ribs.

"Here, darlin'," I said as I placed a cup of water on the sand for her. To hell with science. To hell with research. And my scientist boyfriend didn't argue. She drained it and another and quickly another. We gave her an orange and watched as she held it in her hand, using her front teeth to gingerly peel back the skin before devouring the flesh. Then she stood and slowly climbed up the cliff, perching on a ledge just over our sleeping bags. Tonight we were her troop.

For the next three days we gave her water and oranges so that she'd have enough strength to keep up with the others. If she could just hold on another few days, storm clouds were building. We watched them grow, thinking each day that this would be the day the floodwaters came down. But the river remained dry, and no matter how much water we gave her, Pandora became slower, weaker, weaving like a boxer too broken to continue the fight.

"Oh, my girl. What has happened to you?" Pandora had nearly fallen off the cliff. Her eyes were still puffy, almost swollen shut, but now green slime was running out of her nose and mouth. She stumbled past me, wiping her face with her arm and then tentatively licking it. It looked awful but it was moist. I chased after her with water and oranges. She stumbled on, as if she couldn't see me.

I fell to the ground, wondering what had happened to me. Four years before, I had come to this desert knowing it was a place where I would heal. I'd willed the desert to sweep away the pains of the past and restore my faith in my talents and my future. But on that day, I knew the desert had won. It had destroyed me as surely as it had destroyed our baboons.

Nad stooped down beside me and brushed the hair out of my face. "Gin, come on. We need to get back to the station tonight. You'll see them again tomorrow." I couldn't speak. Limp as a rag doll, I draped my arms over his shoulders and tucked my head in the curve of his neck. He had to carry me back to the Land Rover.

IF ONLY THERE were a letter, I prayed. I needed news of a celebration—a birth, a marriage, a party, even a hangover. I needed to be reminded that there was a world beyond this.

Mail was precious in the desert. Many times it had taken months for letters to reach us; sometimes they never arrived. But that day, there was a letter. News from home, something I needed as surely as the baboons needed water.

I lay down on a mattress under a huge acacia tree and unfolded the letter slowly, wanting to savor the moment. It was short, a single page. I read it once. And read it again. The third time I read it, I was crying. Many of the words were soft and gentle, but I only remembered one—divorce. As in, Sara and I are getting a divorce. And the letter was from Sara's husband. I felt sick. I simply could not believe it. Why? Where was Sara? Why hadn't she written to tell me? What the hell was going on?

I wanted desperately to talk to her, but I had no idea where she was. Covering the war in Somalia or fires in California? Or there'd been talk of a posting in London. She could be anywhere. How the hell could I find her? From the research station our only link to the outside world was a radio-telephone. Twice a day, at 6 A.M. or 6 P.M., we could book a call through the central operator, our call sign "Double Three." But it was a national party line. Every lodge manager and farmer would hear our conversation. I tried to imagine the call.

Why, Sara? Over. The sound of breathing as everyone waited for her response.

I wish I knew. Over.

Through the static I would beg, *What? Oh no, Sara. I can't hear you, you're breaking up, please repeat. Over.*

Then the line would go dead.

The voice of the operator would break through, saying, *Sorry.*

Weren't we all.

It was too much. A dead man, dead baboons, a shattered marriage. Nothing was working out. No explanations, no communication, over and out.

12

SARA (1993)

It was a glorious day in London. After a run around Hyde Park I'd had a quick shower back in my enormous room at the Hyde Park Hotel. In thirty-two years I'd never stayed anywhere half as beautiful as that creamy pink and white suite. I still got a start every time I opened the door—as if I'd walked into someone else's room and someone else's life.

My husband and I had barely spoken since I'd arrived but I tried not to think about it. In calls to my parents I instead focused on all the fun I was having, including a behind-the-scenes tour of "Buck House," as I'd learned Buckingham Palace was called by locals. My sisters were more inquisitive about the impact of career and geography on an already strained marriage and Elizabeth suggested I was "in denial" and "blocking" when I glibly responded to certain questions, but tunnel vision felt right to me. There would be time to figure out home when I returned there. Still anxious to do hard news, I raised my hand to go to Sarajevo. But it had been less than a year since ABC producer David Kaplan, on assignment there with Sam Donaldson, had been killed by a sniper. In the end NBC sent a more seasoned correspondent, to my disappointment.

Still, I couldn't complain. I'd been at the network for less than a year and already had had opportunities to do bureau duty in Atlanta, Chicago, and Los Angeles as well as substitute on the *Today* show. After one appearance, my photographer pal Ken Ludlow had sent a computer note to say they'd watched in London. Working there was a chance to catch up with him as well as so many others I'd met in Somalia. And it hadn't taken long for London to start to feel like a home away from home.

That day when I arrived at the NBC bureau on Tottenham Court Road, things were quiet. I'd read the papers and was having a cup of tea and a chat with my producer pal Justin when someone called out, "Hey, Sara! Phone's for you. You can pick up in Keith's office."

I was surprised. Could it be my husband? My parents or sisters, perhaps? It was so unusual to get a call that I was worried enough to close the office door.

Instead the voice was that of a mutual friend of Ginger's and mine, who was just back in the States from Namibia. I was delighted to hear from him and hoped he'd have news of Ginger and Nad. "Yes, we caught up." He sounded hesitant, then continued. "Actually, Gin asked me how you were. She said she had no idea how to reach you but wanted to make sure you were okay."

The knot in my stomach tightened. I sat down. "What do you mean? Of course I'm fine."

There was another brief pause. "Well, she said she'd received a letter from your husband, a letter saying you two are splitting."

I stood up again, clutched the desk, knuckles white. "Saying what?!"

The next pause was longer. "I gathered that you two were getting divorced. Gin is worried about you, and I just wanted to tell you I'm sorry."

I don't really remember the rest of the conversation. He spoke. I asked a few pertinent questions, including getting a number for Ginger, who was briefly staying with friends who had a phone. Hardly knowing what I was doing, I got off the line and gently replaced the receiver in the cradle.

And then I sat back down. There was a mug on the desk and I tipped it over, poked idly through francs and deutsche marks, lire and rubles. Coins of the realms I'd dreamt of visiting. In those dreams, I'd returned home, pockets stuffed with boarding stubs and receipts, to kick off my shoes and tear open a bag of wrinkled clothes to pull out some treasure I'd brought home for the man I loved. And as every trinket comes wrapped in a story, to tell the tale of how and where and why I'd thought of him and it had to be his. I'd imagined listening to his stories, too, legs entwined, each bewitched by the familiar, reminded that distance can disappear in a kiss. But what I hadn't pictured, until just that moment, was returning from life on the road to find no one waiting.

Why should he wait? a small voice inside me whispered. I closed my eyes to stop the voice but it only grew louder, more insistent. Wait for what? What's left, after all, beyond a dream, a snapshot, a past?

I opened my eyes and leaned back, noting how the watery sunlight that streamed through the office blinds left a pattern of stripes on my left hand that disappeared as soon as I moved it. My wedding ring was still there. But soon I'd take it off, and the stripe it left would disappear just as surely. And then it would be over. Truly over.

I stared at the phone. I needed to know more but I wasn't ready to call my husband. I didn't know what to ask or where to begin and still didn't want to believe it was true. And I wanted to wait until I felt more composed to call my parents. And Ginger? I realized that I suddenly felt anxious and uncertain. I decided to call Linda first.

"Oh, Sara." LP, the unofficial life coach who always knew exactly what to say, was out of words.

"Linda, why would he do it? Why write her? Could it have anything to do with the fact that she's beautiful? Oh my God, listen to me! I'm sure I'm reading way too much into this. I know they'd talked about working on a project together someday. I'm sure he just wants to stay friends. But I don't know if I could stand that. She's *my* best friend."

Using the gentle sort of voice you might use with someone who has unexpectedly picked up a grenade and is threatening to pull the pin, she said, "I realize this is a shock. I'm sure he never anticipated the letter would get to her before you two had a chance to talk. This monthlong assignment of yours was kind of a surprise. But, Sara, be honest, you really *have* known your marriage was ending, letter or no letter. Neither one of you has been happy for a very long time. You need to go forward. And you need to do it on your own."

"But why did he write Ginger?"

"Why don't you call her?"

Instead I sat staring at the phone, chewing my lip until I tasted blood, twisting my rings around and around and around. My stomach felt like I'd swallowed broken glass. I felt a surge of jealousy like I'd never experienced before. Jealous that he would write her. Jealous that she was the kind of person he would want to write. And angry that he'd made me jealous of my best friend.

The shadows pooled in the corner. I'd been through all of the coins. What was it worth, all the money in the world, if you didn't have what you wanted, the things that were most important? Finally curiosity and a certain futile hope that there had been some mistake prompted me to dial.

"Gin?"

"Oh, Sara, thank goodness you called! I've been so worried about you and I've had no idea how to reach you! Where are you? I couldn't understand why you hadn't written to tell me."

And then, finally, I wept. I wept because it was sad and because it was real, for that was obvious before she said another word. And because if I'd been brave and honest with my husband and myself, willing to face a hard truth rather than run away from it, things might not have ended like this. I cried because her voice made me feel better, even though she was thousands of miles away, because I knew she loved me and because we'd known each other so long and because she understood what this felt like better than anyone I knew. At the end she asked, "Oh, Sara, is there anything I can do?"

"You have already. Just by being there."

As I hung up the phone, exhausted and depleted, the person I was angriest at was myself. Clearly my husband had been trying to tell me for months, if not years, that he wasn't happy. I'd always known you can't make someone love you. And yet in a way, that's exactly what I'd tried to do. And because I'd been unwilling to accept that our marriage was in dire straits, unwilling to listen to any talk of divorce, unwilling to face facts, my best friend had found out before I had.

What had I done? What would I do now? How would I make it on my own? And as I wiped my eyes I wondered something else. Was this, then, the terrible price the Fates exact for granting desire—that you could have the odyssey, the opportunities, but the price might be returning to an empty home? Or were we simply two people who had married young after the briefest of courtships only to discover we weren't compatible after all? I had waited too long to ask the questions and in the end the answers would change nothing.

"Sara, I'll come over as soon as I can," Ginger promised. "But I want you to remember something. You have a job you love. Hang on to that."

For the first time in my life I didn't know whether work was a lifeline or a noose. And when I flew home, it seemed that the glittery spangle of Gotham had faded to sepia, and for the first time I wished that New York were merely a transfer, and my true destination somewhere, anywhere, else.

13

GINGER (1993)

I RESTED MY HEAD against the window of the Boeing 747 and pulled the thin blue blanket up around my shoulders. The air was stale, dim light from the movie screen enveloped the seats in a gray cloud, a baby cried, a man snored. Unable to sleep, I tried to remember how many times in the past eleven years I'd made this flight across the Atlantic between Africa and the U.S. It must have been at least eight. Each trip marked either the beginning or the end of an event, a chunk of time dedicated to a project, a relationship, a dream, one that was vital and, though I might not have known it at the time, would turn out to be defining.

By now I was old enough and my friendship with Sara deep enough that our lives were connected in so many ways, in a series of circles—some sad, others crazy, others maniacally wonderful, plates spinning round and round as if in a juggler's act. They might crash, wobble, and come to a slow stop or they might spin forever, but they didn't break. The circles connecting our lives were stronger than that.

For me this trip home was bittersweet for many reasons. For one, it marked the end of our time with the baboons. Rains had finally fallen in the highlands and the Kuiseb River had flowed. One last time we raced the headwaters, swam, and filmed. We felt a strong sense of relief, but it was impossible to feel joy. Cleo and Smudge had survived the long drought, but Bo, their mother, was dead. Pandora had been alive the day before the flood, but we never saw her again. We'd scanned the trees, the cliffs, and then we started counting. Of the fourteen baboons we had come to love, only six survived. Six baboons left to groom, to fight, to mate, to have babies, and to rebuild a troop. They would be doing it alone because for us, this chapter was closed. But at the same time, my trip back to the States would also mark a new beginning. I would try to find funding to finish the film, to complete this circle.

And then I thought about my other reason for coming home. Sara. She had filed for divorce. Another circle completed, time to move on. Too many times I had been far away when she needed me, but not this time. I had been there at the beginning when she said "I do," and I'd be there at the end.

TWO WEEKS AFTER arriving in America, I walked up to Sara and her husband's perfect white Victorian house. Outside at the top of three stories was a widow's walk. In the hundred years that the house had been standing, I could imagine all those who had paced there, watching and waiting, at times in vain, for a loved one to return. With so much history inside those walls, this was just another sad chapter.

Stepping into the house was disorienting. Inside, Sara's grand piano stood untouched against the living room window. Lining the long hallway with its high ceiling and graceful arches were boxes marked "den," "books," and "kitchen," as if Sara and her husband were still in the process of moving in. Stacked neatly on the dining room table were place settings of china and crystals, those that happy, expectant brides select, but now they were divided evenly into two piles. His and hers, all right. It was eerie, surreal, and so damn civil that I wanted to smash everything in sight.

I smiled at Sara. "So where do we start?"

Her lips parted as if she wanted to speak, but in the end she nodded and I followed her upstairs. CD stayed downstairs, quietly out of the way, but his presence was everywhere. It clung to the clothes in the master bedroom; we stepped around it in the bathroom as we picked through toiletries; it was there as we thumbed through the titles lining the bookshelves. To escape it, we delved into Sara's past.

Reaching up to the top of the armoire, Sara pulled down a grass basket full of scarves.

"Oh no!" She laughed for the first time that day. "Look at these. How awful!"

"Sara, I remember that one. You wore it the night we had margaritas in Charlotte."

"Did not!"

"Okay. Maybe I saw it on the billboard."

"Oh no you didn't. I've never even seen it before. These things have reproduced and their offspring are hideous. They aren't mine. I swear!"

"Don't lie to me. You are a closet member of the Junior League!"

It felt so good to laugh. From girlish giggles to lusty, knowing laughs, laughter has always been present in our friendship. In fact, it is one of the keys to our friendship. When Sara's eyes flash with a certain sparkle, I know what she's thinking and I laugh. When I toss my hair, she laughs, knowing there's trouble ahead. Our friend Luca Babini, a gifted photographer and filmmaker with a thoughtful, probing eye and a sharp sense of humor, shakes his head, claiming we even laugh alike. Sometimes we laugh through our tears and sometimes we laugh until we cry, but mostly we laugh because we always have so much fun together. But on that day, we laughed in spite of the situation.

In the midst of all those ugly scarves we lay on the bed, spent with laughter and emotion. It was quiet for a moment, then Sara spoke. "Gin, I have no bearings for this. No references. I don't know what to think, what to feel, except failure."

"Sara, you didn't fail; you tried. And you know what? I'm sure he tried, too. But no one is immune. It just happens."

"It" was divorce, and because we had been friends for so long, Sara didn't have to explain that in her family there were only seemingly perfect marriages. No raised voices, no broken china, and certainly no divorces. In a play she'd never seen, she'd been asked to speak lines she couldn't begin to know. An understudy thrust into a part she wasn't prepared for.

"It'll be okay. Soon. Sara, you couldn't go on like this, and after tomorrow, you won't have to."

After Sara went to bed, I walked downstairs to the den to talk to CD. In this huge house, against the backdrop of what should have been such a happy home, he looked sad, lonely. We talked for a while, tentatively, more like strangers than friends. He asked me about the baboons and the desert. We talked about filmmaking, all safe topics and passions we shared. We had a lot in common. Clearly, he still cared for Sara, just as I did, and ached to see her in so much pain. But there was one difference: I loved Sara and, sadly, he did not.

If this had been a movie, the next morning would have been raining, that steady drizzle through gray skies, the kind of rain that makes you cold, sad, melancholy. But it wasn't. It was beautiful, clear, and crisp, the kind of day you want to celebrate. Instead we loaded boxes. Sara pointed the movers away from what was staying to what was going. Before we climbed into the front cab of the moving truck, Sara and CD hugged each other good-bye. The big, burly moving men and I looked away. The driver made a lame joke as he started the truck, but at least he tried. I gripped Sara's hand and CD stood alone outside that beautiful white house while we drove away, headed for the city, through the tunnel to her new life.

Somehow Sara stayed calm, at least outwardly. At night, in the apartment she'd rented in New York City, I sometimes heard her crying herself to sleep in the next room. By day we each tried to get on with our jobs. I counted my pennies to buy a subway token; often she got picked up in a limo. I fumbled with a mascara wand while Sara had her makeup done for her. Producers didn't return my phone calls; Sara had them lining up outside her door. Maybe, at some other time, I would have been jealous, but it was impossible to be envious of someone so desperately sad.

All too soon I would be headed back to Africa, to a life and a man I loved, but I hadn't sold the film. I had no new work and even less money, while Sara had an amazing career and a life full of possibilities. The only problem was, life, faced alone, seemed to terrify her.

Nothing I could say or do would take Sara's pain away. But I'd known her a long time, and knew she was resilient—that soon her spirit would rise, and she would begin to heal. As for me, I struggled to negotiate my way through a professional trough. I had heard "no" many times. Though rejection hurt, I believed in the baboon film, and felt certain that one day a television executive would also believe in the film. The baboons' story would air, and when it did, I knew I'd make another film. I, too, needed time.

No one reaches their early thirties without enduring disappointment, and Sara and I were no exception. There were jobs we had wanted but were never offered. Men we had loved who had stopped loving us. But we also knew that angst was a temporary state. We had come a long way from that high school stage and, in sacrificing so much, discovered that real gratification is rarely instant. We'd both burned the map a long time ago, forging our own paths in the search for a life we loved. I knew neither of us would give up now.

14

SARA (1993–1994)

He's cute, Sara. What about him?"

"He looks trapped, Gin, like he wants to dash out and check his stock portfolio."

"Well then, what about that man over there?"

"Not my type."

"Have you ever considered that perhaps your type is not your type?" Ginger retorted with an exasperated sigh that only made me laugh. Decked out in velvet and satin, sipping drinks as we whispered critiques of the guys on the dance floor, I suddenly felt as though we were back at the Tucker High School senior prom, and almost expected to hear the falsetto strains of the Bee Gees' "Night Fever" instead of the eighteen-piece orchestra playing for the wedding reception of Ginger's college roommate in High Point, North Carolina.

"You're being way too picky," Ginger continued. "It's only for a dance, not the rest of your life. If you looked remotely interested, someone might ask."

"Well, I just saw that very guy dancing with that woman over there and look at her! She'll probably never walk again."

Ginger shook her head. "I give up. Dad can be your partner. At least all you have to worry about are your toes."

Almost in spite of myself I found I was having fun, and couldn't believe my friend would desert me in two weeks to return to Namibia. Over the past few months I'd come to better understand and appreciate

Ginger and her minimalist approach to friendship, especially since I was the beneficiary. Personally I'd always surrounded myself with dozens of people, as if friends were a collection of spices, with this person or that adding just the right flavor to any occasion. But sorrow had shocked me into recognizing that the variety-pack approach was no substitute for a few stalwarts who, like my family, improved the bitter as well as the sweet. By temperament and circumstance, Ginger had proved the friend most able to help me. She'd spent weeks of her trip back to the U.S. as my de facto roommate, introducing me to her New York friend network and reconnecting herself. Then there'd been the invitation to tag along with her family to Kristy's wedding—an easy decision, as I loved the Mauneys, and Kristy had become my friend, too, since I'd moved to Manhattan.

Ginger and I seemed to swap friends as effortlessly as we traded clothes. As I looked at her, I realized our taste in friends was actually more similar. Ginger usually wore elegant, understated ice blues or creams, and being a bridesmaid was the only reason she was decked out in emerald silk taffeta. Meanwhile I wore a black velvet dress with a matching jacket trimmed in lots of glittery gold braid, accented by large, glittery hoops. After all, I wasn't on TV and the wedding was down South.

"You've got to admit there's something pretty amusing about this," I whispered to Ginger, snagging another mini ham biscuit from a tray of passed hors d'oeuvres. "Coming to a wedding as a way to recover from divorce."

"Maybe tonight will help restore your optimism. Kristy kissed her share of frogs, too, you know—but just look at her."

"She's radiant. And wonderful. But I'm not sure that's relevant."

"It's only been a few months. You don't have to fall in love again tomorrow, you know."

I was ready to change the subject. "And what about you and Nad?"

She hesitated, then replied carefully, "We're working on things."

"Well, you know I think he's great."

"He is." She paused again. "I just want to be certain this time."

I understood.

* * *

BUT BACK IN New York, sorrow returned like an illness I couldn't shake, leaching joy, bleaching hope, and I spent my time alone in an endless round of internal cross-examination. What exactly was I missing? The person my ex could be when he wasn't with me? How pathetic. Or was I missing being part of an "us," even an us less than the sum of its parts, because somewhere deep inside I felt like two against the universe was such better odds than me, myself, and I? I was beginning to realize that I'd forgotten how to be single, perhaps even forgotten who "I" was. There was time to figure it out, there had to be. And in the meantime work offered distraction, direction, and, frequently, perspective.

IN THE LATE autumn of '93, Haiti seemed to be on the brink of imploding. Former members of vicious death squads called the Tontons Macoutes—re-formed as shadowy paramilitary gangs and now known as the Attachés—had thrown their support behind dictator Raoul Cédras and his junta. President Clinton was debating whether to intervene in an attempt to reinstate the country's democratically elected president, Jean-Bertrand Aristide.

I flew from JFK to Miami, where I boarded one of the few commercial flights then still serving the country. We landed in Port-au-Prince, a Graham Greene city, all tropical colors shot through with sharp, poisonous menace. I made it through the shakedown at customs, feigning ignorance as a way to escape blatant requests for bribes, relaxing just a little after I'd managed to round up boxes loaded with tens of thousands of dollars' worth of gear I'd been assigned to bring for crews already on location. Then the waiting driver took me to the Hôtel Montana, an incongruously lovely mountain retreat overlooking the seething capital.

In the evenings, cars loaded with gun-waving Attaché goons patrolled, and even by daylight danger lurked, coiled for a premeditated or random strike. One day a cameraman and I turned a corner in the city's impoverished Cité Soleil neighborhood, a stronghold of Aristide's supporters, looking for a spot to do a stand-up—the segment in a taped story in which a reporter directly addresses the camera. We practically tripped over a dead man whose body had been tossed into the gutter. I was convulsed by a violent shudder despite the heat, sobered by the sight of a person who'd been thrown away. Who was he? What had happened to him? But the photographer waved me vigorously toward the car before I could voice a single question. "Get in now, Sara," he insisted. "They may still be around." "They" made us shiver again a few days later, as we filmed in a remote area outside the city, a strangely lovely place but also, we were told, a killing field. As a breeze stirred the grasses, it was hard to believe that beneath that soil lay the bodies of dozens of men and women slain by Cédras's thugs, until the photographer pointed to what looked at first like a stick. The wind couldn't warm the chill that wrapped around my ribs at the sight of a human bone piercing the rough ground.

At night I'd decompress in the hotel bar with my old friend Linda, who was covering the conflict for ABC's *World News Tonight*. But when I flew home, Linda remained. What's more, she, Ginger, and the rest of my close friends all lived somewhere else, across the country or overseas. Fiona had returned to Scotland, and Julie and her son Tarl had also moved to the UK when Julie's marriage ended shortly after mine. I was only just meeting people in Manhattan and was always delighted when an old friend came for a visit, as Judith did early in the frigid winter of '94. Years before, she'd been my first boss, but over the years she'd become both friend and doting honorary aunt.

"Let's just nosh, shall we? I'm not very hungry," Judith said after we'd hugged hello, so we wandered from her hotel to Gino's, where we snagged a table by the zebra wallpaper and shared olives and a chopped salad, to the disapproval of our convivial waiter. It had been eight years since we'd first dined together in New York, on the trip where I'd reconnected with Ginger, and it felt strange to suddenly be the local. But that wasn't what I found most disconcerting. Like me, Judith had just lost her husband. Jerry, the father of her two children, the man whose license plate read "DaBronx" and whose accent never altered despite twenty years in the South, had died a few months before from a swift, rare form of lung cancer.

"Judith, I can't imagine what you're going through," I said, looking at her drawn face.

"You know, sweetie, I think we have more in common than you think," Judith answered. "It's a loss, either way. And besides, we don't have to compare."

But inevitably we had. We'd shared wan smiles over shedding pounds without dieting, discussed how we sought escape in detective fiction or light novels, and agreed that one of the worst things was being caught off guard by memories triggered by random events—the sight of a car, the whiff of cologne, a familiar profile. Later that evening I'd felt comfortable enough to make a confession. "My biggest fear is that I'll never find love again. Maybe there's something wrong with me. Especially since I'm not twenty-something anymore."

For the first time that night, Judith looked startled. "Sara, you're only thirty-three! Of course you'll meet someone. Even though I can't imagine a relationship right now, my only fear is the opposite—that I'll never find anyone I love that much again." As I trudged home, I couldn't get our conversation out of my mind. Her loss was far greater, yet she was far healthier than I.

I'd rented a pretty two-bedroom walk-up on the city's Upper West Side, but much as I loved it, I hated the silence of living alone. In the Kuiseb with Ginger and Nad, I'd found the evening quiet comforting—the wind stilling, the crackle as the fire popped and died, the cry of a faraway jackal the only punctuation marks. But I was new to the creaks and echoes of the apartment, the clatter of my heels on the wood floor. When Ginger had been in town, we'd filled the quiet with laughter and dinners and parties, with late nights and extra coffee in the morning.

As I changed clothes and got ready for bed, I almost felt as though Ginger were there, I could hear her voice so clearly in my mind. Unfortunately, I wasn't thrilled by what she had to say. *Sara, you need conversations like the one tonight, and you need this time living on your own—time to reflect. Give yourself a chance to heal, okay?* But thinking was driving me nuts. And as anyone knows, just because your best friend is right doesn't mean you must heed her advice.

* * *

FOR ALL MY traveling, it was only in New York that I felt I needed a compass. I'd once shaken my head sympathetically at Ginger's tales of dating in the Big Apple. Now I was the one who felt lost. I went out with an orchestra conductor. A doctor. A motorcycle-riding ad exec. But it seemed as if there was some complicated rule book that everyone had read except for me. Take the night one friend and I both met a handsome, well-connected lawyer. Later that night he slept with my friend. The following afternoon he called to ask me out to dinner. Even though I mentioned I'd heard quite a bit about *their* evening from Our Mutual Friend, he still seemed stunned when I declined his invitation.

By far my best blind date was with a woman. Our matchmaker was my former *Nightside* coanchor Antonio Mora, who was now a correspondent for ABC News based in New York. "Her name is Sharon Dizenhuz and she's the entertainment reporter and an anchor for New York 1. The local cable all-news channel. You'll love her."

I did. Our friendship solidified the night we covered Donald Trump's wedding to Marla Maples, where the eye-rolling of the press was equaled only by the nudge-nudge, wink-wink of the guests. Sharon was battling her way back from an urban dating disaster and, after years of living in New York, had a few trusty tips for a newcomer to the city's social scene.

"Okay, you've got a pager, right, Sara?"

"Of course! For me, getting beeped usually means catching a taxi to the airport."

"Right. Well, let's just pretend you're actually in New York and you're going out on a date at, say, eight o'clock with a new man. I'll page you at eight forty-five, with 666," she said with a mischievous laugh. "If it's a *disaster,* explain that you got paged, head to the phone booth, wait a couple of minutes, and then return to the table and say, 'Sorry, gotta dash—breaking news.'" She flashed a cheeky grin.

"People do that?"

"Look, dating is *work*." She lowered her voice conspiratorially. "I confess,

my secret hobby is to speculate about all the other couples in the restaurant—
you know, is this their first date? Or their last? I remember one night when
I thought the check would never come, I noticed that the cute guy next to us
seemed to be in the same predicament. So when both our dates headed to
the loo, I couldn't resist asking him, 'Blind date? First date?'"

"Sharon, you didn't!"

"But I did! Next thing you know, I'm sampling his french fries."

"And what did you sample later?"

"Sara, I'm shocked, shocked! What kind of girl do you take me for?"
We both started laughing. "Of course what really happened is that we both
saw our dates coming back and that was that." She paused, and a misty
look came into her eyes. "Gives you hope, though. Our guys, they have to
be out there."

I snorted. "Sharon, I don't even know how to do this anymore. The
whole thing makes me feel like I don't know where north is."

Sharon nodded. "They move it at the Lincoln Tunnel. Cross into New
York and—poof—all systems jammed."

"Do you get used to it?"

"Not really. But you have to keep trying."

"Don't you ever want to give up?"

Sharon slid an arm into her sweater, tightened one of her signature
jaunty silk scarves. "Look, a friend of mine wrote an article about the perils
of dating in the city. 'One woman recalls—' 'Then there was my friend
who was shocked to discover—' 'An Upper East Side woman confided—'
Just one horror story after another. But you want to know the worst part?
Every story was mine! Every single one of them."

I started laughing. "She only used you because you could make a date
with Dracula sound amusing. But you still get out there."

"I do. Speaking of which. You have to come with me tomorrow to this
journalist event. Several thousand of your soon-to-be-closest friends will be
there, including some eligible males."

"No way. Absolutely not. I say *nyet* to men."

"I'll call you tomorrow with the details!" With a cheery wave, she vanished into the night.

* * *

THE PERFORMANCE WAS an annual spoof of national, state, and local politics by a New York journalists' group called the Inner Circle. While the following night would be a black-tie dinner for the rich and powerful, this dress rehearsal was for the hoi polloi. As we threaded our way through the crowd of journalists, Sharon skidded to a halt beside a tight group. "Sara, these are some of my friends from the *New York Post*." She smiled her way through the introductions, then stopped. "But you I don't know. I'm Sharon."

"G'day."

When the dark-haired man smiled, his eyes twinkled. I was uncomfortably aware that he was tall, good-looking, and of indeterminate age. Perhaps a month or two younger than I. He turned to me, held out his hand. "And you are?"

"Sara."

"What do you do with the *Post?*"

"Actually, I work for NBC. I'm a correspondent for our evening newscast."

"Well, maybe you can introduce me to Bryant Gumbel and Katie Couric. We get the *Today* show and I think the way you cover news is excellent. Actually, that's why I'm here—to watch and learn."

"How long will you be here?"

"Only a few months. Then I'm moving to Tokyo to be the Japan correspondent for my paper, the *Melbourne Herald Sun,* and the rest of Murdoch's Australian papers."

My heart took a dive. I'd finally met someone who seemed interesting and he was from another country and moving to a third. Time to cut my losses. But while I had every intention of wandering off immediately to mingle, somehow Andrew managed to wangle an invitation to watch the second half of the program sitting between Sharon and me, pleading a combination of ignorance of New York City politics and jet lag. And as the evening continued, I found I'd liked more than his looks. He was observant and plainspoken—if occasionally unintelligible.

"Where are you from?"

"Muckleford."

"Is that near Sydney?"

"It's in Victoria. Way up woop woop." As I looked mystified, he continued, "Even Australians have never heard of it. I'm off a sheep farm about an hour and a half outside Melbourne. My Uncle Norm was a reporter. One day he landed his TV helicopter in the side paddock on his way back from a story and I caught the bug."

"I've always wanted to go to Australia. Kangaroos and koala bears sound good, but aren't there snakes?"

His eyes twinkled, and he leaned forward and said in a stage whisper, "Koalas aren't bears, they're marsupials. And don't worry. I haven't seen a snake bigger than six feet."

I hated making mistakes—nearly as much as I hated the sound of those snakes. "Sounds delightful."

"You've gotta be pretty unlucky to get bitten by a Joe Blake. Though I did shoot one once, out hunting."

Oh, better and better. I was in danger of falling for Crocodile Dundee.

At the end of the evening the three of us stood outside the Hilton Hotel to say good night. Andrew shivered in the arctic air, being from a continent where spring attire clearly didn't include a scarf, hat, or gloves.

"Thanks, you two. Just so you know, I don't know a soul here, which makes you two my new best friends. Do either of you run?"

"I do!" I volunteered with more enthusiasm than sense.

"Great. Just give me your numbers."

AS HE'D PROMISED, Andrew called, and was easy to talk to. But given my schedule with *Nightly News* and *Today,* actually getting together proved more difficult, so he joined the he'll-just-have-to-wait list.

At *Today,* I felt increasingly comfortable with Bryant and Katie, but I was just getting to know Matt Lauer, who had recently taken over for Margaret Larson. I was about to get to know him a whole lot better.

One afternoon as I was heading to Broadway to meet Sharon for a matinee, I got the New York City taxi driver from hell. Despite my protests, the wild-eyed lunatic darted and weaved through traffic, and ultimately slammed into the taxi in front of us. He was clearly, unambiguously in the wrong, so what else could he do? Like any self-respecting psychopath, he leapt out to blame the other driver.

"You a crazy man!"

"What? You rammed *my* car, you idiot. I'm calling the cops."

Late for the play and steamed, I did something I'd never done before. I got out without paying, prompting Psycho Driver to turn his wrath on me. Suddenly I had what's known down South as a hissy fit. "I will not! You are demented and it's your fault we crashed. You're just lucky we're not in the hospital! I'm not paying you one damn cent!"

As I turned to make good my escape, I discovered a traffic jam had built up behind us. My anger fizzled instantly, replaced by southern discomfort, and I was just grateful no one had witnessed my tantrum. That's when I spied a cute guy gesturing me over to share his cab. "Sara?" the Knight in Shining Armor asked in surprise as I got closer. Oh my God. Mortification.

"Matt! Hi! Um . . . thanks for coming to my rescue."

"You looked like you were having a little trouble. What happened?" As I tried to explain, his grin got broader until I realized that I'd been the one who must have looked like a New York psychopath. When he dropped me off at the theater, I mumbled thanks, to which he replied kindly, "Don't mention it."

I badly wanted to reply, *Actually, if you wouldn't mention it, that would be even better.* Instead I said, "See ya tomorrow at the show." Of course, it took Matt less than twenty-four hours to spill the beans about the entire awful episode for the viewing pleasure of millions. As I'd just learned, nobody can deliver a good-natured on-air ribbing like Matt Lauer.

A FEW DAYS later Andrew called again to see if I could meet him for a run. A run led to dinner, then another dinner a few weeks later. I liked his easy manner, his warmth, his accent, his amusing anti-establishment rants. I also enjoyed having a man as a friend. I'd never bought Ginger's theory that men and women can't really be friends. Nevertheless, she wasn't my only girlfriend who pointed out I was on the rebound and consequently needed to be grilled.

"Does he have E.B.?" asked Lynne Dale, a *Dateline* producer.

"No, I'm sure he doesn't! What on earth *is* that?"

"Excess Baggage. You know—an ex, kids, diploma from a twelve-step program."

"Oh no, nothing like that."

"G.U.?"

"Excuse me?"

"Is he Geographically Undesirable?"

"Well, he's from Australia."

She gasped. "*That* is a 10! Now listen carefully. This is *not* Mr. Right. He's Mr. Right Now."

THEN THERE WAS the other nagging question. Andrew had dropped a few hints that he might be younger than I. One night as we met for dinner with Sharon and a few other friends, I cozied up.

"So enough of this dancing around the age question, Andrew," I said, wagging my finger at him playfully. "How bad can it be?"

He gave his broad, lazy smile and pulled out his driver's license. The date seemed to glow neon.

"Oh my God!" I pulled my knee away from his knee under the table and gulped. Too shocked to be witty, I muttered, "At least you had the grace to be born in the sixties."

"Oh, come on, it's not that bad, I'm over twenty-one." His smile was as charming as ever and the lashes around his eyes were implausibly thick, but when he moved closer I pulled back. Unbidden, I suddenly pictured myself as Barbara Stanwyck with red nails, mules, and a breathy, dangerous voice. *A divorcée.* The kind of woman any mother wants kept as far away as possible from her son.

"Andrew, you are twenty-four!" I shouted at him as loudly as was possible in a whisper, anxious not to turn this into a source of conversation for the entire table.

"Yes. I'm aware of that."

"Well, don't be ridiculous. It's impossible."

"What's impossible?" His grin got larger. I flushed.

"You are."

"We'll see."

"WOW, SARA, THAT'S nearly a decade" was Ginger's first comment some weeks later.

"Nad's younger than you, Gin."

"Only three years. But age isn't the point, remember how you were going to take it slow—"

"Hey, you guys!" interrupted my cousin Lynn Templeman, who'd joined Ginger and me on this safari, first around Namibia and now Zimbabwe. "Look, look!"

I turned my head to see hippos cavorting in the shallows and wanted to pinch myself yet again. We'd been dazzled by "the Smoke That Thunders," Victoria Falls, transfixed by rainbows spun hundreds of feet in the air. We'd browsed open-air markets, purchasing elegantly carved wooden giraffes and woven baskets. And now we floated lazily down the Zambezi River, watching a wildlife spectacle. "Actually, let's give that family some room," Ginger suggested, paddling toward the bank. "Hippos can actually be dangerous."

But while it was easy to skirt hippos and even more menacing crocodiles, it proved harder to avoid questions from my friend.

"Remember what we talked about at Kristy's wedding?" Ginger continued. "That was less than a year ago. You're still on the rebound, whether you think so or not. And I remember what that's like."

"I know, Gin," I reassured her, "but we're older and wiser."

Not that those were the first two adjectives that might have been chosen to describe us late that night at a Vic Falls bar where we recklessly entered the karaoke contest.

"Wild thing!" we belted out, tentative at first, then getting into our groove. "You make my heart sing!"

And suddenly Ginger let out a sound, part purr, part growl, which ended in a howl that brought down the house, and we wiped tears from our eyes as we laughed our way through the big finish, "You make everything groovy!"

And as I flew back to New York, still smiling, I held on to that line. Everything would be all right. I'd fall just far enough for this guy and no further. Because even if your best friend is right, you don't have to heed her advice. Do you?

15

GINGER (1993–1995)

GINGER, HEY, GINGER, are you getting up?"

"What? What is it?" Through the fog of sleep, I thought I was dreaming until Nad rolled over and pulled half of the blankets off me.

"Wait a minute. I was just up." I rolled in the opposite direction and fumbled for my watch. The yellow glow of hands pointed out that it was 3 A.M. Sara was probably out on the town, dressed in chic black, dancing and dining with the new man in her life. And me, I was babysitting. Not exactly what I'd dreamed I'd be doing at thirty-three.

"Okay, I'll get up." I looked across the thin bedroll. Nad was already snoring again.

Six months after Nad and I had said good-bye to our life with the baboons in the Kuiseb River, we'd moved four hundred miles north, to Etosha National Park, where Nad had taken a position as the park's only veterinarian. A park the size of Switzerland, Etosha teems with wild animals and wide-open spaces. It is dominated by a vast white shimmering pan—an ancient dry lake bed—fringed with seeps of water and etched with game paths. During the dry season, hundreds of animals file into waterholes to drink. Giraffes approach tentatively, scanning the horizon for one of Etosha's fabled lions. Sometimes it takes hours before they are confident enough to spread their long legs and lower their heads to drink. Herds of elephants approach silently while zebra and wildebeest bray and kick their way to the water's edge. Springbok spar, jackals dart among the other animals, and tiny black-winged plovers stand guard over their eggs. It is live theater at its best. Etosha was where Jen and Des Bartlett made their classic film *The Lions of Etosha,* which I'd seen as a teenager on television in Richmond. One day I hoped to make a film here, too. But right now I just hoped to make it through the night.

We'd taken on a new, rather noisy project—one sick and very hungry baby rhino. At the familiar sound of pounding, the uneasy beat of his head or feet hitting rotting old board, I eased out of the blankets, tossed an old sweatshirt over my shoulders, and tiptoed across creaky floorboards into the next room. "Shh," I whispered, "I'm coming."

Reaching for the matches with one hand, I rubbed the tiny stub on our baby rhino's head with the other. One day its horn, actually a dense mass of hair, would grow long and thick. Once the rhino's protection, it had become the rhino's curse. Decades of civil wars in Africa had created a downward spiral where guns were more plentiful than jobs, where an AK-47 could be traded for a sack of maize meal, and where a bullet and fifty dollars would buy you a life—human or animal, particularly an animal whose horn was desired as an aphrodisiac in the Far East and worn as a sign of manhood in the Middle East. When a desperately poor villager was given the option of taking the life of one rhino in exchange for enough money to feed his family for a year, the choice was tragically obvious.

I lit the gas cooker, turning up the blue flame, and its gentle hiss broke the stillness. While the water warmed, I mixed one cup of maize meal, a cup of milk powder, and a vitamin supplement in an empty old two-liter Coke bottle. Next I filled it with hot water, attached a huge plastic nipple, and gave it several strong shakes, the pounding of the rhino's head hitting the floor keeping the beat.

"Hey, stop that racket. Your food is coming." I sat beside him, lifted his head, and placed it on my lap. The nipple was awkward, large and floppy, but he wrapped his pointed lips around it and sucked greedily. Closing my eyes and stroking his head, I leaned against the termite-riddled wall of our temporary bush house where we were staying in a remote part of the park and wondered: *How do mothers do it?* Every two to three hours for the past five days I had been feeding our baby rhino a concoction of vitamins and protein, but every day he grew weaker. At first his heavy feet had shuffled behind me as we walked around the garden, then he had stumbled. A day later his legs had folded under his weight. After that it took two of us to lift him, and since we couldn't hold him up all day, we'd built a sling for him to stand in. Two long steel poles rested on two 44-gallon drums with a thick green plastic sheet stretched between them and under the rhino. We'd hoped he would be able to place some weight on his legs, to walk the length of the poles and gain strength. It hadn't worked.

Nad had tried drips, drugs, and massages. He'd called a wildlife sanctuary in Kenya, friends from Namibia's Save the Rhino Trust, and dozens of other vets in Africa hoping someone might be able to help. Every day he reached deep into his black bag full of medicines hoping to pull out a miracle. Every night we heard the same desperate pounding.

I felt the weight of the rhino's head in my lap. "What are we going to do with you?" I asked, stroking his thick skin. This little rhino was only a year old. If all had gone according to plan, he and his mother were supposed to be moved to another game farm as part of a progressive conservation program of custodianship designed to protect and ultimately restore the population of this endangered species. Though still in its infancy, the program had been a huge success, with many black rhinos relocated and small satellite populations established on safe, secure private land. This time, sadly, the plan hadn't worked. Snatched out of her natural environment and confined in a small holding pen, the rhino's mother had become so stressed that she'd started pushing her son around, hammering him against the walls and not allowing him to eat. By the time Nad was called to the scene, the baby rhino was dehydrated and nearly dead. Drips, injections, and constant attention brought him back, but all too briefly.

Finally I slept through the night. No more pounding, no more sounds of struggle. Before I opened my eyes I knew that sweet baby was dead. Tears spilled onto my pillow and still, as much as I hated her, I sympathized with his mother. I too felt stressed, trapped in a beautiful though alien world with no one to beat on but myself.

When we'd arrived in Etosha National Park, the first question I was asked was, "What are you going to do here, Ginger, because idle women cause trouble?" With his government-issued Land Cruiser and office at the

Etosha Ecological Institute, Nad's role as the new veterinarian was clearly defined, but as a filmmaker without a film, I was—the girlfriend. What I had sworn would never happen again was happening.

Ironically, in 1993, easing into our thirties, Sara and I had both been thrust back into worlds we thought we had escaped. Sara was living alone, navigating the dicey dating scene in New York City, while I had returned to a small town, to a world dominated by men. She had her promising career for security, for sanity. From my vantage point, she also had freedom. I didn't even have a permit to be in the park. Everything was tied to Nad—his job, his income, his position. I was nearly thirty-three years old and still making the same mistakes. After I had sweated it out in the Kuiseb for nearly four years, the baboon film remained unfinished. I had no job, not even a résumé, nothing except the feeling of being trapped.

Instead of the space and freedom of the Kuiseb where Nad and I had drifted naked down the flowing river, wished upon shooting stars, and claimed fierce possession of thirty miles of desert sand, here we'd been assigned a house, "the vet's house." Number 3918-B, one in a row of large, unimaginative boxes, each a carbon copy of the next. Paint was peeling off the walls, the ceiling was stained, and a previous resident's attempt to add a homey touch, a dado of flowers circling the bathroom wall, looked like Martha Stewart gone mad.

Next to the park's main tourist camp at Okaukuejo with a post office, convenience store, and petrol station, we were living in a small town with all the good and bad that implied. Etosha had stunningly beautiful plains and kind people, but I was having a hard time looking past the bad—the constant stream of people asking for work, the suspicious neighbors, the dreadful party-line telephone. And sometimes the bad were looking back. Two men came to us separately, in confidence, warning that the other was the camp's Peeping Tom.

Nad and I were prime targets. Living "in sin," and frowned upon in a circle of conservative couples, I'd never felt so alone. When Nad put on his crisp khaki uniform and went to work, I stayed in the house writing wildlife and travel articles for a local magazine at thirty dollars a pop, taking comfort in wearing my torn sarongs from the riverbed. Rubbing the thin fabric was akin to shining an Aladdin's lamp. Powerful gems flooded back, like the memory of Nad tying half of this material around my burning feet while we watched my sandals drift down the riverbed with the flood's headwaters. Or how Cleo and Bamuthi used to play tug-of-war with the material now tied around my waist. But I'd wrapped myself in memories only to be told by the neighborhood children—who had no doubt heard it from their parents—that I "dressed tatty."

Clearly I was being tested, and never more so than one night. On our way to Kaokoland, a rugged, mountainous area on the Kunene River bordering Angola where Nad and a few of his colleagues had planned to scout locations for relocating black-faced impala, we pulled into Opuwo, a small, dusty town populated by geologists, road workers, and the stately, ochre-stained, indigenous Himba people. We planned to spend that night at Chris Eyre's house. Chris was the chief nature conservator in the area, and someone with a deep respect for the land and the local people. The next day he'd take us further into the mountains.

When we opened the door to Chris's house, I was hit by the sour smell of rotting flesh. Turned out Chris had an elephant skull soaking in his bathtub. When I asked Chris about it, he said, "Yeah, found the old girl lying in the bush. Need a good look at her teeth to accurately age her. She's been in my tub so long I've nearly forgotten about her."

Obviously Chris had been living in the bush a very long time. Rotting skin floated in coffee-colored water and the eye of the elephant was glassy, vacant. But the stench wasn't the only thing that hit me. I looked around Chris's grimy kitchen, the table now half littered with empty whiskey and brandy bottles, and realized I was the only woman there.

While Chris was welcoming, not all of the men were. As the rowdy party continued, some of the looks I got became increasingly hostile. I felt more and more uncomfortable, and possibly sensing this, one of the men picked up a panga, a long, thick knife designed to hack through the bush, and handed it to me. "Here, Ginger," he smirked, gesturing to the huge solid block of ice on the table, "cut us some ice," certain I couldn't do it.

Mad as hell, I picked up the panga, staring him down as I stroked the two-foot-long blade. Then, with one deft quick stroke, I cleaved off a chunk of ice that went flying from the main block and slid across the filthy concrete floor. I picked it up, placed it on the table, and halved it with another blow. Retrieving the splinters of ice and dropping them noisily into battered tin mugs, I covered mine with whiskey and smiled before looking him in the eye and declaring, "You don't need a penis to cut ice." I might not have known their rules but they didn't know me either.

Nad tried not to laugh. He winked at me and I winked back. Then I thought of Sara. She would have loved it.

In between trips to Princeton, Port-au-Prince, L.A., and London, Sara always found time to call, battling to reach me through our phone exchange. Undeterred by the fact that others could be listening, she implored, "Tell me the truth, how are you?" knowing that I wouldn't be "fine" until the baboon film was finished. Without that visual résumé, letters to commissioning film editors went unanswered, phone calls unreturned. A finished film was my only hope of kick-starting a stalled career. While Sara's calls would lift my spirits, there was little she could do from so far away. When relief finally arrived, it came from two unlikely sources—the 1995 Miss Universe pageant and a stranded elephant.

Hosting the Miss Universe pageant was a coup for Namibia, a chance to showcase the country's beauty, diversity, and infrastructure to an international audience. One junket designed for some of the beauty queens and members of the media was a trip to Etosha National Park. But in order to file their stories, the press needed telephone lines. They got them. When Telecom Namibia installed direct-dial telephone service to Etosha, it meant reporters could send faxes and talk directly to their editors, things they took for granted. For us it meant no more straining to identify your sequence of rings, no more booking calls hours in advance, and no more sharing private conversations with uninvited ears. After five years of connecting to the outside world through radios and party lines, I could finally call my family, Sara, and other friends and they could call me. Person to person. It felt like a lifeline.

The other source of relief was a lifeline in the most fundamental sense.

One day Nad raced into the house shouting, "Come on, grab your cameras, let's go."

I stopped typing and my bewildered gaze prompted him to add, "An elephant needs help. Fast."

Fifteen minutes later we walked around Homob, a waterhole in central Etosha, where black mud treacherous as quicksand held a huge elephant in its grip. Attempting to quench its thirst, the elephant had stepped too far out into the waterhole, landing in a quagmire. The mud gripped him and didn't let go. As the elephant struggled, it opened pockets of air for the mud to expand into, further strengthening its hold on the elephant. The harder he struggled, the deeper he sank. Inch by inch, the mud consumed his massive body until his head, ears, and trunk were all that could be seen. The rest was buried deep in the thick black mud.

"Can you believe it?" We shook our heads and waited as other vehicles arrived, full of men, ropes, shovels, and ideas. The elephant flapped his ears and trumpeted in vain to try to scare us away. A South African cameraman, poised to capture the scene of lions and hyenas ending this struggle between life and death, packed up his gear and drove away, disgusted. Spoiling his day felt good. Now we just had to find a way to get this massive ten-ton elephant out. We started digging.

Hour after hour, we dug. Several of us close to the elephant's body dug with our hands, while others used shovels, tossing thick black mud onto the bank of the waterhole. We backed away, exhausted, while the elephant remained planted in the mud, defenseless. But we had managed to ease the pressure on him, and he was about to exploit this. The elephant strained, pushing through the mud to expose the top of his shoulders. He stopped. It was our turn.

We dug, we pulled, we labored. We waited. The elephant pushed through the mud, turning on his side, exposing part of his huge belly to the open air. Caked from head to toe in mud, we started digging again. I was so immersed in the action that I didn't realize where I was kneeling until I felt something leathery quake beneath me. It was the elephant's leg. And suddenly I realized just how vulnerable I'd been. At any time in the past thirty minutes, he could have lashed out, sending me flying into the bush, but he hadn't. He waited, not moving until we were spent and it was his turn to push through the mud. It was an amazing union of effort and understanding, silent communication and shared purpose.

Six hours after we arrived, we tied ropes around the elephant's body and attached the other ends to a powerful Land Cruiser. "Ready?" the driver called. Tires spun, mud flew, and the elephant slid forward. As soon as his feet felt firm earth, he kicked, righting his body and standing to his full twelve-foot height. And as I looked up at that muddy, towering elephant, relishing his newfound freedom, something released in me, too. I would stop feeling so damn sorry for myself and make things happen, starting with finishing the baboon film.

Fortunately the Bartletts had the same idea. They planned to finish their epic saga of life on Namibia's untamed Skeleton Coast, a series that had been sixteen years in the making. They'd hired editors in England to begin the process, and the baboon film would be the fifth and final film of the series. It was a huge leap of faith. Would our images be good enough to tell the baboons' extraordinary story? With little experience, we'd trusted our instincts, but were they in sync with the international television market from which we were so far removed? There was no buyer for the film and no guarantee there ever would be. The Bartletts would be risking tens of thousands of dollars on our film, on us. It was a vote of confidence I desperately needed. Finishing the film also meant a ticket home. I'd fly into JFK, run around New York with Sara, and then go to Richmond to visit my family, whom I hadn't seen in a year and a half.

"COME ON. It's your last night here, let's go for a drive." Nad and I drove out onto the plains, stopping at Okondeka where a sliver of water disappears into a mirage on Etosha Pan. Zebras filed past, the air cooled, the sun set. A flock of sand grouse descended on the waterhole for a final drink. When they flew away, their chorus of gentle cooing and mass of wingbeats was replaced by quiet, a deep silence that one of us needed to break.

After five years together, we could no longer drift through our relationship without a commitment. From the dramas of sharing the baboons' lives to caring for a dying rhino, we were a good team. Our relationship had a rich, wonderful past, one that stirred feelings of love and respect. But was it enough? It was time to decide if our relationship had a future. To part seemed unfathomable, but then again, so did making a commitment. Our conversation went something like this:

"Should we?"

"I guess."

"It makes sense."

"Yeah, it should be okay."

"Okay."

"Are you sure?"

"Sure as I'll ever be."

"Okay, then, yes, I will."

About as romantic as a thermos flask. No phone call home to ask my father's permission, no falling down on one knee or producing a brilliant diamond ring. An offhand proposal spoken into the wind which would seal our future. Getting married was the logical next step in our long relationship. So now not only was I going home to finish the baboon film, I was going back to the U.S. an engaged woman.

16

SARA (1994–1995)

I WAS STANDING AT the Hertz rental car desk already holding the keys to a bright red Miata. What was the fun of being in California if you couldn't drive a convertible? With the story finished, this part of my trip was for pleasure. A few months before, my trip to the West Coast had been drastically different. I'd been in Los Angeles covering devastating wildfires for *Nightly News* and the *Today* show when *Dateline* executive producer Neal Shapiro had asked if I could report live for his broadcast as well. It turned out to be a sort of unofficial audition, and now *Dateline* had assigned me to profile a quixotic, charming pioneer by the name of Peter Bird who hoped 1995 would be the year he'd finally accomplish his goal of rowing solo across the vast Pacific. The shoot had gone well, and now Andrew had joined me in San Francisco for the weekend. As Katie Couric had quipped, "He can be the transition guy." Besides, I now found it easy to ignore the nine-year age difference. Most of the time.

"So there's your license, Miss James, and I'll just take a quick look at yours, sir," said the man behind the desk. Seconds later his official smile sagged into a frown.

"I'm afraid Miss James will have to do all the driving."

"Sorry?" Andrew replied. We'd been dating for about a month and it hadn't taken even that long to learn Andrew was expert behind the wheel of any and everything, from trucks to cars to the occasional motorcycle, which drove my mom crazy.

"Sorry, you have to be twenty-five to drive a rental car in the U.S. And it says here—you're twenty-four." Andrew looked at me ruefully and we both laughed. Transition Guy, Boy Toy, I was having too much fun to notice.

BUT THE CONTINENTAL drift became harder to ignore. A few months later Andrew moved to Tokyo to become Japan correspondent for the *Melbourne Herald Sun* and the rest of Rupert Murdoch's Australian newspapers. I ran the numbers. There was the twelve-hour time difference. The thirteen-hour flight. The fact that I was thirty-three years old. The hundreds of attractive, eligible women he'd meet. Ever the optimist, I gave the relationship a 7 percent chance of success.

But somehow we didn't break up. We talked virtually every day, and every few months one of us got on a plane—including one flight courtesy of *Dateline*. Hearing that I had a boyfriend in Tokyo, Neal decided I was the perfect correspondent to send to Japan and China to report on a notorious World War II prison camp in Manchuria known as Unit 731. My boss turned out to be a lot more understanding of my relationship than many of my friends, including Ginger. Unable to lecture me in person, Gin sent a series of increasingly urgent e-mails before reluctantly accepting the situation with, "Just as long as it's nothing serious." The P.S.—"But don't say I didn't warn you"—didn't need to be written.

But I found having a long-distance boyfriend actually fit perfectly with my pell-mell life. In those days, it seemed I was always on a plane heading somewhere, and I loved it. Almost all of the time. April 19, 1995, was one of the exceptions.

News of the explosion at the Murrah Federal Building reminded me of the bombing at the World Trade Center in New York two years before when a truck carrying explosives had gone off in the basement of one of the buildings. Six people had been killed and another thousand injured on that day, and my throat tightened as I wondered what the death toll would be in Oklahoma City.

But no one knew. "From the look of that building, there may be a lot of victims," the assignment editor told me. "And, Sara—the bomb went off just after nine local time. A lot of parents had just dropped their kids off at the day care center on site."

I felt my stomach lurch. The fact that adults had lost their lives was terrible enough. I couldn't bring myself to think about the children.

I hung up and dashed for the airport, catching an NBC News charter with Tom Brokaw and several producers. *Who could have done this?* I wondered, and could only imagine it must have been foreign terrorists. I was wrong, of course—most of us were—but only about nationality. As America learned that day, any ideology stoked by hate and fed on anger is combustible. And terrorism can happen anywhere.

Before and since Oklahoma City I have covered many disasters. Too many, I think, now that I am older and the cumulative weight of them seeps into dreams, makes ordinary anxieties loom larger than they otherwise might. I have never grown accustomed to the metallic, bloody taste of fear. Worse yet, the plot is invisible until long after the fact. Sometimes it feels as though you're driving through Spanish moss, trying to glimpse the truth through trailing vines. It's not always clear who the good guys are, much less whether they'll carry the day.

After so many years as a journalist I find I've grown less certain, less confident than I was back then, but I know this much: I became a reporter because I hoped the plot would be clearer if I saw things up close and could do my own detective work. Because I was young and brazenly certain I was fair and objective and could report anything without exposing the flank of my own feeling. Because I was nosy and passionate, because I liked to read and write and ask questions. Because I loved roller coasters and caffeine and downhill skiing and scuba diving, but the rush wasn't enough. Because I held some twisted belief that life lived in the shadow of guns would prove more real, that in such a crucible I'd be forced to make choices which would reveal who I truly was. Because I wanted to be reporter Martha Gellhorn or pilot Beryl Markham and see the rough, tattered edges of the world before they were mugged of mystery. And I also became a reporter because I was an idealist and thought travel would confirm my prejudice that we humans have much in common and can resolve our differences if we choose. I still count myself an idealist but a chastened one, because along the way I've learned too much about the unenlightened self-interest of the human species. I've been forced to witness a creative potential for extraordinary evil which all too often obscures our enlightened, but sluggish impulse for good.

When I landed in Oklahoma City that day, I teamed up with two *Dateline* producers I'd never met before, Marsha Bartel and Lisa Semel. Years later I can still hear the scrunch of our shoes as we picked our way through the broken glass from the blown-out windows of the federal building. I can still smell the acrid, sickening, poisonous air, still remember how I gasped upon seeing that once-imposing edifice up close for the first time, its façade ripped away to reveal crumpled walls, mangled steel, a desk teetering over the abyss. What had become of the man or woman who sat there, who'd been answering the phone or typing a letter? Had they survived? Who had done this? And how could it have happened?

Fueled by adrenaline and desperate for answers, we worked day into night into the frosty, bitter dawn, emerging to rub our eyes against the glare of a sky stained like broken ice. I was unaware of what I ate, when I slept, especially since sleep was little more than a three-hour collapse, still in my suit, onto a hotel mattress, to arise, shower, and head for the next assignment.

Because the story in Oklahoma City was immense and multifaceted, *Dateline*'s executive producer and senior staff in New York assigned different teams to cover each element. While our colleagues handled the investigation, Marsha, Lisa, and I reported on the search for the missing, the vigil of the waiting.

Appearing as streaks of blaze orange and brilliant yellow, rescue workers combed through the treacherous rubble, using their dogs to search for survivors. I jumped at the wail of sirens, and ached at the sight of heads bowed in prayer. Each action, each sound became intertwined, until the hours turned into days, the temperature plunged, a cold rain fell, and as the term "rescue" gave way to "recovery," it became clear these men and women risked not only their lives but their equally fragile hearts. When we caught up with a rescue worker named Russ Bovay, he pulled aside his breathing mask to talk and his bright blue eyes were ringed in red. "If my family was in there I would want . . ." He paused, composed himself. "I'd like every last effort made. But after it gets so long and this type of collapse—it's tough."

After four long days, a devastating answer could be better than no an-swer at all, as we learned from Betty Lewis after the body of her forty-three-year-old daughter Charlotte was found. With great composure Betty told us, "I feel better now we don't have to worry that she's there in the cold with all those bodies. So I have more peace."

I thought it couldn't get any harder. I was wrong.

Our team was assigned a story about the first day in a new location for the children who'd attended the day care center in the basement of the Murrah building. Counselors were on hand, including one who had brought a pet monkey. I thought of Ginger. She would have loved how the bright-eyed chimp captivated the little boys and girls and helped them settle in. And while it was hard to see so many little kids with bandaged heads and bruised arms, multiple stitches covered by Lion King Band-Aids, we knew they were the lucky ones. Nineteen children had been murdered that day.

Twenty-three-year-old Edye Smith was a secretary for the IRS, and her children attended the America's Kids day care center just a few blocks away. When the truck bomb exploded, Edye's three-year-old son Chase had died immediately. Two-year-old Colson was pulled from the wreckage but died in a rescuer's arms.

"Since they had to die, I'm glad they died together," Edye told us bro-kenly. "I couldn't have dealt with seeing one of them grieve over the loss of the other one, and it would have been hard to try to explain it, especially to the older one."

As I listened to this young mother, a woman ten years my junior, speak of her beloved sons, I found it increasingly hard to breathe, and felt I might suffocate from the weight of so much sadness. But Edye wasn't finished. She told us that as difficult as it was to talk about losing her boys, it was also a way for her to heal. And she wanted to pay tribute to her children, both for all they had been and for all they had not been allowed to become.

In the warm, inviting home Edye and the boys shared with her parents, Kathy and Glenn Wilburn, we were entrusted with precious home videos to use in our story. There were the boys, splashing at the beach. Making their first snowman. And, just two weeks before the bombing, toting twin blue baskets as they hunted for Easter eggs.

"You know, Chase always wanted to be a star," Edye confided. "So everybody is going to know what he looks like, and know who he was, and that he was special."

But it was when she spoke about dropping them off at school that morning that I thought I might splinter like the windows of the federal building. She spoke of how the boys had been eating donuts all the way to school, and how when she'd dropped them off and prepared to leave, Colton at first had refused to give her a kiss. "So I pretended to cry and I turned around to walk out and he goes, 'Kiss, hug, Mommy kiss.' So I gave him a kiss and he wanted to kiss me again so I kissed him again and I got crumbs on my face." As she paused, I could imagine it all, my tears stung, then she continued, "I walked over to where Chase was playing on the floor with the other children and he wanted to give me a kiss, and he gave me a hug and he said, 'I love you, Mommy.' " By now the broken voice had faded into a whisper. "I turned around and that's the last time I ever saw them."

I could barely hold it together as we said our good-byes, overwhelmed by this intimate encounter with grief. What had happened was senseless, tragic, devastating, wrong. But those were words, just words, clumsy and insufficient. Words could not return those two darling boys. Words couldn't give their mom snuggles under the blankets and Christmas mornings, unexpected kisses and class photos and refrigerator art. Words couldn't replace T-ball and soccer practice, high school dances and diplomas, milestones now marked by some other mother's child. In the end nothing could make up for buckling a pair of sandals on a squirming toddler, tousling his hair and bundling him off, only to see one of those sandals in the rubble, your child gone. Your children gone. Hide and seek never to return.

I wasn't the one who had lost a child, but interviewing this young mother left me feeling unsettled, queasy. She was so raw and vulnerable. I knew how vulnerable and uncertain I still felt, and all I'd suffered was a recent divorce. Was I guilty of exploiting a grieving woman, preying on her pain? I didn't think so. She had chosen to talk about her sons, and her poignant story would make viewers understand all that had been lost that day in a way that the dry, sterile facts and figures of a disaster never could. The faces of Colton, Chase, and the others who were killed would make this story real. But still I couldn't help but wonder if that was merely a rationalization to make it easier for me to sleep.

I thought about Ginger. I remembered watching the rough cut of her film, quizzing her about missing scenes, scenes I knew she'd witnessed of her beloved baboons tearing each other apart, dying. Scenes she admitted she'd never filmed because they were too painful, too raw. She'd sacrificed material that would have made her film stronger to keep her integrity. But had that been the right decision? After all, she'd watched those very baboons dying of thirst and chosen not to give them water. Science. Journalism. Who made these rules?

And what about me? True, there were the pressures, unstated but clear, for any reporter anywhere. You had to cover the story and in this story people had lost their lives. But what was the line between good journalism and exploitation?

I found I was thinking about Andrew, wishing I could see him, even just hear his voice. But what a foolish thought. I had a boyfriend who lived thousands of miles away.

Late that night, as Marsha, Lisa, and I looked through videotape at KFOR, the NBC affiliate which had become our temporary base, I confided, "I don't know how much more sadness I can take."

"I know what you mean." Lisa nodded.

Marsha paused. "I have two boys myself," she said. "This is tough."

Lisa and I looked at her. We were both single and neither of us had kids.

"They're about the age of Chase and Colton. I gotta tell you, I just want to get home. Hug them. Hold them."

We sat there for a few minutes.

"But we have got to finish this story," Marsha continued. "That's all we can do, for her, for anyone here."

And suddenly I knew she was right. We had met civil, dignified men and women, and we'd been entrusted with the stories of those they had loved, and lost. As the night rolled into morning, and as we agonized over the right shot, the right line, the right tone, something happened. We shed inhibition as well as tears, and began to share our own stories. And as we walked out of the station in that pale hush between starlight and dawn, I discovered that two women I'd barely known had become friends, overnight.

17

GINGER (1995)

Against the crush of New Yorkers window-shopping on a Saturday afternoon in SoHo, I braced myself, remembering the first time I'd returned to Manhattan after leaving for Africa. It had been four years earlier, Sara was still living in Charlotte and Kristy had moved into a new apartment at East Forty-seventh and Second. After a thirty-hour journey through seven time zones and countless cultures, I'd dropped my bags on Kristy's living room floor and turned back to the bank of elevators. I had longed for fresh air, to walk the streets of New York, to see the city through different eyes. Yet when I stepped out onto the sidewalk, I'd nearly passed out. Overwhelmed by rotting garbage, car exhaust, and fresh flowers in the bin at the corner store, horns honking, neon signs flashing, pizza baking, crushed ash and tobacco, a beggar muttering, and, rising above the tide, the nasal, strident voices of businessmen in an animated exchange. Blindsided by excess, my senses had been attacked, suffocated. Before I'd reached the corner of East Fiftieth, I turned and ran back to Kristy's. A hot shower and an hour later, I was fine. It was a quick acclimatization, and one that was getting quicker with each trip home.

This was my fourth trip back to New York City since I'd moved to Namibia, and one of the joys was seeing how Kristy and Sara had connected. While both were busy, they'd become friends, too. And now another old friend from Richmond of both Sara's and mine, Beth Worrell, had joined us. Strolling the streets, Beth and Sara walked ahead of me, their heads tucked together in intimate conversation. I lingered, eyeing a brocade coat and long, buttery leather boots with four-inch heels on display in a shopwindow. I remembered how I'd once been able to run in high heels. Back then, stilettos had felt natural. But after years of walking barefoot in the sand, my feet had spread. They might be tough enough to trek across hot dunes and over thorns, but they were no match for a pair of Manolos.

The crowds drifted past, a backdrop dressed in black, breaking up the image, and then I got a good look at myself. Suntanned in the middle of a New York fall, skin lined after years in the desert and with more than a few scars underneath, but eyes opened wide to take in a city I couldn't see clearly when I'd left six years before.

I had planned to be away from the U.S. for a year. My life in Africa was an intermission, nothing permanent. It was meant to be an interlude, an adventure, maybe I'd find strength, purpose, maybe not. Either way I'd return home. Now I wasn't sure where the bush ended and my soul began. Yet as much as I needed the peace of the wild, at times I craved the pulse of the city, a dichotomy that was at once confusing and invigorating. I found I needed the extremes. My body craved sand, heat, wind, adventure, but at the same time it needed a dose of that parallel reality—a world where people talked about an executive producer's style and ate food that wasn't covered in sand. A world in which I cuddled up with my niece to read her a bedtime story, and where friends weren't voices on a crackly international line, but a warm, wonderful presence.

"Hey, Gin, what do think?" Sara waved, a New York Yankees baseball cap dipped over her eye. I ran to catch up with her and Beth.

"Looks great. Beth, how about a Mets cap for you?"

She scanned the tables and laughed. "Don't they have anything from the Richmond Braves?"

The street vendor stared, then, with a flash of recognition, grinned. "Braves, Atlanta, yes?"

"No," we laughed, pulling each other further down Bond Street.

In a city of 8 million, we only needed each other. When night fell, we headed for the China Grill, ate scallops, drank champagne, including a round sent by a group of smiling men at another table, and laughed until our sides hurt. We never glanced at the clock. When we got back to Sara's apartment, it was 4 A.M.

"That blond one was really cute, wasn't he?" I giggled.

"Yeah . . . cute, rich, and oh, Gin of the Jungle, you had better be careful!" laughed Beth, the sole married one among us. She'd left her two children, Elisa and my godson Trent, at home with their dad, our old friend and her high school sweetheart, Danny.

"No, don't worry. I just haven't seen another man in years . . . does it show? Anyway, it's fun, and remember, I'm engaged."

"Engaged, sure," added Sara. "I'll buy that. But married? That's the picture that gets blurry when you're here. I think you'd better watch out."

"Yeah, and where did you disappear to for an hour? Please don't tell me you were on the phone the entire time."

A look of disbelief passed over Sara's face, followed by a mischievous grin.

"Oh no! Sara, do you get some sort of special rate to Tokyo from a pay phone?"

"He called me back!"

But I'd successfully changed the subject. "I think you're the one who'd better watch out."

Lying on the floor in Sara's living room in our pajamas, mugs of tea and a bag of cookies at our elbows, we could have been thirteen again, back at that long-ago slumber party, telling secrets. Only a few wrinkles gave us away. But who was counting? Certainly not us. Old friends know precisely which lines appeared during a stressful time in a relationship, which are reminders of too much time in the sun as kids, and know, too, the other lines that appear as time slips away. But good friends also know that you wouldn't trade most of them. Especially the laugh lines, which we added to during that wonderful weekend in New York.

"I can't keep my head up. I think it must be noon in Namibia." Kissing them on their heads, I said, "Good night, you two."

As daylight crept through the curtains, I drifted to sleep to the sound of Sara and Beth's quiet laughter.

The next day, after hugging Beth good-bye at the train station, Sara and I walked back to her apartment. Those fifty blocks gave us plenty of time to scheme ways to continue the fun. It wasn't hard. Invitations, miniskirts, and desire—what a potent combination. With Sara's confidence restored and her television star ascending, I found myself on the fringes of a very glamorous world, even if sometimes that meant not going to bed at 4 A.M., but getting up then.

"Gin, the car will be here in fifteen minutes. Are you coming?"

"Wouldn't miss it. I'll be quick." Sara was dressed in a deep red suit; her hair was wet, her face freshly scrubbed, freckles showing. I tumbled out of bed, slipped into my jeans, and followed her to the chauffeured car. She was filling in for Katie Couric on the *Today* show, and it was my chance to visit the studio. For me television programs came in blocks of three-year projects; now I would have a chance to see it live. No bits of film spliced only to fall on the floor, no forgotten sequences, no mistakes. Backstage in a whirl of hands holding blow-dryers and makeup brushes, Sara sat unfazed, reading the latest news and story updates for the show from a tiny computer. A final fluff to her hair, a smack of brick red lipstick against tissue paper, and we were off to the set.

During a commercial break Sara came out of the lights to where I was standing in the back of the studio.

"Gin, I'd like you to meet Bryant Gumbel."

"Hi. Sara tells me you live in Namibia. Never been there, but I was in Kenya last weekend, playing golf. Great place." Though he spoke of his trip in modest terms, I could only imagine the first-class travel, five-star safari lodges, and pristine golf courses. How different his Africa must be from mine. We watched Sara deliver a story directly to camera, her eyes bright, brimming with intelligence and warmth. It was clear that in the past two years, while her heart had healed, work had helped to soothe and complete her, as my life in the bush had for me.

But I found that life in Manhattan could be both exhilarating and utterly disorienting. I'd left New York with only two thousand dollars in the bank and no sense of myself. But now when I came back, I found that I had some sort of weird cachet. Not only was I accepted, I was treated like some

rare bird that had flown in from Africa to tell stories of her exotic life.
People listened, especially men.

"DON'T LET HER fool you," Sara laughed. "Gin's life isn't all about chasing elephants and sunsets. Tell them about the time you nearly drowned."

Several men, some wearing gold cuff links, others leather jackets, clean-
shaven or sporting the latest in facial hair, edged closer.

"Oh, Sara, it wasn't that bad, more ridiculous really, given the fact that
I was sucked into a whirlpool in a river that rarely had water." And yet,
though I had no intention of admitting it, I had been terrified. But in the
middle of Manhattan, the agony of waiting for water, and the relief I'd felt
when the floods finally arrived, a relief interrupted by fear when I'd been
pulled below the surface in a whirlpool, was impossible to explain. It would
seem exaggerated, if not pure fantasy. But I remembered it clearly. Underwater, holding my breath, for how long I have no idea, but long enough to
think of my parents, my sisters, how much I still wanted out of life, and
then to have my very rational thoughts about life and death fuse into one
important question: Would the whirlpool push me out onto a bank of sand
or throw me violently against a jagged wall of rocks? I shook the memory
from my mind, doubting that this group of urbane, sophisticated men with
soft hands and padded pockets could begin to understand my life in Etosha, much less the years I'd spent living with a bunch of baboons.

I started to raise an empty glass to my lips. "Wait," said one man, lightly
touching my elbow, "let me get you a drink, then finish your story."

Sara raised her eyebrows. I knew what she was thinking.

I looked at the collection of men in the room. Advertising executives,
independent filmmakers, and company presidents, each more handsome,
more successful than the next. These were the men I had once wanted to
define me, and now they were attracted to me. Or at least the image of
me—a baboon-grooming, sand-surfing, lion-stalking filmmaker. It all
made for good dinner party conversation and a great deal of temptation. In
my wallet there was a business card from a handsome television executive
who, handing it over, said, "If you need any help, any contacts at stations or

with distributors, just let me know." He paused a second, gave me a sly smile, and added, "I just wondered, how long are you staying?"

For the first time, I acknowledged a question that had been brewing for the past two months: What if I did stay? I wasn't the same injured girl who had run away to Africa. I was stronger, tougher, and, dare I say it, more marketable. There were options that hadn't existed before. After six years away, was the pull of family, of friends, and of the possibility of new adventures here stronger than the pull of the bush? My head was spinning, so was Nad's, and Sara became the lightning rod, the unwitting focus of his fears.

I knew that Nad liked Sara, but "like" is such a benign, misleading word. He respected her talents, was awed by her ambition, and appreciated all that she had done to help my career. But was he jealous of our friendship? Was he threatened by the lifestyle she shared with me when I stayed with her in New York? Was he afraid that ultimately the combined allure of big-city glamour and our close friendship would tempt me away from him? I think, at times, the answer to all these questions was yes. I could hear it in his voice. And yet he never said a word.

It had been three months since I'd packed away my cameras, put the Land Rover keys on the kitchen counter, and left Etosha. Three months since Nad and I had decided to get married. In Namibia this had seemed right, the sensible next step, but now that I was back in the U.S., it was beginning to feel horribly wrong. The wedding invitations sat untouched on my parents' dining room table. My mom looked at the calendar and shook her head, but was willing to give me more time than southern etiquette allowed. I took full advantage, ignoring the invitations and focusing on work.

Six weeks before our wedding day, I took a train from Richmond to Washington, D.C., to formally pitch the baboon film to National Geographic Television. The screening was like stepping back in time. Images of Cleo dancing down sand dunes, SP reaching out to touch her kidnapped baby, and finally the flood restoring life in the riverbed and completing our film. The room was dimly lit, but still I watched the faces of Keenan Smart, the head of the Natural History Unit, Alexandra Middendorf, an associate producer who had become a friend and an advocate of the film, and Jenny Apostle, the head of acquisitions, while they watched the film. They laughed and sighed deeply at all the right moments. As the end credits rolled, we talked about what additional footage we hadn't included which could be used to bolster important scenes, how to involve their host in the program, and how the film could be marketed. They even asked me how much money—real money—I wanted for it. The meeting ended with their pledge to talk to the executive producer of *Explorer* who would make the final decision, but everything seemed to have gone so well that when I left their offices I pinched myself, thinking I just might have my dream of becoming a National Geographic filmmaker.

A month later, two weeks before I was supposed to get married, I picked up the phone at my parents' house to hear that word had come back from the executive producer. It was quite simple, really. "Thanks, but no thanks." My dream had been destroyed with one phone call.

And the dream of marrying Prince Charming was shattered, too. A life I'd lived and loved suddenly became a commitment that seemed too much. I felt like I was being asked to give up everything—to choose Nad was to choose his world, his life, his continent. Although part of my soul had belonged to the bush from the first moment I stepped on African soil, being home had reminded me that the other half was firmly rooted in America. For Nad there was no division, no confusion. He was complete. I felt completely torn. Saying yes to him would mean giving up part of my identity. I'd done that once with Kevin and it had nearly destroyed me. I didn't think I could survive it again.

A flurry of international phone calls followed, but even with the direct line, there were still so many mixed messages. *Yes, no, I don't know, maybe* . . . I couldn't commit to the time of day. Nad seemed to be the only one with resolve. As far as he was concerned, we had made plans and we were going to keep them.

During long sleepless nights between days full of fittings for my wedding gown, selecting the right color roses for my bouquet and the menu for the reception, I dug deep, trying to get to the core of my discontent. Undoubtedly there was the continental divide—feeling pulled away from my family, my history, and my identity—but there was more, and it was closer to the heart of falling in love. No degree of tossing and turning altered the fact that Nad was a wonderful man. But I feared that by marrying him, I would never again feel that extraordinary rush of falling head over heels in love.

I remembered Sara telling me about a friend who, though excited to get married, lamented, "I'll never again have a first kiss." I knew what she meant. My stomach no longer tightened when Nad walked into a room; my skin didn't tingle at his every touch, feelings that had started to stir during some of my more reckless nights away from him in the city. Nad made me feel secure where once he had made me feel giddy. Our love had changed, shifted onto safer, more predictable, and less exciting ground. I should have been mature enough to realize that this was a natural evolution and accept it thankfully. Yet in the middle of the night, I found myself wondering if this was what Kevin felt when he said, "I love you like a sister." I loved Nad, but I panicked at the thought of standing up in front of God and my family and making a pledge I feared I could not keep.

Running away from reality, from Richmond back to Manhattan, I felt Sara's voice drift over me. I was trying not to concentrate on her questions, just focus on the reassurance in her voice. But the more she probed, the deeper I sank into the couch in her office. The rich maroon fabric was enveloping, a perfect embrace for my desire to simply fall asleep and have someone wake me up when it was all over. But Sara was relentless in her questions.

"What do you want?"

"What will make you happy?"

"What is so wrong with waiting?"

"Do you love him?" That was the $64,000 question. I wondered if she was acting as a reporter, a friend, or a shrink.

When Nad arrived in Richmond, we sought out Sara's father for advice. A professor and an ordained minister as well as an extremely kind man, Dr. James was supposed to marry us in two days. Walking through a blaze of autumn leaves to the door of the Jameses' house, Nad and I drifted apart, each lost in our own thoughts. Dr. James must have sensed this because after greeting us warmly, he asked to speak to each of us privately. While Nad waited in another room, I talked to Sara's father in hushed tones about my feelings and my fears, whether I could possibly vow to make my divided life permanent. With the same warm, intelligent spark in his eye that I'd always seen in Sara, he told me many things, but the words I clung to were: "It is okay to try." This simple message, delivered so sincerely and without any sense of judgment, made me feel as though I'd been pardoned. Instead of being handed a life sentence, I'd been given permission to love Nad as best I could. I didn't know what he said to Nad, but less than forty-eight hours later, Nad was brave enough to stand beside Dr. James and in front of the mantel in my parents' living room and wait for me to walk down the aisle.

As the harpist played, as Beth's son and my godson Trent lifted the end of my heavy Victorian veil, I felt blinded by details. I saw the band of wax flowers and lace that ran the full length of my satin dress. I saw Beth, my matron of honor, waiting downstairs, smiling reassuringly at Nad. Saw my mother, my Grandmother Hall, and two great-aunts, Ise and Virginia, the surviving matriarchs in a family of women who had nurtured me and my sisters, sitting quietly on the sofa. As I edged down the stairs, closer to the living room, I saw my sisters. Tish stood hand in hand with her wonderful boyfriend Mark and smiled. Marsha, who would play for us later, held her guitar, and Dona held Maggie, my precious six-week-old niece.

My closest friends were there. Kristy, who at nine months pregnant had convinced her doctor and her husband, Gordon, that she could make the drive from Tennessee to Virginia for my wedding, since no airline would be crazy enough to take her. Every three hours throughout their ten-hour journey, Gordon had stopped the car and waited while Kristy stretched her legs. Standing against the banister, Kristy looked beautiful and amazingly rested. I caught a glimpse of Stacy, whose friendship had outlasted tennis, as well as changes in boyfriends, continents, and careers. She and her fiancé, Ian, had just arrived from Los Angeles, suntanned and radiant. And there was Sara, with a tall, dark, handsome man standing behind her, his hands resting on her shoulders. She knew better than anyone what it had taken to get to this point, smiled up at me, ready to run with me if I fled or toast Nad and me if I stayed.

At the bottom of the stairs, I took my father's arm and saw his brothers, my uncles Harry, Darryl, and Ralph, who must have been remembering when they too held their daughters' arms, perhaps supporting themselves as much as their girls as they made that symbolic walk down the aisle. I knew that along the way they silently vowed that no matter how much they liked the young men waiting for them, they would never give their daughters away. Candles glowed. The harpist played. Nearby, Nad stood tall, flanked by his family. With dark hair and dark eyes, their physical connection was obvious, but it was their deep feelings for one another that bound them most completely. I thought of Nad's sisters, Mel and Gin, and their families back in South Africa and knew how much they longed to be with us today. Tim, Nad's brother, best friend, and best man, was here, standing shoulder to shoulder with Nad. I spied Tim's beautiful wife, Megan, who was so much fun and so true that I couldn't have handpicked a better sister-in-law. Then I saw Nad's parents, Bob and Laura. Dressed in an ethnic print, Laura brought a fresh touch of Africa to our wedding while Bob brought along his trusted Rolleiflex camera, ready to document the moment when their youngest son said, "I do." Nad smiled. He looked so handsome in his tuxedo, so sure in his love for me and, even now, in my love for him.

The ceremony was brief. Afterward there were toasts, congratulations, kisses, and handshakes. Champagne flowed, and along with the rushing sound of laughter, Marsha's guitar, Dr. James's trumpet, and the harpist's fluid music filled my parents' home. I finally relaxed. I'd made a vow to try and I would keep it. From the beginning, when Nad had swabbed my bleeding nose on the gravel plains in the desert, he'd nurtured our relationship, treating it and me with respect and love. With his help we would work this out.

I moved from group to group, bending down to speak in Aunt Ise's ear, sitting for a while with my Grandmother Hall, and finally meeting the handsome man by Sara's side, a man in some ways I felt I already knew, her

Australian boyfriend, Andrew. He'd just flown in from Tokyo, suddenly immersed in Sara's parents and my enormous family, but he seemed unfazed. He was funny and relaxed, but as he and Nad fell into easy banter, I remained guarded. If I could shield myself from his charms, perhaps I could protect Sara from having her heart torn in half. But standing with Sara and Andrew, laughing as they laughed, feeling the electricity between them, I couldn't help but worry that this New York–Tokyo relationship was destined for heartache; that the schizophrenic nature of wanting to be on two continents at once that had haunted me would soon haunt Sara.

18

SARA (1995–1996)

Sara, can you get me another drink?" I poured Ginger another glass of Moët, eyeing the level of the bottle with alarm. Champagne might be the nectar of celebration, but it was obvious she didn't taste anything except anxiety and dread. How had it come to this? She was dressed the part of the radiant bride—the vintage gown of ivory silk, antique lace veil glowing against her golden hair. But Ginger's brow was puckered, her smile forced. "Is everyone there?"

For a moment I had a weird premonition that if I said no, she might hike up her train and climb out the window. As if she hoped that out there in the dark a stranger would be waiting to steal her away.

"Yes. And Dad's ready, too."

I didn't recognize my friend in the role of Damsel in Distress. She was thirty-four years old and marrying a man she'd lived with for five years. Nad was smart, caring, and funny. Not to mention an elephant-darting, rhino-wrangling pilot. I exchanged a worried glance with Beth, our mutual high school friend and Ginger's matron of honor.

"Ginger, you look beautiful, and wait till you see Nad. He looks so handsome. I bet this is the first time you've seen him wear a tie!" My weak joke prompted the barest upturn in her lips, but it was time for me to head downstairs. I gave her one last hug and promised, "You'll be fine." I wondered if I was lying or just trying to hope her into happiness. Given the knot in my stomach, I could only imagine the one in hers. Clearly, reinventing your life wasn't easy, especially when you opted to marry the man around the world instead of the boy next door.

Ginger's turmoil over reconciling two continents, two lives—family here, work there, love there, friends here—was painful to witness. Did she hanker for the romance of the new as opposed to the dependability of the known? I could relate to that. Was it that she feared trusting her heart to any man? We both knew that a love which seemed certain could prove false. Or was it the endless horizon of forever?

I'd asked countless questions hoping to help her figure it out, to no avail. Perhaps I hadn't asked the right ones. Or maybe I'd asked too many, should have just sat quietly and listened. Only weeks later would I acknowledge the obvious. This wasn't about what I had or hadn't done, wasn't a question of how good a friend I was. Ginger wasn't entirely sure herself what had prompted this crisis and would have to figure things out on her own.

THE IDEA THAT there was nothing I could do ran counter to my personality and to my working model of friendship. When times were bad, I believed the best friend's job was to be a marine—storm the beach, brave the sniper fire, rescue your buddy. The job of Wait and See left me frustrated. Frustrated because I wanted my friend to be happy. Frustrated because that was beyond my control. And frustrated because Ginger's cataclysmic ambivalence made me worry about the path I was taking.

What exactly did I think I was doing with an Australian beau nine years my junior who'd moved to Japan? A beau whose ultimate goal was to return to Australia, probably to one of the picturesque towns in Victoria, near where he'd grown up? How opposite could you get from working for the network in the largest U.S. city? I'd looked at Andrew, bending over to talk to Ginger's grandmother. He had also looked handsome that night, so good you'd never know he'd just gotten off a long-haul flight. During that visit he'd charmed both Ginger's family and mine, including my mom's mother, reigning matriarch of the Marple clan, Grannykins. But I had promised myself after my marriage broke up that I would learn from my mistakes, take my time the second go-round. And I wasn't sure I'd done that. Like Ginger, I clearly had a weakness for a man with a passport and an accent. But that didn't mean I had to marry him.

·

"SO YOU TWO'LL be next, I'll bet!" said one of Andrew's many relatives with a broad wink a few weeks later, as we left the quaint but steamy church in the beach town of Cairns, in far north Australia. It was Boxing Day, the day after Christmas, and Andrew's brother Trevor had just tied the knot with a lovely young woman named Helen.

"You never know!" I responded playfully, then tried to duck out of the family photo. To no avail. The entire rambunctious Butcher clan was on hand, and Andrew's mum, dad, and sisters Chrissie and Kate, as well as a host of tall, tanned aunties, uncles, and cousins, were as warm and welcoming as any visiting Yank could wish. Of course it only made me feel my predicament more acutely. Just what were we doing? Increasingly, it felt like acting in a charade.

Afterward Andrew and I escaped to the nearby Tablelands, where I rented a horse and galloped through the tropical rain forest, emerging wet and laughing but none the wiser. On New Year's Eve we had an early dinner, then watched a crowd of raucous locals howl in 1996.

But as much fun as we were having, I couldn't see where we were going. And I didn't want to repeat the mistake I'd made in my first marriage of hoping that if I ignored unpleasant facts, they'd simply go away.

"What are we doing, anyway?" I asked.

"Having fun. Or we were. But we aren't so much anymore, are we?" Andrew met my gaze with a level one of his own. When my amusing boyfriend got serious and remote, I felt his appeal more keenly.

I braced, took the plunge. "Not so much. It's too hard, you being in Tokyo—"

"—you being in New York—"

"You need to have fun, be young and single, date around—"

"We both need to have fun—"

"It could never work."

"Exactly."

And then, because it was such a mutual, friendly, and thoroughly ludicrous conversation, we both burst out laughing.

"So we feel exactly the same way?" I said cautiously.

"Apparently." Andrew's smile got even broader.

"What a relief!"

"I agree."

I settled down to work out the terms of the treaty. "Now, I'm guessing we shouldn't keep in touch. That would be foolish, wouldn't it?"

Andrew amended, "We'll give it a few weeks off, see how we go. Maybe we'll talk occasionally."

"I'm not sure. Next thing you know, you'll date some gorgeous Japanese woman and I don't want to know about it."

Andrew's smile got broader. "What of it? You'll be dating Yanks, so fair's fair. But okay, if that's the way you want it, so be it."

Then he leaned in to seal the deal with a kiss. "But there's no reason not to enjoy the next few days before you get back on that plane for New York."

"HAVE SOME MORE champagne," urged the handsome blue-eyed former marine and devout vegetarian thirty years my senior. Once again I was celebrating, but this time I wasn't toasting a bride and groom but reveling in my official promotion to correspondent at NBC *Dateline.* The new title came with a bigger salary and an office with a view of the Rockefeller Plaza skating rink.

"Are you pleased, Sara?" pressed my dinner companion and agent, Stuart Witt. "A job on a network magazine show, filling in on *Today.* Not bad for thirty-four. And you're not upset about that Australian guy, right?"

"Stu, I'm thrilled. And being single was my choice. Well, mutual."

"Good. What's wrong with the men here? You dating?"

"I've been out a bit. No one special."

"You're a jogger. Join the New York Running Club, do the marathon."

My agent as yenta—I wasn't ready for it. "Look, Stu, you're the marathoner, not me. I'll be all right, don't worry. I'm enjoying being single."

And I was. When I looked back on just three years before, it was hard to believe the married woman with the stately home and the shaggy dog in a New Jersey suburb had been me. While it felt strange to be single—as even before my marriage I'd usually seemed to go from boyfriend to boyfriend—I was increasingly grateful that my ex-husband had forced a split, which liberated us both.

As for work, my new contract afforded me the chance to purchase a home of my own, an apartment on the city's Upper East Side. New friends like *Dateline* producer Andi Gitow and *Nightly* producer Susan Morris salvaged my decorating disasters, and with the apartment freshly sponge-painted, with flowers resting on the piano and a tiny table and chairs on the terrace, it was time to invite friends and colleagues over for a housewarming party.

Better yet, Ginger was in the U.S. for a few weeks and arrived in New York carrying a small suitcase and a large Virginia ham. I was relieved to see that her woebegone expression had disappeared and that her infectious laugh was back. She seemed like herself again. When I tentatively asked about Nad, she replied, "It's going much better than I had expected," with a smile before changing the subject by retrieving my to-do list. "Now what's next?" I had asked enough questions on her last visit; this time, I would wait and let her tell me more when she was ready.

On a warm, brilliant night, wearing a cool pair of cropped white pants and a sleeveless mint green silk shirt, I looked around to see my living room filled with pals new and old. I still smile when I remember the sight of an old UVA pal, Ward Johnson, in animated conversation with a journalist I'd met through Andrew, Pilita Clark, not to mention the circle of puppy-eyed would-be suitors crowding around *Dateline* correspondent Elizabeth Vargas. Another mutual friend of Ginger's and mine had designed the quirky invitations to the party. Glenn Zagoren quickly made friends with everyone else in the room, too, inviting many of them to his traditional Turkey Bowl party. The laughing and dancing lasted until the wee hours of the morning.

"Can we call it Ginger's Room?" said my friend as she made the bed in the guest room and prepared to leave.

"It's yours anytime," I replied as I hugged her good-bye. But on that occasion when Ginger left, while I missed her company as much as ever, I no longer felt disoriented and desolate on my own. Sipping a cup of coffee on my terrace on the eighteenth floor, I surveyed the city, wide and noisy and full of promise. I had no one to support but myself. I had great friends who were also single, excellent company for movies or theater or dinner, even trips. On weekends I could run or lounge in bed and read. I could throw my clothes on the floor, drip on the carpet, squeeze the toothpaste in the middle, and leave half-filled teacups strewn everywhere. I could let the food in the fridge turn radioactive. There was always delivery. Or spend a night out on the town. I was free to date anyone I wanted. I went out with a dot-com guy. A couple of lawyers. My friend Ann Curry even played match-maker, setting me up on a blind date. It resulted in a few enjoyable evenings at the theater and more than a few questions from Katie, Matt, Al, and Ann herself on the set of *Today*. But there were no headlines, nothing serious. And that was fine with me.

Mostly, I just traveled. And loved it. Loved the airport, with all those beautiful planes dressed up in their team colors, from stately British Airways to the rambunctious upstarts. I'd flown so often that I'd earned "gold" status on three airlines and platinum on a fourth and could usually upgrade to first class, where I would read the research packet the producer had supplied about the latest story I was about to cover. Then I'd arrive in an often unfamiliar city and settle into a Hertz car, figuring out where the trunk latch was hidden and whether the gas tank was on the left or the right, before driving to an interview. And at the police station or attorney's office or university or home, I'd sit down in a room that had been transformed into a television studio for the kind of frank chat you never have with a stranger. Except on TV.

And at the end of what was always a long day, I'd drive to the hotel and open the blinds to check out a vista glittering with streetlights. And if it wasn't too late, I'd have dinner with the producer and crew downstairs or in a nearby restaurant or else cuddle up with a book and room service, enjoying the solitude, enjoying eating whatever I wanted with no one to comment. And then I'd fly back to New York, trying to wangle a seat on the left side of the aircraft if we were landing at LaGuardia for the first glimpse of Gotham, that neon Welcome Home.

But as the months passed, an occasional fluttery feeling of panic became more frequent. At thirty-five, there was no way to deny I was in my "mid-thirties," a time when many of my friends were already married or about to be. My friend Sharon, who'd had so many dating disaster stories of her own, now had a wonderful boyfriend and didn't sugar her sage advice. "Sara. If you want to get married, sweetie, not to mention have kids, you need to get going." I tried not to think about it, but increasingly, weddings and baby showers gave me the heebie-jeebies.

And the truth of the matter was, there *was* a man in my life. Sort of. Although I never saw him, given that he lived 6,760 miles from New York.

Two weeks after we'd officially broken up, Andrew had called. Before long we'd resumed our daily chats, and thanks to the Internet, we could also correspond by e-mail. After all, what was the harm? We were Just Friends. I figured it wasn't a problem because it didn't stop either one of us from dating. But I did wait a while before confessing to my girlfriends, especially Ginger. When I did, their response was swift and unanimous. This was Not Wise.

Perhaps not, but I still appreciated his warmth, intelligence, and kindness, and the distance made our connection feel safe. Plus I had too much to think about. It was the spring of 1996 and I was about to leave on another assignment, one that, while important, was anything but safe. It would take me back to Africa. I wasn't so sure about telling my parents, but I couldn't wait to tell Ginger.

19

GINGER (1996)

It was 1 a.m., and I couldn't sleep. If I had been in New York with Sara, I might just be getting back from a night out with her friends at some exotic restaurant, about to peel out of my little black dress. But I wasn't in New York. I was in Etosha, where I was once again babysitting in the bush. I heard the sound of branches breaking, feet stomping, the fence giving way. The toddler in my charge was having one massive temper tantrum, wrecking my backyard. I rolled over, put the pillow over my head, and moaned. "Elee, please. Stop it. I'm trying to sleep."

I tried fading to black, counting sheep. All I saw were elephants. I tried listing all the things I loved about my life. Space. Not having to answer to a boss. Learning new animal languages. Freedom. Capturing beautiful images on film. Drifting naked down a flowing river. Investigative work into animal behavior. Driving out onto the plains at sunrise. Still being there at sunset. Storytelling. I loved my life, I truly did. I had fought hard for it. But at 1 a.m. with my thoughts clouded by sleep deprivation, suddenly my friend Sara's life looked better.

She owned her own apartment. I lived in a government house. She could write a Zagat restaurant guide to dining out in New York, London, and L.A. My cookbook would be called *300 Ways to Cook Pasta for Under $1 a Serving*. She could order takeout, a different cuisine delivered to her doorstep every night. I brought food supplies in monthly bulk with no one to cook but me or Nad. She had a substantial salary that would come in month after month, year after year, without break while she developed new story ideas. Not an assurance in the freelance world. She had benefits—hospitalization, dentist, stock options. Not me. She could keep an audience riveted with the stories of her travels, the knowledge she'd plumbed from years on the road from the White House to Whitehall. I talked about baboons. My life was removed, completely out of touch. Sometimes I felt like I had only one story, one life, while my friend had many and each was more interesting than my own. Sometimes it was hard not to compare. And many times I longed to trade places with Sara . . . for a night or two . . . or two thousand and two.

"Dammit, *stop it, Elee!*" Starting with tonight.

The next morning I refocused on my life, conjuring up all the magical elements that had drawn me to the bush and kept me there. There was this great wild world to explore, ephemeral bonds formed with animals which could turn on you in a flash but didn't—moments of clarity when, after years of observation, an animal's behavior suddenly made sense and a story took shape. Unique to my world, these were gifts I never would have discovered in New York. And there were more. There were gifts with names and faces—baboons like Pandora, Smudge, and sweet Cleo; a baby rhino; my husband, Nad; and when I saw who was waiting for me at the fence, I added another name to the list, Elee.

"Come, Elee, come." I started walking to the fence in our backyard. From behind the shade of a mopane tree, a four-hundred-pound baby elephant came running toward me at full speed, one elephant alone without a herd of elephants in sight. "Hey, sleep well?" I laughed. "Listen, you kept me awake half the night, and there is something I must tell you, since your mom isn't here . . . Elee, you are a diurnal creature. That means you are active during the day. And it means you sleep at night, so I can sleep!" I rubbed his head. "Okay, Elee? Please? Thanks. You can have some water now."

After I'd filled his trunk with water from a hosepipe, Elee reached out to me with his trunk. The thin skin dividing his nose quivered, reminding me that this long, dexterous tool, strong enough to push over a tree and sensitive enough to lift a grain of corn from the sand, was also an elephant's nose. I placed my hand over the end of his trunk. It was wet, with short, spiky hairs, and ticklish. He blew hot air into my hand. "You are a very sweet Elee," I laughed while scratching his head, his thick skin reminding me of our little rhino. After the rhino's heartbreaking death, this would be my second chance at animal motherhood. I just hoped that this time it would end more positively, as his story was also rooted in sorrow.

Elee came from Damaraland, a dry, dusty area a hundred miles west of Etosha. Against a vast backdrop of flat-topped mountains and baked red earth, elephants were forced to travel long distances in their search for food and water. The humans for whom this harsh land was a birthright stayed put, eking out a meager living as subsistence farmers. Inevitably the two intelligent species met, and for Elee's herd, conflict had led to crisis. A water reservoir had been smashed, crops were trampled, and a baby elephant had squealed in fear. To protect their livelihood and possibly their lives, one farmer had fired a shot. The bullet had lodged in the chest of our little elephant's mother. She'd turned and run with the herd, dying later, her youngster by her side.

Namibia's game capture unit had found him, alone, standing over his mother's dead body. Without the protection of his herd, he never would have survived. Nevertheless, he refused to leave his mother without a fight. He had run for twenty miles, until the game guards had gotten close enough to throw a rope around his neck, stick a needle into his backside, and finally, once the sedative had taken effect, load him in a truck. Hours later, when he ended up in our backyard in Etosha, he was angry, tired, and lost. He had nothing. Nothing but us, a pair of humans he had every right to hate.

It had taken several days of constant care from Nad and me, but soon he began to trust us. Just us. The scrapes and cuts Elee had suffered while running through the bush had healed. But those were superficial injuries. What about those scars deep inside? Elephants are sensitive, intelligent creatures, animals that live with and learn from a protective herd. As a male, at around fourteen years old, he would ultimately have left his family, moving alone or joining other bachelors for company and in a time-honored search for females to mate. But that break was only supposed to happen in the next decade, not now. As much as we loved him, there were things he needed to learn that we could never begin to teach him. We could only give him a shadow of his real life. He needed to be with elephants.

"Elee, we are going to find you a family. Nad is flying right now, trying to find you a herd." He shoved me, settling his shoulder against the fence and my chest. "It's taking longer than we thought," I explained. "Please just be patient."

In his search for a breeding herd of elephants, Nad flew for hours, criss-crossing the entire park, all 22,000 square kilometers of it. He didn't see a single suitable surrogate family. Though curious as to where these massive animals might be, we couldn't wait any longer to relocate Elee. He needed to be moved quickly, before we became even more attached to him.

With permission from Namibia's Ministry of Environment and Tourism, Nad phoned the owner of a private game farm with a resident breeding herd of elephants. He offered Elee a home. Two days later, without drugs, darts, or drama, Elee walked past Nad into a game capture truck. He was relaxed, eating bits of grass and stripping mopane leaves from branches we'd cut for him. Nad reached through the slats of the container and injected him with a sedative to keep him calm for the trip. After he'd fallen asleep, I walked in and rubbed his head for the last time, reassuring him once again that it would be all right.

Unlike my unwittingly false reassurance to the baboons, this time I was right. We released him on the game farm and within two days the resident herd of elephants accepted him. Elee had a new family.

Nad and I returned to Etosha, to our empty backyard. At night, I would lie awake listening to jackals cry and genets screech, hoping for the sound of an elephant trumpeting. I had to settle for silence, knowing ultimately that both Elee and I had a wonderful life—perhaps not the life we had imagined, but a life we could learn from, one that would complete us.

My list of reasons for living in the bush was growing. I knew that if Sara had a list for doing the job that she loved, fame and fortune wouldn't be on it. They were by-products of many years of honing her talents, of hard work, and of real sacrifice, making tough choices to tell tough stories. Which was why she was about go to Sudan. I might envy Sara's life at times, but I didn't want it. All I wanted was for her trip to Sudan to end safely. And then all I wanted was her here.

20

SARA (1996)

YOU DON'T HAVE to go," said Neal Shapiro, *Dateline*'s executive producer. "I want to make that clear to both of you. This assignment is entirely optional."

Producer Lisa Hsia and I looked at each other. We were in a meeting with Neal, as well as with NBC vice president David Corvo and NBC's lawyer in charge of network standards David McCormick. Everyone looked grave.

"I know," Lisa said.

"We want to," I added.

"Do you have visas?"

"We'll have passports but we won't be clearing customs in Sudan," Lisa said. "As far as the government knows, we won't be there. They don't want anyone to document what's happening in the south. If we are going to prove there's slavery, this is the only way."

"Now let me get this straight," Neal continued. "Once you get there, you will be on your own. No car, no truck. You're hundreds of miles from anywhere. If the militias strike, how do you get out?"

"We'll use our satellite phone to call the pilot at the air charter company," said Lisa, who'd researched the trip meticulously.

"And how long will that take?"

"A day."

Everyone was quiet. There were some things research couldn't fix.

Then Neal said, "I can't tell you how careful I want you to be. Both of you."

I appreciated Neal's warning, but it didn't lessen my resolve to journey to the largest country in Africa, to cover an outrage which had gone virtually unnoticed.

The background went like this. Civil war had racked Sudan for thirteen years, and the Muslim fundamentalist regime in the north had declared a "jihad," or holy war, against Christians in the south, a tribal people known as Dinkas. But now international rights groups, including Christian Solidarity International, were reporting that thousands of women and children in the south were being bought and sold as slaves. Chattel slavery in 1996. It was almost incomprehensible. Since President Omar al-Bashir's regime denied the charges, we decided to sneak into the country to learn the truth for ourselves.

As committed as I was, the timing was terrible. During my years as a reporter I'd missed my share of Thanksgiving feasts, family gatherings at Christmas, and New Year's Eve toasts. There was always next year. Except this time. In 1993 my Richmond roommate, Lisa, had married Lewis Powell, a boyishly handsome, intelligent attorney who wore the mantle of being the son of a U.S. Supreme Court justice lightly. They'd just had a daughter, and I was honored to be Hannah's godmother. But going to Sudan meant I would miss the christening. While Lisa was supportive, I could hear the disappointment in her voice, and it was clear she worried about me and didn't entirely understand my desire for yet another dangerous assignment. Not surprisingly, neither did Mom. As for Andrew, he urged caution but sounded increasingly preoccupied with his single life in Tokyo. I tried not to think about who might be keeping him busy as I headed to JFK.

My producer, Lisa, and I flew to Sudan with a team including a South African camera crew and Baroness Caroline Cox, Deputy Speaker of the British House of Lords and president of Christian Solidarity International. We landed on a dirt strip where a group of tall, thin men and women waited. Everyone pitched in to help carry the numerous boxes of gear back to the village, a collection of huts on a tributary of the Blue Nile. The surrounding countryside was bleak, as most trees had been cut down for firewood and there was no need to fear lions. Game in this part of Africa had long ago been killed for sport or sustenance. When I spotted a pretty bird and asked its name, I felt a wave of sadness for both the people and their wildlife when the gaunt translator replied, "Food."

We pitched our tents next to a bullet-riddled shell of a building, eating a dinner of military rations, or MREs, as the baroness explained the situation in the south. Several times a year, an army train would rumble through the region, flanked by well-armed but unpaid Arab militias for whom human beings were often the spoils of war. "They tend to kill the men and they tend to take women and children as human booty," the baroness explained in a voice of quiet indignation.

"And when will the train come through?" I asked.

The translator hesitated. "Sometime very soon."

That night, as I had so many years before in Nicaragua, I slept with my boots by the door of the tent flap.

WE KNEW THAT the only way for families to rescue loved ones was to buy them back at a slave auction, which was held in a small market eight miles away. As there were no cars, we set out on foot, carrying heavy gear, for the three-hour hike. We started out at daybreak to beat the heat.

As we trudged along the path across the baking earth, we chatted with our Dinka porters, some of whom had learned a good bit of English. At one point one man paused to talk to a few local herders, and by their gestures I realized I was the subject of conversation.

"What was that all about?"

"I am not sure you wish to know."

"I wish to know."

"Well then. That man wants to know if you are for sale."

"What!!" I stopped in my tracks to stare at him. "We're on our way to do a story about slavery—and you're talking about selling me?"

His laugh was loud and immediate. "Oh, this is very different! This man wanted you as a wife!"

"Oh yes, that's *totally* different."

"Besides, he made a good offer."

In spite of myself I was curious. "Purely from an informational point of view, what was my price?"

"Twenty cattle." I gave him a sharp, probing look, and clearly thinking he'd offended me with a low-ball offer, he hastened to continue. "He has several wives already but was willing to make such an offer because you are—different."

I'd considered many dangers in taking this assignment, but being traded for cows hadn't been one of them. But as I smiled, ready with a quick retort, he added, "The man did have one question. He wanted to know how many children you have."

"I'm not married. I don't have kids."

He looked shocked. "What? No children?" He shook his head. "That is very sad. You are a poor woman indeed."

And suddenly an amusing situation wasn't funny at all. In fact, his comment stung like a slap in the face. I opened my mouth to argue that I was an independent, successful professional woman. But what was the point? It wouldn't change his opinion. Besides, infuriated as I was, I was also alarmed at how much his offhand comment had shaken me. With nothing to say, I took a shot of already warm water from my canteen and tried to remind myself why I'd wanted to come to Sudan in the first place.

For me the assignment wasn't just professional—it was personal. At thirty-five years old, I'd lived in New York for four years, long enough for the city to feel like home, especially since my mom had been born there. But I was also a daughter of the South. During the Civil War, Richmond, just two hours south of Washington, D.C., had served as capital of the Confederacy. Even today the city's most beautiful street, Monument Avenue, is a Southern Hall of Fame, with statues in honor of Robert E. Lee, Jefferson Davis, Stonewall Jackson, and J. E. B. Stuart. In fact Ginger's younger sister Dona married Stuart's handsome, upstanding great-great-grandson.

Richmond has changed over the years. Indeed, the most recent statue on Monument Avenue is of an African-American man armed only with a tennis racket. Once banned from the city's whites-only courts, tennis great Arthur Ashe now shares an address with those who fought to create a country in which he could have been a slave. Much as I loved Virginia and being a Virginian, for me being born in the South also meant feeling both sorrow and shame regarding the disgrace of slavery. The thought that slavery might still exist was not just barbaric, it was obscene. After all, a Virginian had written the Declaration of Independence, with that stirring promise that all men are created equal, and my own liberated life made it impossible to imagine one person owning another.

I THINK I expected some Hollywood version of a slave market—a wooden platform where the overseer cracked his whip while men, women, and children were paraded. But this auction was clandestine. At the edge of a large open market where the local Dinka people came to buy sugar, flour, and cattle, a slave trader aptly named Chain lurked under a copse of trees. While he was dressed in long, flowing white robes, the bony, sickly-looking boys and girls huddled together in the shade were dressed in rags, as if they might still be wearing the clothes they'd had on when they'd been kidnapped, as long as five years before. Nearby, families had gathered, hoping to find long-lost children. But buying a child's freedom cost hundreds of dollars, and most of these families were penniless. That meant Baroness Cox, an outspoken opponent of slavery, would now be in the awkward position of becoming an unwilling participant in an ancient, ugly transaction. She had brought thousands of dollars raised overseas to purchase as many slaves as possible. Now she must haggle with Chain.

"What price freedom?" she said in a voice choked with outrage, each time a child was brought forward and a wad of money changed hands.

One little boy told us, "We were forced to herd livestock. If we complained, they beat us."

I asked another, "When was the last time you saw your mother and father?"

He looked down, kicked at the dust, and I saw the scars on his ankles left by the ropes which had kept him tied to a post so he wouldn't run away.

"Four years ago," came the desolate reply, and I thought I would weep. No chance to run or chase or kick a ball. No one to hug him when he tumbled, no one to kiss him good night. Four years. Half his short, tragic life. The little children told of how they'd been fed little more than scraps thrown to a dog, how they'd sometimes been so hungry they'd eaten grass. But some stories were too terrible to tell, and could be glimpsed only in the haunted look in their eyes. Beatings. Rapes. Murders. Memories of fathers who had been shot, of brothers and sisters lost, never to return.

As the bartering continued, it felt indecent, as if some sort of stain were seeping into me. I wanted to crawl out of my skin. Chain was every bit as ruthless as I'd expected, snatching bills, shoving children. I wanted to jump in, grab that little girl with her dirty brown hair and knobby knees, that little boy with his wobbly lip, scoop them in my arms, and flee. How could my ancestors have done this?

When the whole awful business was over, Baroness Cox sighed with relief. She had liberated fifteen little boys and girls, paying the equivalent of five hundred U.S. dollars for each, and the children were now enveloped by waiting mothers and fathers. "It's such a distressing situation to be part of that words cannot convey the distaste of being part of that transaction, but what do you do?" she told us. And yet she had no qualms about what her organization was doing, dismissing any suggestion that paying to free the children would increase the number of children kidnapped and enslaved.

"That's rubbish. Slavery was going on before we ever came."

The baroness told us the best chance of eliminating the slave trade would be to bring world attention to the plight of those in southern Sudan, in the hope that international pressure might bring an end to the wretched practice.

I looked at the faces of these children, and thought of my new god-daughter Hannah back home, whose life was so different from the lives of children here. I thought of all the stories I'd covered overseas and at home where defenseless children had been the victim of trauma and tragedy—in Somalia, in Oklahoma City, and now in Sudan. And suddenly the pressure I felt wasn't international but personal.

I had an impotent urge to rescue them all, especially one girl of about nine. She and her mother and sister had been taken during a raid two years before, as her father, Apin Apin Acot, watched helplessly. She sat on his lap, head tucked into his shoulder, as he protectively held his arm around her. "Look at her leg," Apin told us, gesturing. The girl's leg had been broken but never reset, so that she would walk with a severe limp for the rest of her life. "She was not born like this. This happened when they took her." His face showed the anguish of any father unable to protect his child from a desperate fate. And then he told us of his older daughter, who remained in bondage, reserved as a future concubine, and his eyes filled with tears. "She told me death is the only bad thing in life. As long as you are alive, I know you will try to get me out." I thought I would split apart with the weight of it all.

Yet, to my surprise, as Apin turned to look closely at the little girl on his knee, his worn face creased in the barest of smiles, and there came over his face an expression I could only identify as hope. Hope in spite of the fact that his wife had been raped repeatedly during her captivity, in spite of the fact that his daughter would be crippled for life. And then I realized. He had hope because they were alive. What's more, Baroness Cox would give him money to purchase his older daughter, and then his family would be united once more. And that was enough for him to believe that, in spite of a bleak past, the future might be better.

As I looked around, I saw the same expression on the faces of others who had been reunited. This was a hope wilder, stronger than I'd ever encountered, a hope powerful enough to crack through an arid wasteland of despair. While they had lost the most precious gift of their lives, that gift had been found. Their children were home. Anything was possible.

THE FOLLOWING DAYS passed quickly, days in which we worked from dawn until the sun slipped over the edge of the world, when we crawled into our tents for a few hours of hot, fitful sleep. One morning we heard the sound of shouting as a group of men came carrying several injured men. It turned out the dreaded train and its trail of bandits had arrived in the region the day after we had, and their village—just fourteen miles away from us—had been attacked by those militias.

One of the men had the most gruesome wound I'd ever seen. He'd been hacked with a machete and he was missing half his face. Without a mouth he was unable to speak, but the agony showed plainly in his tortured, pleading eyes. The others explained that he'd been attacked when he tried to prevent the marauders from kidnapping a child. We managed to get him airlifted to a hospital but he soon died. Only when that same plane returned for us two days later and we took off for Kenya did I dare to relax.

But as the plane rose sharply and danger both receded and compressed, I had an immediate, uncomfortable realization. There had been no time to think of something so inconsequential during the past week, but suddenly I realized that I stank. The smell of my own body made me nauseous, the smell of days without a bath, the smell of greasy hair, and worst of all, the lingering scent of fear. I was trapped on that tiny plane with my own rank odor and equally intense thoughts.

As we flew over that shimmering East African landscape, I suddenly felt lost, as if the cerulean sky were instead a vast, nameless sea and I was alone in a dinghy, shouting for help, but no one could hear me. I was thirty-five years old and alarmingly adrift. I had a new job, a lovely apartment, a life I loved. I had felt independent and free. But after this harrowing, isolating experience, I realized again that I wanted someone, not just something, to call my own. What use was freedom if you became so shackled to autonomy that you couldn't share your life with someone else?

I'd tempted fate in Nicaragua, the Gulf, Somalia, Haiti, and now Sudan. I'd seen people who'd been shot, macheted, stabbed, beaten, tortured, raped. I'd frightened my parents and sisters more times than I cared to remember, and this world of hard living and too-easy dying was losing its allure.

High above the African plains, it was possible to see life from a distance. And as I looked out the window I finally acknowledged just how badly I wanted to have a child of my own. To feel the kind of love I'd seen on that father's face. Suddenly everything I had, all that I'd accomplished, seemed insignificant in the face of his blazing devotion. Once I had thought having a child might spell the end of chasing my dreams, but my time in that crucible had reminded me that for many people around the world, having the love of a child was the most important dream of all.

And then there was the question of Andrew. I missed my ex-boyfriend far more than I wanted to admit. He was not a Boy Toy any longer but a grown man who was clearly moving on without me. I needed to make my own plans.

Fortunately, I knew that there was someone I could turn to, someone who could guide me through this turbulence, and I'd see her in just a few days. What's more, this trip, my third to Namibia, wouldn't be purely social. When I'd learned about the Sudan assignment, I'd suggested another African story to *Dateline*'s executive producer—a story about a gorgeous filmmaker who'd spent years documenting the lives of a remote troop of baboons. Neal had loved it, and smiled when I mentioned that the filmmaker was my best friend. So now I would have the chance to talk to Ginger in person about what felt like clashing emotions I was only beginning to explore.

Sara, eighth grade.   Ginger, eighth grade.

Sara crowning Ginger "Miss Tucker," 1978.

The fragile beauty of Kevin's Ginger

Newspaper coverage of Ginger's romantic life, July 1983.

Ginger mending a broken heart.

Sara reporting for WWBT-12 News, Richmond, Virginia, 1986.

Sara on the cover of *Charlotte* magazine while she was news anchor for WBTV-3, 1989.

Complete acceptance:
Ginger with Cleo,
Smudge, and Pandora,
1990.

Baboons of the Namib
Desert, 1992.

Ginger with Cleo,
1993.

Ginger naps with the
baby rhino in her care,
1993.

Sara living among the troops in Saudi Arabia during Operation Desert Shield, 1990.

Sara with the 1454th Transportation Company (Concord, North Carolina), whom she covered during operations Desert Shield and Desert Storm for WBTV-3.

Sara on the *Today* show with Katie Couric and Bryant Gumbel, 1992.

Sara interviewing child slaves in Sudan, 1996.

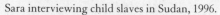

In Etosha National Park for
the *Dateline* shoot, 1995.

Leisure time during the filming of
Legends of the Bushmen for Turner
Original Productions.

Sara and Ginger at Victoria Falls,
1995.

Sara interviewing Afghani refugees
near the Pakistan-Afghanistan
border, 1999.

Nad and Ginger on their wedding day, November 4, 1995.

Kimber growing up behind (2000) and in front of (2004) the camera on the National Geographic film *Born Wild*.

Sara and Andrew on their wedding day, December 26, 1998.

The *Richmond Times Dispatch* covers "Living with Anthrax," which aired on MSNBC's *National Geographic Explorer* on December 9, 2001.

"Safe Soph," 2001.

Sara and Jacqueline, Easter 2006.

Kimber and Smokey, 2006.

Sophie and Jacqueline, 2005.

Kimber, Nad, and Ginger, July 2003.

Sophie, Andrew, Sara, and Jacqueline, July 2005.

21

GINGER (1996–1997)

Seven years in Africa had taught me to listen to the sound of the wind, the snapping of branches, and to listen especially hard whenever I heard the whisper of instinct invade, then overwhelm my thoughts. On that particular night, it was quiet, too quiet, even for the middle of the night in the bush. No plaintive owl hoots, no crunching of hooves on rocks or gentle bays as animals moved closer to the waterhole for a midnight drink. Nothing. Beside me Nad was asleep. I peered into the darkness, listening to the silence for a few more minutes before closing my eyes. Then a wave of sound shook the ground. It was the same sound that drove our ancestors into caves, that inspired them to make and master weapons, a sound that a million years later caused the hairs on the back of my neck to rise. Danger was not only audible, it was stalking us, coming into focus and taking shape.

"Sara. Lisa. Wake up. They're here." As much as they needed sleep after their Sudan ordeal, Sara and Lisa needed to see this even more, to be reminded that Africa was also a place of wonder and astonishing beauty, where power had a purpose and wasn't always abused. I rolled over onto my belly, propped myself up on one elbow, and ran a hand through Nad's hair.

"Sara will be so happy." He smiled, his eyes still closed.

Fifteen feet above us in the tower hide at Gobaub waterhole in Etosha, I heard the ruffle of nylon sleeping bags, then saw the dim light from two tiny beams scanning the bush. "Gin, is that what I think it is?" The lights met and reflected off one large tawny animal. Before I could speak, Sara's question was answered by one tremendous roar. In this part of Africa, Lion was still King.

Nad had been right. This camping trip into the wilds of Etosha was just what Sara and Lisa, her friend and producer from NBC, needed. When they'd arrived a few days before, the strains of their most recent assignment were evident, not so much in what they said as in what they didn't say. As if the horrors were still unspeakable. At night, around the fire, I saw Lisa withdraw, lost in thought, her arms wrapped protectively around her slender waist. One minute Sara would be laughing, then she'd bite her lip and rub her eyes as if to erase a memory I could scarcely imagine. With this camping trip we hoped they could replace their visions of appalling suffering with those of elephants dust-bathing and springbok pronking, of toasting fiery sunsets and drinking ice-cold beer. Sara and Lisa could finally relax; it was my turn to worry.

I—or at least the *Dateline* segment about me—was the light diversion in an otherwise horrific trip for them. The only problem was, now I was scared. Not for my life, but for my career. Ratings for natural history programs were up, and because the costs of making wildlife films was low compared with sitcoms and dramas, television stations around the world were responding to the demand by buying more and more programming. Jen and Des Bartlett's *Skeleton Coast Safari* series, with our baboon film included, was riding the wave. The series had just sold to Channel 4 in the UK and PBS in the U.S. Now *Dateline* was covering our story. I was thrilled but nervous, remembering all too well the words of one commissioning editor after he'd seen a short scene from our film: "I don't like baboons, and I would never, ever watch ugly baboons on TV." So the question remained: Would viewers watch our baboons, and my life with them, as told by Sara on NBC?

With Lisa directing, a South African cameraman and soundman stayed at my shoulder, recording my every move. For three days I did as I was asked, finding it mildly amusing to be on the other side of the camera.

"Gin, walk out onto the pan, put your camera down, and pretend to shoot. Turn, turn. Okay, now pick up your camera and walk to my right. No, *my* right."

"Okay," came the voice from the walkie-talkie, "drive toward me, past the camera. Great. Do it again."

"That's a great tree. Would you please climb up there with your binoculars and pick them up, turn around, then put them down. Can you do it a couple more times?" And so it went. From sunrise to sunset, I scouted locations, gazed deliberately through my binoculars, pulled focus, zoomed in, zoomed out, and did a meaningful scene in our spinach patch. It wasn't long before I yearned to be on the other side of the camera.

Sara and Lisa had ticked off the shots, giving me time to relax in front of the camera, until there was no more avoiding the interview I'd dreaded from day one. In her career, Sara had grilled politicians and executives, famous celebrities and infamous murderers. She probably couldn't count the number of interviews she'd done. Hundreds? I could count the times I'd been interviewed. Zero. For my first, there would be no peeking at the questions beforehand, no Cliff Notes, no warm-ups, just a call to be ready first thing in the morning. Rise and shine.

"Sleep well?" Sara asked while we dodged each other, vying for space in front of the small cracked mirror above the sink in our bathroom, the only mirror in the house.

"All right," I muttered.

"I like your shirt. Pink is a great color on you, and that shade isn't too pale for TV."

"Thanks." Also muttered.

"Want to try my lipstick?"

"No thanks."

Applying a final stroke of mascara, she smiled. "Gin, would you please get me a cup of coffee?"

"Get your own damn coffee," I snapped. What a way to start the morning. Did I look like a maid? This wasn't fun anymore. Everything I'd enjoyed over the past few days—the filming and relaxing around the fire at night with the crew—now seemed like a chore. All I could remember was that, behind the scenes, I'd been the one doing all the cooking and cleaning for four extra people. And now, coffee. Sara obviously didn't have a clue what was going on with me. Couldn't my friend tell that what I needed was reassurance, not lipstick. For her, this might be a simple interview, a few questions, but the thought of it had kept me awake at night. I knew my panic was ridiculous but it was also real—I was afraid I'd embarrass my friend and myself. But instead of sharing those fears with Sara, I did what was predictable with me: I kept them inside, expecting my friend to understand, then, when she'd asked for coffee, I'd cracked.

"Sure, Gin." Sara's quiet voice brought me back. "Can I get you some coffee, too?" And when I'd shaken my head, she'd said, "You'll do great, Gin. Don't worry."

When we pulled the Land Rover up in front of a grove of trees where the cameras were set up and two chairs were placed in the long grass, facing each other, Lisa walked calmly toward us. "Sara, don't panic, but we just saw a snake." Clearly Lisa also knew about Sara's phobia. The morning was only getting worse.

Finally the cameras were rolling. Sara looked me in the eye, tilted her head slightly to the side, and asked, "Had you ever shot a film camera before?"

"No."

"Had you ever taken a professional photograph?"

"No."

"You came on a wing and a prayer."

"Absolutely."

"And about two thousand dollars."

"That's it."

And those were the warm-up questions. The fact that I was nuts was established up front. From there it got worse. Two cameras and endless questions fired at me by my best friend, who was trying very hard, if not always successfully, to pretend she didn't know me at all.

"How did your family feel about you living in Africa? It is a very different world from the one Dona—"

"Cut!" Lisa shouted, leaping to her feet. "Sara, who is Dona?"

I cut in, "She's my sister."

"But we don't know she's Ginger's sister, do we? Now you two stop talking to each other like you're friends!"

Chastened, Sara shuffled through her notes. "Did people think this was a whim, this is gonna pass, Ginger's on a long safari, she's coming home soon?"

"I think so."

"She'll get sick of it?"

"I definitely think so. A lot of people thought, She'll get over it, maybe New York wasn't for her but she'll come back and she'll find out what is. But I found what it is right here." My voice cracked. Was I making any sense at all? I couldn't keep my nervous hands out of my hair. Meanwhile, I should have worried less about my nerves and more about what was coming out of my mouth.

When Sara asked me about our relationship with the baboons, I told her about Nad and the black spitting cobra, how little Cleo had rescued him. "She looked him in the eye and said, *WAHOOOOOOOOOOOOOO!*" My eyes darted sharply toward the camera I'd been told to pretend wasn't there. Would somebody please, please tell me I hadn't just barked like a bloody baboon. What the hell was I thinking? And what was Sara thinking when she pitched the idea of this segment to her boss? Clearly promotion hadn't been on her mind.

Two numbing hours later, after the interview was finished and the cameras packed away, Sara and Lisa drove back to our house with the crew, leaving me alone. When I started to breathe normally again, I confessed to myself that I knew exactly what Sara was thinking. She had thought she could help her friend. Simple. She had contacts, clout, access, and she had used them to help me and other friends repeatedly. It was Sara's friendship with Julie Bruton-Seal that led to my introduction to Jen and Des Bartlett, and that eventually led to the production of the baboon film. In New York, Sara had introduced me to her agent, to executive producers, to network vice presidents, without expecting anything in return. No quid quo pro, no tit for tat, no keeping score, and even now, no apparent regret. Never once had I felt indebted. Sara had shared the perks of her hard work willingly, and with such enthusiasm that it seemed there was nothing better for her career or simply nothing more fun than lavishing eight minutes of prime-time network television on a friend.

I hoped she would be just as pleased when the *Dateline* story was completed. There was one more interview, this one with Nad and me. It was brief and, after my solo interview, painless. Sitting under a huge camel thorn tree waiting for the sun to set, Nad told Sara, "I was actually quite skeptical when we first went out because it *is* rough. I really thought she'd take one week of it and that would be it." But that hadn't been it, I thought. I was still here, seven years later. While the interview was over, I knew Sara still had a lot of questions—but questions which weren't for a national television audience. They would come later when we were alone.

"DO YOU LIKE this one?"

"No, it isn't right for the shape of my face. How about this style?"

Lying together on the carpet in the living room that Sara and her cousin Lynn had given us after their African safari, we flipped through back issues of *Vogue* magazine. Perfume, makeup, haute couture. All a million miles away. Yet despite Sara's recent adventures in turning a bombed-out house in Sudan into a temporary salon, *Dateline* was prime time, *Today* show opportunities beckoned, and on those stages, a great haircut was essential.

"Here, this is the one. It would frame your face beautifully. It's perfect, Sara." She tore out the page, added it to the others in the pile, and laughed. "So what is happening? You look so happy. I keep thinking, How did you get there? It was only a few months ago that I thought we'd lost you for good. You were the most desperate bride I've ever seen."

I sighed. "Desperate is putting it mildly. How about crazy, mad, insane."

"Okay, you win. So how did you do it? What was the path from there to here?"

"Nad left." I smiled.

"He *what*? Talk about bury the lead! You never told me that."

"No, he didn't leave *me*; he left Namibia. He went to South Africa for three months to study for his commercial pilot's license."

"Why didn't you go with him?"

"He never asked. I think he was trying to punish me, to get me back for all I'd put him through before we were married."

"Would have served you right," Sara replied with a chuckle.

"Maybe, but ha-ha, little did he know leaving me alone would turn out to be the best thing he could possibly do for me. It was just me. All I had for company was a pride of lions. Lazy beasts, they sleep about twenty hours a day, so I had a lot of time just to think. Finally, after all the years of having Nad to fall back on, I had the challenge of making myself feel at home alone in the bush."

"Gin, when you were in New York I had the sense that you were tired, that maybe this life had become—too hard, too many fights. I mean, it may be beautiful but the weather here is brutal. It's almost as tough as what you face when you're looking for funding for your projects. And you must get lonely. That would do me in right there. Anyway, all those things people don't think about when they romanticize your life. I still remember when you were so broke you described a glass of Coke as good food."

"I'd forgotten that."

"Not to mention in New York there were all those guys who flocked around you, like Mr. Deep Pockets—"

"He's a wonderful man, but . . ."

"What about that handsome admirer who—"

"Who called *you* as soon as I got on a plane."

"Mostly just to talk about you."

"Anyway, he hardly knew me."

"Nad and you know each other very well. It still doesn't explain why you were so afraid to marry him."

I turned over and watched the fan whirling lazily above us. Sara was quiet.

"I was afraid of losing myself in someone else's life again."

"That was a long time ago, Gin."

"I know, but that's why being on my own here was so good for me. I realized I'm much stronger now. I'm not the twenty-year-old girl who polished her boyfriend's trophies. I've fought damn hard for this new life. I miss you and my family like crazy." I paused trying to explain my epiphany to myself as well as to my friend. "But I love the bush and I discovered that the challenge of life here and those lazy lions were all I needed. I didn't need another man and I didn't need Nad. So when he came back, I realized that I wanted him."

Sara smiled and I wondered if she was thinking about Andrew. I rolled over onto my side and continued, "Remember what they used to say when we were kids? 'Sara will interview the senator and Ginger will be married to him.' It sounds ridiculous now, because it's so selfish and immature. But I think I had to forgive Nad for not being the person I had expected to marry. Once I'd gotten beyond that, I realized he was so much more than I had ever expected. It was like shedding skin."

FAR TOO SOON, Sara and Lisa had to return to New York, back to the world of keeping in touch by telephone and e-mail. But when they called a short time later to say the story had been edited and they just needed information for Stone Phillips's in-studio tag to the taped piece, I had an update. With uncanny timing, our baboon film had just been nominated in the "Best Newcomer" category at Wildscreen, what's known in the industry as the Green Oscars. It was the perfect ending.

A month later my parents invited a few friends over to watch the broadcast that included my life story in eight glamorous minutes. Sara's boss was pleased, and in spite of my fears, Mom and Dad weren't the only ones watching. My cousin Missy called to tell me that she'd heard a group of young women in a bar talking about the segment. "Gin," she told me, "those girls loved it. They said, 'Heck, if she can change her life, so can I!' I was so proud of you."

I found that the story was almost like an extra résumé, showing people what I had done and what I could do, including the brass at Turner Original Productions. Suddenly a project that *Wild!life Adventures* executive producer Thom Beers and I had been developing got a green light. With *Legends of the Bushmen* in preproduction, there would be a professional life for me after the baboon film after all. This one would include an interesting role for me on the other side of the camera. But first we were off on a reconnaissance mission, a reccee. I needed to scout locations, gather ideas, and find talent for the film, to see if we could turn *Legends* into a reality.

STATIC CRACKLED IN my ears and for a moment I hadn't a clue where I was. I looked at Nad, who was spinning a dial on the airplane's instrument panel.

"Good snooze?"

"Where are we?"

"About a hundred miles out. Go back to sleep."

Instead I rested my head on the scratched window and gazed down below. Etosha Pan was a hundred miles behind us; below lay gentle hills, clusters of tall trees, and small depressions in the sand, a monotonously beautiful landscape. From a thousand feet up, it looked soft, pristine, safe. The reality was very different. Black mambas slithered through the sand, sharp thorns jutted off the branches of seemingly benign trees, while leopards stalked silently under the cover of darkness. How ironic that this land, a place of rare beauty, fantasy, and deception, is home to the Bushmen, a group of people shrouded in the same mystique.

The original people of Africa, the gentle people, the first people, hunter-gatherers, the Bushmen are many things to many people. Traditionally, their lives are rooted in the earth, at one with the animals in a relationship of respect, harmony, and predation. Today, some Bushmen still hunt with incredible skill; they still gather foods from the bush, and for the most part, they still understand and revere the land as if their lives depended upon it, because sometimes they do.

But in a world rushing into the twenty-first century, the Bushmen haven't been completely left behind. Sadly, they've been propelled into the margins by land laws that declare areas off limits, stripping them of their ancestral hunting grounds, driving them from the bush into squalid townships where, without formal education and training, alcohol abuse and complacency have created a culture of deep, dark depression. The myth of the wild, gentle Bushmen is just that—a myth, and not one we wanted to perpetuate.

I turned from the window to the backseat of the plane, refocusing on why we had flown here, and mentally ticked off our gear: video camera, stills cameras, film, tapes, a box of canned tomatoes, a six-pound bag of pasta, and two boxes of wine, our provisions for the week. When I turned around, the ground was rising up to meet us.

After coming to a stop, the airplane was surrounded by familiar faces, shy smiles, and laughter. We climbed out of the plane, passing boxes and cameras into willing hands. "*Kaiza,* Nica?" Are you well? the only word I knew in Ju/'hoan Bushmen, but it worked. Nica, a strong Bushman woman and respected tracker, stepped forward and shook my hand. "Ah, lovely," I smiled, touching a collection of ostrich-egg beads twined around her slender wrist. Nad greeted Gui warmly, looking over his tiny frame to where the bow and arrows hung low on his back. As was now the norm, the Bushmen were dressed in clothes that reflected the uneasy meeting of the Western and Bushmen worlds, a torn Nike T-shirt worn next to soft duiker skin, brightly colored beads against faded plaid skirts, a visible reflection of a cultural clash.

"Howzit, Flip." Behind the Bushmen, wearing his standard khaki shirt, blue shorts, and cap, Flip took his pipe out of his mouth and grinned. "Hi, how was the flight?"

Dr. Philip "Flip" Stander, a colleague of Nad's, had been working with this small team of Bushmen trackers for the past five years. A Cambridge graduate, Flip was humbled by the Bushmen's knowledge of animal behavior, likening their wisdom to "the equivalent of many Ph.D.s." A year ago, when Nad and Flip were flying a game census in the area, I'd made a tentative connection to this small band of Bushmen trackers. Now, two months after my original meeting with Thom Beers in Atlanta at Turner Original Productions, Nad and I were back to discuss the filming project with the Bushmen.

Our goal was to make a film that celebrated a positive part of the Bushmen's history, one that is very much alive today: their connection to the land that remains beautifully deep and true, resonating in their legends. In a culture with no formal written language, the Bushmen's spoken words passed from generation to generation, gaining in power and significance.

Their legends speak of a rich history and a proud heritage with gentleness and humor. They are the links to their past and a way of guiding their children forward in a world where it's increasingly easy for them to lose their way. We were asking the Bushmen to share something that was essential to their spirit, and it was important that they felt they could trust us to tell their stories with reverence and sparkle.

Under a canopy of shade offered by a large leadwood tree in Flip's camp, we gathered with an extended clan of Bushmen. I had a notebook and pen. The cameras were still in their boxes. This was the Bushmen's chance to watch us. I looked down at the questions I'd listed in my notebook, and up at expectant faces. I wished that Sara were here, for many reasons, not least of all to share her interviewing skills.

I began, "Who is stronger, the lion or the lioness?"

Flip translated my words into Afrikaans, and then a Bushmen tracker, Kachee, in a series of staccato clicks, spoke to the gathering. Laughter spilled out and Kachee shook his head. The interpretation was reversed until Flip told me, "They said, 'You must be crazy. One is not stronger than the other. They need each other to survive.' " As I got to know them better, I would see that this is how—when times were good and when alcohol hadn't interfered—Bushmen men and women respected each other, gently, unselfishly, without chauvinism.

I looked around at the open faces of the men and women. Many of the men had small black dots of ash between their eyes. I nodded and asked, "Why does Toma have a dot between his eyes?"

The answer came back, "It is so Toma will have the same keen eyesight as the animal he is hunting."

"Are there any other animal markings used by the Bushmen? Anything for strength or beauty?"

This question was followed by silence, until Old Dixo slowly raised her long patchwork skirt.

"You see the markings there, the stripes on her legs?" asked Kachee.

I nodded, mesmerized by her slender, strong legs. A running pattern of black lines burned into brown flesh, and now partially hidden by aging skin, was etched across her thigh.

"When Old Dixo was a young girl, she thought the zebra was the most beautiful animal in the bush. Even now she wears the stripes of a zebra on her skin."

I imagined a zebra bounding across the plains, a black-and-white blur of strength and grace, an image so inspiring you wanted to hold it, feel it, be it. Old Dixo dropped her skirt and looked up at me. The sun and a long, hard life had left her skin worn with the patina of old leather, but her eyes shone brightly, and on her legs she wore the memory of her youth, her beauty, and her kinship with zebras. It was ageless, timeless, and so was she.

In the five days we spent with the Bushmen, their answers became more animated and more voices were heard as lines of a story were passed around the fire. I was told an old person who doesn't know a story doesn't exist. It was impossible. Life was about sharing—sharing meat, sharing fears, and sharing stories. To be selfish was the worst sin of all. Against the firelight, the children's faces glowed as the legends came to life, their history to be absorbed and retold around other fires as they grew older. Old Dixo said, "Telling a story is like taking an old skin, adding beads, and making it new each time."

We left the Bushmen with the promise that we'd be back. Three months later we were, and with us was a small film crew from New York City and Windhoek, Namibia's capital city, eager to capture the legends on film.

"GINGER, GET UP."

"It's too cold. I can't get out of bed." I pulled the blankets up over my head. Nad pulled them down.

"Come on, get up. You're the star."

"I am not. The Bushmen are the stars of this film."

"Well, they are out of bed and waiting for you, so get up."

"Throw me my jeans."

I got dressed under the covers, layering a sweater and jeans over long underwear. When I went outside to wash my face, the water in the bucket was frozen solid. "So much for makeup. Let's go."

The shooting script revolved around scenes that, added to the wildlife footage I'd shot in Etosha, would help us tell the Bushmen's legends. Before sunrise until long past sunset, the crew trailed the Bushmen and me as we dug for roots to eat, prepared the bows and arrows for hunting, and played games with the children. Spilling yellow beads in the sand, Dixo told us how the giraffe helped the sun find its way across the sky. Young Gui, a respected hunter, told us how the cheetah was rewarded with great speed for its unselfish acts. And Old/Gui, such a gentle, wise man, told us the story of how the Great God created life. The Bushmen were so animated on camera that it made it easier for me to relax and enjoy my on-screen role as the film's guide and narrator. There was a special connection, one that I'm sure Sara had made with interview subjects through the years. The camera was forgotten and a trust was born. It was of such depth that it took my breath away.

On our last evening, Old Old/Gui, soft, beaded leather draped around his waist and a long white ostrich plume jutting out from a band around his head, pulled a thick root from the fire. Its smoke would drive evil spirits away and prepare the backdrop for the three traditional healers to dance. Dance is an ageless ritual, designed to bring the community together. If a healer reaches a trance state during the dance, it can bring about healing. As described by Old/Gui, dance is "the highest form of prayer."

That night, for the first time, they invited an outsider to be a part of the healing circle. Long into the night, I clapped alongside the other members of the community as the healers circled the fire, their feet beating rhythmically in the sand, dancing, chanting, reaching out to the Great Gods. When Old/Gui reached the trance state, he stopped in front of Gao, a Bushman hunter who had been sick for a long time. He ran his hands up and down Gao's body while the other healers stood between him and the fire. They wouldn't let him fall. They were protecting him as he was healing Gao. There was such power and trust, such faith and serenity. It touched my soul and finally I found the peace I had been longing for. For the first time, my connection to Africa felt complete. It didn't feel like a betrayal of the life and lives I loved back in the U.S. It was as much a part of me as they were, not disconnected, but reconnected, creating a better whole.

The next day as we prepared to fly out, Tsessaba, one of the Bushmen trackers, gently touched his wife's full belly and said, "If it is a girl, we will name her Ginger." I loved the thought of a little bright-eyed Bushmen child toddling into her mother's arms and fingering the beads around her neck, answering to the name of Ginger.

Three weeks after leaving Bushmanland, Nad and I were shopping for supplies in Windhoek. I lingered in front of a pharmacy's window. Shampoo, vitamins, lip balm, the basics.

"Do you need something?"

"I think so," I whispered. "I think I'm pregnant."

"Wow." Nad beamed and I shook in awe and happiness, grateful to all those we had been blessed enough to learn from before this moment—a baby rhino, Elee, and now the Bushmen. I remembered so clearly that when Kachee's youngest child crawled into his lap, he told me, "When you hit a child, it locks away his heart. It is better to teach them through example, through the legends." I prayed to hold tight to Kachee's words, and I prayed for strength in the months ahead.

At thirty-six years old, I faced two daunting tasks—having amniocentesis and having to tell Sara. Sara would understand my need to know if my baby was healthy. Living through the pain of my sister Tish's mental illness had been enough for me. The impact of her destructive moods when you never knew if she would lash out physically, call the police to complain of abuse at the barest slight, or fall down the stairs when a seizure struck had ripped at the core of my family until it had almost torn us apart. Bravely, within the physical, emotional, and mental limits of her illness, Tish struggled on. But I knew I wasn't strong enough to go through it again, not with a child of my own.

But I was also aware that my pregnancy would be hard on Sara. Two years after my wedding, she and Andrew were still trying to figure out their relationship. Had my angst over getting married cost them these years? Years where they too could have started a family? Sara was on assignment to Australia and Andrew had moved back there. I knew what that meant. I picked up the phone and got ready to track her down.

22

SARA (1997)

I OPENED THE DOOR and smiled in delight. The honeyed cream room of the Park Hyatt was stunning, but having a balcony with a view of the astonishing Sydney Opera House was pure bliss. I sighed and threw myself onto the luxurious pile of pillows on the bed, craving relaxation after a month in which I'd been ricocheted around the globe.

I'd just completed an assignment in Tokyo and was at Narita Airport when I'd learned of the tragic car crash in a Paris tunnel which had killed Princess Diana and her boyfriend, Dodi Al-Fayed, as well as their chauffeur. I'd immediately volunteered to go to London, where I'd covered the aftershocks of the death of the enchanting, complicated princess. Rich, royal, and an international superstar, Diana was nothing like me except in one way. We were both thirty-six years old—far too young to die. The fact that in her mid-thirties this gorgeous, entitled woman had finally appeared self-confident, reveling in hard-won independence as well as giddy romance, made her death especially poignant. But it had been her charitable endeavors, first with AIDS patients and more recently calling for an international ban on land mines, which made me admire her. I'd interviewed inconsolable men and women who'd regaled us with tales of her kindness and her convictions, but tall, handsome Ken Rutherford had a story that walloped me for a different reason.

Ken had been working as a loan officer in Somalia back in 1993, just a year after I'd been there, trying to rebuild the country's shattered economy. His vehicle had hit a land mine and both his legs were blown off. As I listened to him speak passionately about the Landmine Survivors Network, the group he'd cofounded, and the princess's tireless support, I willed myself to stop the shiver which raced from my neck down to my toes as I thought about my time in Somalia and Nicaragua, and about how very fortunate I had been.

Now, just a few weeks later, I was in Australia, depleted, jet-lagged, and feeling stretched taut as a piano string for the simple reason that I was actually on the same continent as Andrew and would see my ex-boyfriend as soon as I finished my *Dateline* assignments.

Recently Andrew had finished his two-year stint in Japan and returned to Australia, where he now worked in the capital of Canberra, three hours from Sydney, as chief political reporter for the largest newspaper in Australia. That job had taken him to New York a few months before on a trip with Prime Minister John Howard, and when our "just friends" lunch had turned into something more, we'd agreed to sort things out when I came across. The situation was entirely romantic and hence wildly improbable, and the thought of his slow grin and long-lashed gaze made my stomach hurt.

But my stomach was about to hurt even more. The phone rang and it was Ginger, who'd tracked me down to deliver news which left me gasping.

"You're pregnant?!"

"Kind of a surprise, isn't it?"

"Kind of. Wow!" I was gripping the phone so tightly I thought it might implode, but at least I was able to hold back the selfish tears which had filled my eyes. "I mean—you must be really happy, Gin."

"I am. Just a little nervous. Are *you* okay, Sara?"

"Of course." With effort, I pulled myself together. "Congratulations, Ginger. And to Nad, too. I'm so happy for you. I wish I could talk longer, but I'd better dash—I've got to meet my producer."

But when I hung up, I couldn't seem to move. My best friend would be having a baby. What exciting news. She would be a wonderful mom and the pregnancy seemed yet another sign her marriage to Nad was secure. So why hadn't I screamed with joy? Why hadn't I at least asked how she was feeling? Why had I been tongue-tied instead of supportive? I could only imagine she must be anxious about raising a child in the middle of nowhere, about trying to juggle being both a mom and a wildlife filmmaker. I knew it was hard enough for her to straddle two continents as it was, and couldn't imagine how much more difficult it would be with a child in tow. What's more, Ginger had acknowledged being nervous, which I could understand, especially given her sister Tish's complicated medical history, and she'd needed reassurance. But I hadn't been able to offer it.

Most of my old friends had children already. The photos taped to my refrigerator back home told the story: Beth's son, Trent, now with little sister, Elisa; Scottie's children, Logan and Conner; my college roommate Carol's girls, Maria and Monica; and Lisa's new baby, Luke, cuddled by big sister, Hannah. It was a gallery of gorgeous children, including my two darling godsons, Daniel, flanked by sister Sarah, and John. Recently both Linda and Fiona had discovered they were pregnant. Now Ginger. While I felt unequivocally thrilled for all of them, occasionally I also felt sorry for myself, and even, in some strange way, abandoned. I wasn't ready for yet another pal to choose diapers over deadlines, *Sesame Street* over Mary Chapin Carpenter, being sleep-deprived over being jet-lagged, even though such behavior was entirely understandable.

Ginger's defection felt especially treacherous. For some reason I just hadn't expected her to get pregnant. Not yet, anyway. We'd known each other so long, our lives were so intertwined, our timing in many ventures so uncannily similar despite the geographical distance, that watching her embark on this journey, solo, seemed like a violation of the unwritten Friendship Code of Conduct. Who would I play with now? In spite of an expensive new haircut and chic, updated wardrobe, it was only with good friends who led similar lives that I could kid myself into thinking I was still twenty-something instead of thirty-six.

Thirty-six. Ten years older than my mom had been when she'd had me. I'd been an adult when Mom had revealed how she'd been forced to quit her job as an elementary school teacher early in her pregnancy because she was "showing." To lose your job because you were pregnant was so outrageous it almost hid a second indignity—that she'd then taken a job as a secretary, even though she'd graduated Phi Beta Kappa from Smith College. Over the years sometimes Mom mused about how she would have gone to law school if she'd been born a few years later. Instead she'd become a sought-after piano teacher and accompanist, juggling students and performances with raising three girls. I felt like my childhood had a score as I listened to Mom play Schumann's *About Strange Lands and People,* a Chopin prelude, or Bach's *St. Matthew Passion.* A devoted mom, she was married to a man who still charmed her and us forty years after they'd met aboard the *Liberté.* We loved the story of how the band had taken a break one night, and our outgoing dad had jumped onstage with his trumpet. My reserved mother must have been impressed, because she promptly joined him at the keyboard.

While Mom had no complaints about her life, secretly I had two major reservations. I felt she'd been denied a broader choice about career, as well as greater economic opportunity, by virtue of gender and generation. How could I fail to take advantage of all the choices that beckoned women my age, especially since the doors had only opened recently? I not only had the right but the obligation to succeed in my career.

But it had taken me nearly fifteen years to get where I was at NBC, and now biology was a factor I just couldn't ignore. What if professional achievement came at the expense of having a family? It almost seemed as if there had been a currency exchange at some invisible border and I'd been fleeced, only to discover my error too late. I had so much. And yet I couldn't help but feel that so much was missing.

With enormous effort I rose from the bed and stumbled toward that beautiful balcony. As I watched the boats bob in the harbor, I thought about how a collision of one egg and one sperm on one particular night had started that exponential fizz-bang of limbs and libido, elbows and attitude, marrow and mind which would change so many lives, especially Ginger's, and by extension my own. This was no mere concept, but conception. And at that moment somehow everything I'd created seemed like little more than words howled into the wind.

My feelings were all the more unsettling because they clashed with my thoughts. I'd never believed you needed to have a child to lead an interesting, meaningful life. No woman should be judged by whether or not she had a child, not to mention that the real test of parenthood wasn't having a child, but raising one well. But watching my unconventional friend choose this time-honored path seemed to highlight the topsy-turvy nature of my own existence. Deep inside a voice shouted, *Wait for me!* then selfishly continued, *And if I don't catch up, don't do it.* A third grader's notion of friendship. Me too. Or neither of us.

I headed back inside to get ready for dinner, caught sight of my woebegone face, and shouted, "Grow up!" at the mirror before turning away in embarrassment. Clearly I'd spent too much time on my own. Besides, I was now late to meet Sandy Dennison, a *Dateline* producer and new friend. I'd call Ginger back later. Her gentle tone had indicated she'd known how difficult our conversation would be. Sometimes it seemed she knew me better than I knew myself. And I had work to do.

"WE COULD SEE one anytime now," Steve Irwin whispered. The two of us were tiptoeing across a scorched, pockmarked expanse of desert, hundreds of miles from Sydney, searching for a delightful creature known for its venom, fangs, and attitude.

"Are these snake holes we're standing on?" I asked anxiously.

"Perhaps. Underneath, the ground here is like a subterranean labyrinth . . . These snakes can travel from here, three miles over that way."

Sandy and I were in the middle of shooting a *Dateline* profile on Steve Irwin, owner of a wildlife park in Queensland and host of an increasingly popular American show then on the Discovery Channel called *The Crocodile Hunter.* We'd chartered a plane to Windorah, a tiny outback outpost, in search of the deadliest snake in the world—the inland taipan, more commonly known as the "fierce snake."

Steve told us that local lore had it, if you got bitten, forget phoning the doctor. Just call the undertaker. The fierce snake was so deadly that the venom from one bite was enough to kill one hundred people. Years before, I'd slept in the back of a Land Rover in Namibia to avoid spitting cobras, yet on this assignment I was walking two steps behind a manic Australian snake charmer who'd actually survived having a taipan lick him on the nose. I'd always been best able to confront my fears when I looked at them through the prism of a work assignment. Just then I spotted a ripple of black straight ahead.

"That's a fierce snake!" I yelped, not whispering anymore.

"Let's get down as low as we can," Steve instructed, moving closer to the serpent. "If I say move, just go straight back that way, or if your instincts tell you to freeze, just freeze." My instincts were telling me I was going to die of a heart attack before the snake got any closer.

"What's he doing with his head?" I asked.

"He's really grumpy. See that body posture, his mouth open? He's a particularly aggressive snake. I'd stay right where you are." I didn't need to be told twice. Finally the snake darted down into a hole.

I breathed deeply, trying to slow my heartbeat, but a few minutes later it thumped like a helicopter rotor when we saw another glistening streak.

"You can see that this one's a lot longer and thinner," Steve said, all excitement, taking small crouching footsteps forward. Meantime my legs wobbled and the gap between us widened from two steps to four as he continued, "I'd say this is a young male."

But there would be no more science lesson because suddenly, just a few steps from the snake, it turned and lunged. I screamed. Fortunately the cameraman was made of sterner stuff and held steady as Steve executed a backward leap—half pirouette, half tae kwon do—and the indignant reptile wriggled off at full speed.

"If you got bitten by that snake, Steve, you're dead," I said, panting.

Steve merely grinned, barrel chest heaving. "I'd be in a lot of trouble." Steve Irwin was, as they say, great TV.

SEVERAL DAYS AND several thousands of miles later, we'd graduated to larger reptiles. "So what do you think he'll do next?" I asked Sandy, as a dark green dinosaur lunged toward Irwin, who leapt back in his sturdy Blundstone boots.

"Who knows, when you spend the day with the Crocodile Hunter," she replied drily. We'd traveled into remote northern Queensland's Cape York Peninsula with Steve and his lovely, calm, and capable American wife, Terri.

Sandy and I shared one tent, the cameraman and soundman another. The communal shower was a bag with showerhead attached, a blanket strung for privacy. But I'd learned a thing or two since Nicaragua, and not just about eluding desperados. By now I knew that I needed to look camera-ready regardless of field conditions. So I pulled out my handy sidearm—a mini Conair blow-dryer—and plugged it into the cigarette lighter of the SUV. A girl's gotta do what a girl's gotta do.

Despite its idyllic appearance, the lake was home to a number of crocs, including one notorious behemoth. "Old Faithful" had recently been stalking local fishermen, who were increasingly tempted to kill him. Anxious to save this prehistoric troublemaker, Steve had attempted a sort of "Scared Straight" rehabilitation project. Now we'd venture onto the water to see if it had worked. But I had little faith in Old Faithful and sat down carefully so as not to tip the motorboat.

"Steve, how long is this boat?" I asked.

"Fourteen foot."

"And how big is this crocodile?"

"Fourteen foot."

Perhaps even less comforting were the wavy skid marks on the bank, which indicated Old Faithful had been on the prowl. "Interesting how close he is to our camp," Steve noted with characteristic Australian understatement. Later that evening when we took a second boat tour to assess whether Irwin's Crocodile Obedience School had worked, what I thought was a floating log turned out to be the taciturn beast himself. "He's sitting there watching us watching him," Steve mused before revving the engine and pointing our bow directly at the croc, an attempt to remind the monster who was master. Old Faithful dove like a nuclear sub, to my mind unrepentant and unreformed.

When we finished our shooting and sat down for dinner, a campfire feast of fragrant coal-cooked bread called "damper" and enough red meat to feed even a hungry crocodile, I unwound. Fears and worries had charred to embers, then died out. After years of covering dangerous, complicated humans, there was an honesty in the battle between life and death in the animal kingdom, and though it was scary, it was at the same time incredibly refreshing. And I reminded myself that life had a way of working out, even if you couldn't always guess how. Now in my mid-thirties and four years past a failed marriage, I realized I felt a resilience and contentment I'd lacked in my twenties.

As twilight surrendered to dusk, then slipped into a brilliant Australian evening, Sandy and I contemplated the stark beauty of the Southern Cross, the clarity of all those stars winking and twinkling. Our voices stilled against the emptiness. I thought of the New York skyline I loved, its jagged neon outline obscuring any celestial view. There was a tranquillity here I craved. And suddenly I understood how Ginger had left home for a country and a way of life, rather than a person. Away from the noise and chaos of a big city and a busy life, it almost seemed possible to feel the pull that guides a compass. Thousands of miles from home and in the southern hemisphere, I realized I might finally be figuring out where true north really was.

LATER THAT NIGHT, lying side by side in our tent, Sandy and I exchanged confidences.

"So you're in the same spot?"

"We're trying to figure things out, too. But at least we're in the same city—not to mention the same continent."

"Do you think you'll work it out, Sandy?"

"I think so. How about you and Andrew?"

"I wish I knew. We were broken up. He'd had another girlfriend, I'd had another boyfriend. But when he came to New York a few months ago, he dropped by for lunch and stayed for a week."

Sandy gave a wicked giggle I'd only gotten to know on this trip.

"So you guys are great together except for the fact that you're never together."

"Exactly. The situation is impossible, and somebody's got to do something because I'm too old to waste any more time on this."

"Then it's good that you're getting together. You can see if it will work or not."

"We'll see. Thank goodness we have another story to do first."

INTERVIEWING DEB CHEETHAM felt like talking to one of my friends back home. She was attractive, smart, and single, a teacher and opera singer who'd grown up in a middle-class Sydney suburb. Early on Deb's parents had told her they'd adopted her from an orphanage when she was three weeks old.

"They'd told me I'd been abandoned. And that I'd been found by a Salvation Army officer. In a cardboard box in a field," Deb explained as we stood in the front yard of the rambling house which had once been the orphanage. She looked down, kicked a clod of dirt. "That kind of means I was left to die, doesn't it?"

But Deb wasn't finished. She was telling me about how, a few years before, she'd given a concert that had changed her life. "I looked out into the audience one night. And I saw a woman who was the spitting image of me."

It turned out the woman was Deb's cousin, and they were both Aborigines. While the first white convicts came to what was then an English penal colony in the late 1700s, the Aborigines are the original people of Australia and have lived on the continent for forty-five thousand years. The cousin took Deb to her birth mother, who gave a dramatically different story of Deb's adoption. Monika Little explained that she'd been an eighteen-year-old mother, abandoned by her husband, when a woman at the orphanage offered to care for her newborn while Monika earned money for essentials. A heavyset woman with a face that had mourned a thousand sorrows, Deb's birth mother could barely speak as she told us what happened when she returned just a few weeks later. "I had clothing for her. And a brand-new pram. I was so happy. I turned up to get my baby and she was gone."

"Shh, shh," Deb crooned, stroking her mother's hair as the tears rolled down Monika's face.

As we discovered, Deb was just one of an estimated 100,000 children who'd been taken between 1900 and 1969—some torn from their mothers' arms, some spirited off from school—in a comprehensive and, for many, devastating attempt to assimilate the indigenous population. In the view of the patrician white government and church leaders of the time, it was in the best interest of the children to be removed from what was officially considered a doomed culture, and instead placed in orphanages or adopted by white families.

But of course the Aborigines hadn't vanished, and recently the policy had been widely criticized as a human rights violation. Meanwhile the now-grown men and women—dubbed the "Stolen Generation"—were left to sort out a complicated past as best they could. I couldn't help but ponder how in this magnificent country, past injustice had sown seeds of modern woes, just as was true in America.

"What did you lose by having this happen to you?" I asked Deb.

"My identity. I was given another one, it just didn't fit. You ever walked around in shoes that were too small for you? That's what I did for twenty-nine years."

Deb knew she'd received significant material advantages by virtue of being adopted. Her mother flinched but Deb did not when I asked, "What do you make of those people that say we were just trying to do the right thing?"

"You can say we were just trying to do the right thing but you must finish the sentence," Deb replied with great passion. "We were just trying to do the right thing but we were wrong."

And then, in the dusty yard outside that house of shadows, Deb threw her arms around her mother and they rocked back and forth, locked in a fierce, desperate embrace—an embrace to make up for all the months, all the years they hadn't had, to hold fast to a love lost, then found.

I turned away, overwhelmed. To have a second chance. A second chance at life, at love. The chance to say everything you felt. If you dared. To show who you were, how you'd changed. If you were brave enough. But sometimes reinvention takes two. My toes were curling in their boots again. I had to be bold enough to tell Andrew how I felt, all that I hoped for, regardless of my fears.

The thought of our upcoming reunion sent a bizarre electrical current coursing through me, a reckless giddiness, short-circuited by trepidation. What I'd just witnessed was exactly what I wanted. I wanted to be embraced just like that. I wanted to be held by someone who would never, ever let me go.

INSTEAD WE SAT side by side in the car, silent. We'd just spent a week together, and after a quick visit with his folks had lolly-gagged our way along the Great Ocean Road, giving a cursory nod to the stone obelisks just off the southern coast known as the Twelve Apostles, before zeroing in on each other. We'd gotten sunburns, eaten Thai so hot we sweated, discovered time hadn't diminished our mutual attraction, and each said the three words which acknowledged our passion had proved enduring. But "I love you" wasn't enough anymore, and so far Andrew had managed to evade any remotely serious conversation. Now we were driving northeast from Melbourne to Canberra, where I'd meet Andrew's colleagues and enjoy a few more days of fun before I flew home.

But I was sick to death of fun. All I wanted were answers.

I took a deep breath and plunged in. "So, Andrew, what do you think? Are you willing to move to the U.S.?"

He paused a long time, eyes on the dead-straight road ahead, considering. "No."

I took a deep breath. There it was. An answer, but not the answer I wanted. I felt the stomach punch of unexpected disappointment, but it was surprisingly brief. Because I also felt like my hair would burst into flames, I was so white hot with anger. This had been our second chance, a chance I'd been willing to take. But there wouldn't be another. "I understand," I said, controlling my voice with the greatest effort. "Then please take me to the airport. This instant."

"Calm down; keep your shirt on," Andrew replied, reaching out for my arm while keeping his gaze on the road.

I yanked my arm away. "You'd better drive to Sydney, now. I'm catching the next plane to New York."

"Listen, Sara, don't be rash—"

I shook my head, my mouth a tight line, fed up. "Andrew, we can't continue to see each other every few months. It's not enough. I've had it." He looked over, and in that instant his expression told me he knew I was serious.

There was another long pause. Then, as if he'd changed his mind about something as trivial as whether to have sugar in his tea, Andrew said, "All right, yes."

"What?!" If possible I was even angrier now, because it seemed he was toying with me.

"Yes! I said yes," Andrew repeated. Even more infuriating, he was smiling.

But I was suffering whiplash and was unwilling to accept his new answer, even though it was the one I'd wanted all along. "Andrew, I'm not trying to force you. I do *not* want to hear later how you're miserable and you've ruined your life by following me. If you come, this is your choice. No recriminations."

"Listen, Sara, I love it here," Andrew explained with annoying self-control. "My family's here, I've got a great job, I love the place. It's a lot to leave."

I took a deep breath. I thought of Ginger, raising a child in Africa. I thought of how I already felt bewitched by this ancient, beautiful country. I thought of how a career I adored meant little if I lost the man I adored even more. I weakened. "Andrew, I love it here, too, and if you want me to move—"

"Look, as we've discussed, it's easier for me to move to the States. I can get work as a journo there—I've already done it once—and it's going to be harder for you to get established in Australia with your funny accent . . ." The grin got bigger, and he patted my hand. "But if we do wind up getting married, down the road I want to come home to Australia."

I felt breathless and shaky, reeling from a conversation in which dreams had been shattered only to be resurrected. Slowly, I nodded.

"And there's one more thing."

It figured. Just when we'd nearly signed the deal. "Which is?"

"Where do you want to be buried?"

This time I was stumped. What did death have to do with it? With us?

"I have to say, I haven't given it a lot of thought. I don't really care."

"Good." His relief was obvious.

"May I ask why?"

"Because I want to be buried in the Muckleford Cemetery. My ancestors are there. It's my family's land. I already have a couple of burial plots there. I know it may sound dumb, but I have an Aboriginal-style attachment to that land. It's where I'd have to be. And I'd want my wife buried with me."

My guy. My lighthearted, funny guy. My guy who looked handsome in a suit, who was successful and connected. But down deep my guy was first, last, and always the son of a farmer—the son of eight generations of farmers, all of whom had raised their families within a stone's throw of the Muckleford Creek. I thought of the cemetery only a field away from his parents' farm. I thought of Muckleford with its tawny fields, the occasional roo helping himself to hay in the back paddock, of the musical sawing of the magpies, of the shrieks of the galahs and cockatoos as they showed off their stunning plumage. I thought of dirt, of that antipodean earth, old bones decomposing in an old land. I thought of spending eternity in Australia rather than Virginia or New York and realized that was okay with me. I wasn't from one place, after all, but several. I thought of being with someone and his whole family forever and ever. That was okay, too.

Joy seeped slowly through me, tentative but undeniable, a tapped spring allowed to flow at last. We'd have to figure out the rest at another time, in another country. But we'd taken the first clear steps, and I almost felt like singing. "I can't think of a better place to be buried."

Apparently that cheery postscript to our complicated conversation had sealed the deal, and Andrew wasted no time. By the time I was New York bound, he'd met with his understanding editor in chief, Peter Blunden, and worked out the details. Andrew would quit his job, even though his career was on the rise, to come to the Big Apple and the uncertain world of free-lance. He'd have his place, I'd have mine. No promises. No guarantees. But I was elated. I knew we were taking a chance, but I think part of me had known all along that Mr. Right Now was really Mr. Right.

23

GINGER (1997–1998)

Welcome home!" I yelled, flinging open the door to Sara's apartment and embracing her.

"Oh my God, Gin, you're fat." She laughed, pushing me back to arm's length. "I don't think I've ever seen you fat."

"I'm nearly five months pregnant! I have a right to be fat! Now come in and tell me everything!"

I'd been in New York working on the edit of the Bushmen film, staying in Sara's apartment with no Sara, counting the days until she returned from Australia. Finally she was back and my home away from home felt complete. She dropped her bags in the middle of the Oriental rug and sprawled beside them. As spent as she was after the twenty-four-hour journey from the other side of the world, Sara beamed.

"So how was it?"

"The stories were interesting."

I raised my eyebrows. "Right."

"Steve Irwin may be crazy, but he knows what he's doing."

"Yeah, okay, I'm waiting."

"And the 'Stolen Generation' story I told you about is utterly heart-breaking."

"Sara, don't you always caution me not to 'bury the lead'? Tell me about the stories later, first I've got to know what's going on with you and Andrew."

She rolled over, rested her head in her hands, and smiled a weary, giddy smile.

"Nothing much. Except—he's moving to New York!"

This was what the past two years had been leading up to. Two years of dancing around each other, then moving cautiously together, hand to hand, cheek to cheek, before letting the force and fear of their feelings propel them apart. Sara and Andrew were going to try again. This time it would be different. No more mention of the age gap, the continental divide, the cultural differences. Those issues that had kept them apart had been dealt with either over the phone or in the quiet of their own hearts, or had been pushed aside as if ultimately unimportant. And this time they'd be in the same city, where they would confront the not-so-simple question of whether they could make their relationship work, day to day, week to week, year to year, approaching the "till death do us part" part.

"One of his friends told him I'm a 'good catch,'" she laughed. "I guess he believed him." A roller coaster of emotions, fueled by jet lag, took her plunging back to earth. "He's giving up a lot to be with me. Stepping off the fast track at work, leaving his family, his country, and moving to New York. Andrew's not exactly a fan of big cities."

Then she gave a smile that told me the ride was going up again.

"If it all works out, later we'll move to Australia."

Said so confidently, so innocently, that I nearly choked. I couldn't say a word. Like a record scratched and skipping, a painful refrain played over and over again in my mind: *You've made a pact with the devil, you've made a pact with the devil.*

We'll move to Australia, the refrain echoed again. For a week, a year, two years, a lifetime? I thought about the eighteen hours I'd spent crying on the plane when I'd returned from Africa to say good-bye to my grandfather. I didn't get to hug him, to feel the scratch from his unshaven face on my cheek, to smell the richness of earth on his clothes. I had arrived in time to meet my mother dressed in black and join the crowd of mourners at the church, to say good-bye to a body in a box. I thought about my godson Trent, the Little League games and church choir performances I'd never been to, and about his sweet little sister, Elisa, children I loved but barely knew. And there was my beautiful niece, Maggie, crawling, growing, walking, and I'd seen it all in pictures. Returning home every year or two, changes that are imperceptible on a daily basis resonate. More gray hairs. Laugh lines etched deeper. Slower down the steps. Having to "speak up." Age taking its toll on all of us. The only person who never changed was Tish. Her medications might vary, she might have a new counselor or a new roommate, but her illness kept her trapped in the life of a needy child. What would become of her, of my parents, of Marsha, of Dona and her family? And where would I be? Had I consciously run toward a new life or run away from the old, escaping my share of responsibility, choosing the role of distant sister, daughter, aunt, rarely home to help, to play a more meaningful part?

Was love worth this cost? Did love plus adventure—a two-for-one bargain—make it somehow more palatable? When I'd married Nad, I'd said yes to him, his life, and his world. Now our baby would be born in Africa, which meant he'd feel his strongest connection to the earth on a continent that wasn't my own. With our families thousands of miles away, our child would grow up without the protective envelope of an extended family. Who would cheer and clap their hands when our baby took those first memorable steps? Who would hold her when she fell? Whose history would my child absorb that would help define the person he or she would become? As much as I'd made peace with my decision, I also knew that home, a real home, meant having roots and vines which twisted and trailed through generations, drawing you back, and half my child's birthright would be far, far away.

"Gin, I said, aren't you happy for me?" Sara held my hand, a worried look on her face.

How could I presume to decide Sara's fate? She was my best friend, not an appendage. Just because I suffered from the feeling of estrangement, even when I was happiest, didn't mean she would, too. These were my fears. She knew them all, had heard them too many times. To hell with continents and cultures, to sisters becoming mothers and parents growing old; sometimes love is all you need. I didn't believe it, of course, but this time it was Sara's choice, her chance to grab happiness and spin it into life. I wouldn't ruin it.

"Yes, of course I'm happy for you. Now get some sleep and we'll talk later."

She patted my belly and said good night.

The next morning I slipped out while Sara slept. Underground, waiting for the N/R train to Times Square, I started to feel dizzy. When the doors of the subway opened, I was caught in the crush of people getting off, pushing me so far back into the masses that when I finally boarded the subway and searched for a vacant seat, I was met by stares, people looking up at me and without expression looking back down at their newspapers. Maybe they also thought I was just fat.

But already my baby was rebelling against this unnatural world. With one hand I clung to the pole and wrapped my free arm protectively around my belly. A minute's blur in the darkness, and when the doors of the subway opened I joined the flood of people pushing out into another station. Changing trains, I found a seat on the 1/9 line to Hudson Street, then stripped off my coat and put my head between my legs, hoping I wouldn't faint. To calm myself, I thought of the bush, the cool air, the quiet, and then thought again for the hundredth time, *What the hell am I doing back here?*

This was the flip side of wildlife filmmaking. After years spent in the field nurturing an intimacy with wild animals, understanding their story, and capturing ephemeral moments on film, making a documentary also meant spending time in dark edit suites where there's no escape from cigarette smoke clinging to the air, the computer's incessant humming, and the power plays of office politics. Whether you are a baboon or human, it seems there is no getting away from those who try to dominate by pulling rank. When it comes to filmmaking, rank is determined by who decides which pieces of footage end up in the trash, which bits of dialogue make the sound edit, and whose name receives which credit at the end of the film. I found life in an office bizarre, or perhaps I was just bizarrely out of touch. For eight hours I flipped between the edit suite, where pieces of film were being cut into a beautiful, touching story by a very talented editor, then flopped into the outer offices, where cuts were made with unkind words and sharp put-downs. Then it was back on the subway, gasping for air the entire way home.

At the end of the day, I collapsed on Sara's sofa.

"Here you go." Sara smiled, passing me a mug of herbal tea.

"Thanks. Wish it were something stronger."

"That bad?"

"Yeah, that bad. It was so easy with the baboon film. Jen and Des gave us carte blanche to make the film we wanted. They trusted us. I guess I've been spoiled. But I just don't understand why everything has to be a fight. They can argue about anything, even things that seem obvious to me, like who will voice-over what scenes and who should get what credit. I am so new to this, I'm not familiar with some of the terminology and sometimes I simply feel taken advantage of. They treat me like I'm stupid."

"Gin, don't be crazy. You're far from stupid."

"It's nothing new. I've been treated that way most of my life. Airhead, dumb blonde. Pretty, but simple. That's me."

"But you're not!" my friend said, jumping to my defense. Then she paused, nodded. "I guess it's true. In some ways your looks probably work against you."

"Listen, I know they have also opened doors, and it's not that. It's being arbitrarily defined. I hate it."

"I know what you mean, because back in school I was labeled 'the smart one,' even though anyone who said that obviously never saw my math grades! Besides, what I wanted to be told was that I was pretty."

Now *I* was surprised. "Sara, look in the mirror. Why do you think you work where you do? You look great."

"Are you kidding? I always want to lose five or ten pounds and I think this is hairstyle number 186, and I can never hide the circles under my eyes. But what I'm trying to say is, when do we get to shed these horrible, left-over tags from childhood? Why do we still have to be clever, pretty, a jock, whatever label somebody else pinned on us back when we were twelve?" I smiled as Sara revved into one of her "change the world" soliloquies. "Why do we feel stuck with it, Gin? Isn't part of getting older supposed to be figuring out who we are for ourselves?"

"It should be, and lucky for me, I escape most of this when I'm in Africa."

"Exactly. Look, Gin, you should be taken seriously for everything you've brought to this project. Finding the story, writing it, even shooting it for goodness' sake—you don't need this pettiness. None of us do." And then she paused again. "But, Gin, you've also got to try not to take everything personally. These people aren't friends, they're work associates. If they are professional, they also want what's best for the film, but that doesn't necessarily mean they want what's best for you. Look out for yourself, but don't be afraid to compromise."

I found myself thinking about our conversation for the rest of the night. After twenty-five years of friendship, we were still finding out new things about each other, and through each other, about ourselves. I could never have imagined that Sara didn't see herself as beautiful because she was. That she found me smart was also a revelation, and a welcome one. But I was troubled by something else she'd pointed out. It stunned me to realize that I viewed compromise as a novel concept. I didn't compromise with the rising sun or my alarm clock when it rang at 4 A.M. so that I could be out in the bush before first light. There was no bartering with 100-degree heat, no way to trade a violent death for a cautious life in the bush. The forces of nature didn't play "let's make a deal." For almost ten years I'd lived this wild life, accepting it fully, protecting it fiercely, so much so that I'd forgotten about give-and-take. Animal behavior that took years to understand, years to capture, and months to craft into a story was cut down to a half hour of television, twenty-three minutes including commercial breaks— fifty-two minutes, if you were lucky enough to score an hour on television. Of course there needed to be concessions, the truth compacted, scenes shortened, others falling into oblivion on the editing room floor, but the tricky part was knowing when and where to deal, recognizing when a decision improved the project or when it was a matter of greed or an overgrown ego.

I looked at Sara—my smart and pretty friend—with new admiration. This creative minefield was her world, one she had successfully navigated for years. While moving up the ranks from Tupelo to Richmond to Charlotte and finally New York City with her fancy office and fancy title of *Dateline* correspondent, Sara had stayed true to herself and continued to lobby for stories she felt passionately about. But she also knew that there were many ways to tell a story honestly, layering multiple visions of inspiration. The next day, when I regaled her with the latest chapter in our editing saga—where I'd given ground, where I'd held firm—Sara said with a sly grin, "Gin, welcome to creativity by committee, the *other* real world of television." Now it was my turn to laugh, and it felt so good.

LAUGHTER HAD BEEN largely absent from my life in the past month. I was finding out that waiting for the amniocentesis results was as stressful as the test. After the age of thirty-five, testing for Down's syndrome and other birth defects through amniocentesis is routine for expectant mothers in the U.S. A test tube of amniotic fluid can tell you part of the history of a baby's developing life—its health, its age, its sex—a wealth of wonderful information. And yet there are risks, grave risks. The needle could puncture the amniotic sac, spilling the protective fluid and potentially ending the baby's life. A woman lies down on a cold table in her doctor's office with a life growing inside her belly, and minutes later that life is extinguished, through circumstances nearly as random as the baby's conception. The baby shifted, the needle slipped. One prick of a needle, like one sperm, can change your life. Yet I knew that daily, thousands of these procedures were performed safely. A routine, optional procedure. But practices considered routine in the world often aren't typical in Africa.

Nevertheless, for me, there were no options. I wanted desperately to know if my baby was healthy or not. I love my sister Tish, but I wouldn't want my child to have her life. And I knew, selfishly, that I wasn't strong enough to endure those trials again. Having an amniocentesis would give me the answers I needed. The test had been the first step, a step I couldn't forget.

"Ginger, Nad, come in. How was the drive down?" Dr. Baines had asked in his rich, distinctive baritone. "Any rain?"

Rain. It had reminded me of my grandfather, standing in his tobacco fields, looking up at the sky, watching the clouds build and recede, saying a silent prayer that today they'd bless his land. I often thought of my grandfather, because in an arid country, rain was always a topic of conversation. Some things never change, others do.

Normally we met Dr. Baines in his office in the city center, but on that day we drove straight to the State Hospital, where he'd been waiting for us in a large, sterile operating room. The walls, once white, were aged yellow. The overhead lights were bright, the linoleum floor chipped.

"Ginger, put this gown on and come lie down."

When Dr. Baines had patted the table beside him, I'd thought I'd seen a slight shaking in his hands. Could I have imagined this? There had been sweat on his brow and sharpness in his normally easy movements. Was it possible that he was as nervous as I was? After decades in which he'd delivered hundreds of babies with the amazing gift of making each mother feel like her baby was the first, the most special baby in the world, Dr. Baines had performed just a few amnio tests. Older mothers, especially first-time mothers, were rare in Africa. I was clearly an exception.

I'd climbed onto the cold gurney and lain down. Nad had held my hand while Dr. Baines squirted cold gel from what looked like a diner's ketchup container onto my stomach.

"I'll just rub this around a bit and then we'll get a look at your baby."

The image that had appeared on the antiquated sonar machine was fuzzy, a black-and-white soup with little definition that I could see.

"Okay. Nad, I'm going to ask you to stand outside now," Dr. Baines had said, taking one last look at the screen.

When Nad had left the room, the image of our baby had disappeared, too. Dr. Baines had turned off the sonar and marked a dot on my stomach with a blue ballpoint pen.

"Lie still."

Wiping his brow, Dr. Baines had then begun to push a long, thick needle through the dot on my stomach. I'd looked away, squeezed the stiff sheet beneath me, and felt the first painful stab before he'd pulled the needle out.

"Sorry."

The next time the needle went straight through, and as he'd pulled the plunger slowly back, the tube filled with amniotic fluid, a dense, opaque liquid that held our future as a secret.

Dr. Baines had squeezed my hand. "You are fine, and I'm sure your baby will be fine, but don't drive back to Etosha today if you don't have to. You need to lie still, to rest, and phone me immediately if there is any spotting or leaking. We'll let you know the results as soon as we get them."

Lying on a plush bed in a hotel room we couldn't afford, I'd instinctively rubbed my belly. At the time I didn't allow myself to remember the passages from the baby books about amnio—how the doctor used the scan throughout the process, monitoring the baby's movements, making sure the needle never got too close to the baby. There was no mention of a ballpoint pen, a cracked ceiling, and a steel relic posing as a sonar machine. But I trusted Dr. Baines. I hadn't been worried about the procedure; I feared the results: a tangle of chromosomes that could create a heartbreaking pattern.

And now, four weeks later, after thirty agonizing days of waiting, the phone rang in Sara's apartment.

"Gin, it's for you." Sara hugged me. "It's Nad."

"Hi. We got it." The line cracked.

"Got what?" My voice cracked.

"The pram. I just got back from South Africa with the new Land Rover. Your big blue pram."

"Oh, right, the four-by-four stroller. Great. Did we get anything else?"

"Yes, Dr. Baines phoned."

"Stop this."

"What?"

"Tell me now."

I hid behind Sara's richly upholstered chair, curled up in the classic fetal position, willing myself to hold on to the phone.

"The test results were negative. Everything is fine."

"Gin?"

"I'm here. I can hardly believe it. I am just so incredibly happy." Through laughter and tears, I pressed him for more.

"Are you sure you want to know?"

"Listen, I've waited a month for this. I deserve to know more."

"Sure?"

"Sure."

"It's a boy."

I hung up the phone, and in that moment of silence Sara crept back into the room and put her arms around me. "Gin, are you okay?"

"Oh, Sara, he's okay. He's a he. He's a boy. Can you believe it? I'm going to have a boy! I don't know a thing about boys!"

"Me neither, but we'll learn." I'm not sure who cried harder, but at that moment, when I finally gave myself permission to love my growing child completely, I realized that I already did. From the very first moment I'd suspected I was pregnant, I'd loved my baby intensely, but now I could do so without fear. He was healthy, and I was headed back to Etosha armed with hope and a lot more baby books.

"NAD, HOW MUCH change do you have?"

"A couple of dollars' worth, I guess."

"It says here that you should be sure to have enough change for the taxi to get to the hospital for the baby's birth."

"We'd need a Brink's truck."

"And you must make sure the champagne is on ice."

"We'll have a five-hour drive to Windhoek, that's enough time to cool it down."

I handed Nad my book and caught his eye. "Check page 298. Have you been practicing your breathing exercises?"

"Who? Me or you?"

"Both of us. Says here that we should be going to special birthing classes by now, learning all kinds of things like how to breathe."

"I know how to breathe, and besides, I don't think they have those classes in Namibia." Clearly the book I was reading voraciously, *What to Expect When You're Expecting,* was not subtitled *In Africa.* But it was all I had. After visits to my wonderful doctor every six weeks, I was now seven months pregnant, and the next time I planned to see Dr. Baines was when I delivered the baby.

"It's too hot. I'm taking this book to the bath with me."

"Only 105 today, it's cooling down."

"Shut up."

It was the hottest February in living memory. Temperatures averaged 99 degrees in the shade. I'd get up in the middle of the night and lower my body into the splash pool to cool down. My belly was huge, my feet were swelling, and I seemed to be gaining weight by the minute. My friend Mike Hearn told me, with awe, that I looked like I was carrying a four-year-old. Hey, just as long as he was potty-trained.

Then I heard from another old friend, my dear old roommate who'd also been pregnant the last time I'd seen her.

"Gin, hey. It's Kristy. How are you?"

"Enormous, but fine. How are you all, and how is little Emma? She must be four months old by now."

Without hesitation, Kristy plunged in. "Gin, I hate to do this. I know you are pregnant, I know your family, but we are telling everyone now, this week, and I have to tell you something."

"Kristy, please tell me. What's wrong?"

"Emma is sick."

"Oh no, Kristy. How, what happened?"

"I picked up a virus early in my pregnancy and passed it on to Emma. In me it was like the flu, but for Emma it is much worse. It's called cytomegalovirus, and basically it affects everything—speech, hearing, motor skills, all parts of her development. Some cases are more severe than others. Right now we don't know how badly she'll be affected, but regardless we'll deal with it."

"I have no doubt."

If anyone could deal with a grave illness, it was Kristy. She was strong to the core. In New York, Kristy could have stayed in her grandfather's luxurious three-bedroom apartment at the Carlyle, ushered off Madison Avenue by a liveried doorman, gliding up in an elevator alongside Warren Beatty or another rich, successful tenant, then turning the key and stepping into an apartment filled with treasures. Instead she schlepped up four flights of stairs to our tiny apartment and used a cardboard box as a bedside table rather than ask her father, who owned a furniture manufacturing company, for help. Through sheer force of will, packed into her petite five-foot-two-inch frame, Kristy would go to battle. She'd find the right doctors, ask the right questions, and face all the answers, even those hardest to hear, with determination. But I also knew just how much she had to deal with, including caring for her firstborn, a son who was just three years old.

"Kristy, I am so sorry. I know you must be worried about Gordy, but I can tell you he will learn so much from Emma, about himself, his friends, about life. He will be fine. With you and Gordon for parents, he'll be more than fine."

"Thanks, Gin. I knew you'd understand, now I'll just have to get on with educating half of Chattanooga."

"They had better watch out."

To hell with airs and phony social graces, with people unable to cope with anything less than perfect, Kristy would put her children first. As I'd learned from the generations of women who nurtured me—my mother, my great-aunts, and my grandmother—this is what mothers do. Yet I couldn't have known I would have to do it so soon.

"DOCTOR, DOCTOR," SOMEONE cried while pounding on our front door.

"Dr. Nad, please."

I fumbled for the bedside light and checked the clock. It was 2 A.M.

"Just a minute." I slipped on my bathrobe and turned on the hall light.

"What is it?" I said, opening the door.

The front porch light was broken, so it took a moment for my eyes to adjust to the dim light outside.

"I need Dr. Nad." It was Frans, a young man who had once worked in our garden, standing in the rain, jeans hanging from his slim hips, his chest bare, drops of water clinging to his hair, and light rain mixing with blood running from his skull down his face.

"Oh, Frans, Nad is away."

"What? Where is the doctor?"

"I am sorry, Frans, he's gone and I can't help you. Go to the nurse, you know where she lives. It's just two streets away." He held up the palms of his hands, pleading, sniffling and not moving.

"You can't come in. Go to the nurse." I switched off the interior light so he couldn't see my stricken face, and watched him disappear down the street into the darkness.

What had I done? This was another woman's son. Injured, bleeding, shivering in the rain, and I'd told him to go away. I hated myself. But I also had a son to consider. Nad had taken the medical kit with him, and without surgical gloves, I wasn't going to touch Frans, to take the chance that his blood might mingle with mine and my unborn baby's. Frans had made it to our house. He could make it to the nurse's home. She had gloves, training, and knew the risk of contracting AIDS in Africa as well as I did. She would help him. I couldn't. I had to put my baby first, and I had. But I sat in the living room, curled in a chair, and cried until the sun came up.

I HAD TO get out of the house, which was why, at nine months pregnant, I took on a job filming cheetahs. One day I followed a Heikom tracker named Johannes Kapner as he darted a cheetah. I held on to my stomach with one hand and the back of the Land Rover seat with the other as we tried to keep up with the fastest animal on earth. We bounced over burrows in the ground, dodged termite mounds, flattened small trees, until finally the drugs took effect: the cheetah slowed down and fell into a deep sleep under a tree. "I'll set up the camera, Johannes. Then I want you to walk into frame."

I kicked open the back door of the Land Rover, lifted the fluid head and tripod out of their boxes, and screwed the camera on tight. Twenty-five pounds of equipment rested above my belly as I pushed myself out of the vehicle.

"I'm ready."

For the next hour under the blazing midday sun, I moved around Johannes and the cheetah, positioning the camera for the most interesting shots. It was so much fun I nearly forgot I was carrying around an extra thirty-five pounds.

But the calendar told a different story. There were no more doctor's appointments, no more filming engagements, and just two weeks to go before my due date. Still, that was plenty of time to plan our trip down to Windhoek. We'd decided to go down five days early, stay with friends, and wait for our baby.

"Good night, Gin. Sleep well." Nad kissed me, then turned out the lights. I tried to get comfortable, rolling my enormous stomach from side to side. Finally when I settled on my back I felt something wet and warm running between my legs. "Oh my God. Nad, wake up. My water's broken."

"What? Quick, grab the books."

I made a dash for the living room with Nad running behind me.

"Oh, shit."

"What was that?" I spun around to find Nad lying on the floor. He'd slipped in a pool of his baby's waters.

"I'm okay. Just tell me, what does the book say?"

"I'm looking, okay, page 295. It's here. 'Each case is different, a few to twenty-four hours before delivery after rupture of membranes.' My contractions haven't started yet, so that gives us time. I'll just lie down a minute."

It was midnight, Easter morning, and pitch black outside—the time when kudus graze beside unlit roads, when jackals dart across the bush, when no one should drive. The roads are desolate, the towns spaced hundreds of miles apart, the only obvious sign of life the glow of wild animals' eyes. We phoned Dr. Baines, who with extreme hesitation and kindness said since labor is usually longer with the first baby and since contractions hadn't started, we should get some sleep and leave at first light.

Ten minutes later my contractions started. They shot from my back down my legs with such piercing intensity that I screamed. Sixty seconds of pain followed by ten anxious minutes until the pain struck again.

"I can't stand this. We have to go." Nad loaded our big blue diesel pram with a mattress, blankets, and plenty of water. I packed a bag for my baby and myself. So huge was my stomach that I stuffed the baby's bag with clothes for a nine-month-old infant.

It was half past twelve when we began what should have been a five-hour drive to the hospital in Windhoek. Two minutes later we stopped.

"Get out of the road, you beasts."

"What is it?"

I lifted my head and saw two black rhinos standing in the middle of the road, several tons of immovable animals.

Nad eased the car forward.

"Are you crazy? Don't hit them."

"You want to wait?" Finally the rhinos snorted, turned, and melted into the bush.

"Let's try this again."

Nad gripped the steering wheel tighter and drove on, scanning the side of the road for the telltale glow of eyes. If a five-hundred-pound kudu antelope darted across our path, we might not survive . . . much less our baby.

Three hours into the drive, Nad had seen no vehicles, but he'd counted fifty-two kudus and had listened to me moan and then scream every ten minutes. We were approaching Otjiwarango, the town that marks the halfway point between Etosha and Windhoek, where there was a small regional Medi-Clinic hospital.

"I want to stop, just to make sure I'm not bleeding, before we drive on to Windhoek."

We pulled up at the hospital. It was completely dark, shut down for the night. No twenty-four-hour emergency room bay, not a single light burning inside or outside. I tried the doors but they were locked. Nad tried to open a window. Finally a lone nurse appeared.

"Come in, come in. Are you okay?"

"I'm fine, I think. We want to get to Windhoek, but may I first use the bathroom?" Five minutes later we were back on the road. It had been nearly four hours since my water broke.

Two miles outside of town, I bit down on a blanket, feeling the pain of another contraction starting to rise. And then we saw the police roadblock, a typical sight on Easter weekend, when traffic is unusually heavy. Just as we pulled up, I let loose with a bloodcurdling scream. Suddenly a routine check must have sounded like high drama, because when the pain eased, I looked up to see four policemen with their weapons drawn, pointing at Nad. "Sir, we need you to pull over." Then one policeman edged closer to our vehicle and peered inside, perhaps looking for weapons or proof that our Land Rover was stolen. He clearly wasn't expecting to spy a panting, wild-eyed woman in labor. When he saw my big belly, he yelled, "Go, man, go! Get that girl to a hospital. She can't have a baby here!"

Thankfully I didn't. We drove for seven hours, and the sky had turned pink with daylight when we reached Windhoek.

"Well, I see you made it."

I would have recognized that voice anywhere. "Hi, Dr. Baines."

"Must say I'm relieved to see you." He grinned. "How are you feeling? In any pain?"

"Constant."

"I see." He and Nad exchanged glances.

"Have you considered having an epidural?"

"I'd rather not. I'll be okay."

A half hour later I'd changed my mind, and leaned into Nad's arms as the shot was prepared.

"Now this may hurt a—Nad? Are you okay? Nad?"

I felt Nad's muscular arms slacken, and when I lifted my eyes, I saw that he'd turned as white as a hospital sheet.

My husband, who had darted elephants while hanging out of helicopters, captured charging rhinos on foot, pulled calves from their mothers' wombs, who had even delivered eight human babies during his days as a medic, couldn't stand the sight of a thick, six-inch-long needle being plunged into his wife's back.

But Nad was strong and alert ten hours later when our son, Kimberlin

Myles Brain, was born. He seemed to fly into the doctor's arms. He never cried. He simply looked around and had a big wee, sending a stream of urine flying high into the air. I laughed at the thought of a champagne cork blowing and bubbly spraying in celebration. When Dr. Baines placed him on my chest, I had more to celebrate than I could ever have imagined. At thirty-seven years old, for the first time, I held six pounds six ounces of pure joy. Welcome to the world, my boy.

24

SARA (1998–1999)

Sara?" her voice sounded thick and slow, drugged even.

"Gin?!"

"Hey." In her exhaustion, she pronounced the word the way we had as children, with two syllables.

"How are you? How is he? When was he born? Tell me everything!"

Her chuckle seemed to restore her strength. "I'm fine. A little tired, but fine. He was born two nights ago. I'm so sorry I couldn't call till now. But he's wonderful. He was six pounds six ounces and he's got big eyes, and Sara, I know I'm his mom, but he's gorgeous."

"Oh, Gin, I'm sure he is, and I'm so happy for you." And I was. With every part of my being, I was. All those tangled feelings of jealousy and fear for our friendship had evaporated, replaced by the equally powerful longing to pick up her little boy, hold him in my arms, rock him, croon to him. At thirty-seven, my life had changed dramatically, and my perspective with it. We were both quiet for a few seconds. The line gurgled with the swampy, underwater sounds of an overseas call. In the background I heard the echo of sounds in a corridor. When I could trust my voice again, I blurted out, "Was it a long—"

"How's An—"

We both started laughing again. "We can talk about Andrew later," I said, arching my eyebrow at the tall man standing across the living room. After all, he'd been in New York for a few months. "But what about you? How did it all go? Was labor long?"

"Mmmmmmm. Kind of. It started in Etosha."

"*What!?* What happened to your plan to be in Windhoek a couple of weeks beforehand?"

"My water broke late one night, so it was a bit tense and uncomfortable by the end, but—"

"*Tense and uncomfortable!?* And you did that drive *at night*??? Gin, we nearly hit a kudu in broad daylight." I shivered, thinking of all the things that could so easily have gone terribly wrong. "Good God, Gin, did Nad think he was going to have to deliver Kimber??"

"He did, and I did, too. But we made it, and thank God for epidurals. The only thing was at the end they had to use a forceps to pull Kimber out, so he has a bit of a cone head. But he seems fine." She paused. And because I knew she was thinking of her baby's brain, so fragilely encased in his soft skull, I could think of nothing to say. "He *is* fine," she amended, her voice stronger.

"I'm sure he's perfect, Ginger."

"Listen, Sara, I wish I could tell you more, but—"

"I can call you back! Just give me the phone number for your room," I interrupted, anxious for more details but knowing the call must be dreadfully expensive.

"I wish you could, but actually it's impossible. There's only the one phone for the entire floor and it's down the hall. And there's another mom behind me who wants to call her family."

I pictured Gin, two days postpartum, in maternity nightgown, robe, and slippers standing in line on a cold cement floor of a Third World hospital to call family and friends. Forget birthing suites, special dinners, everyone coming to see you. Forget balloons and baskets of flowers, baby showers, baby nurses, and nannies. Kimber just had Ginger and Nad. Thank goodness Gin's mom and dad would be heading over soon for a few weeks.

"I understand. I just wish I could see him, see you. I can't wait to see you as a mom."

"I wish you were here, too. I'll have Nad send a picture as soon as I can."

"Give him a kiss for us."

"I will."

"So is everything all right?" Andrew's voice brought me back.

"Everything's fine. Sounds like a scary trip to the hospital, but Kimber is great and Ginger's tired, but so happy."

"Everything went well. So naturally you look depressed."

I laughed. "Fair enough. It's just that they feel so far away."

"Sara, they are far away. But I'm not. Come over here and I'll take your mind off your misery."

I walked over, snuggled for a bit. Then poked him.

"What's that for?"

"Just making sure you're really here. Living on Barrow Street no less. Although you may be the only person in the trendy West Village wearing a Tasmanian devil T-shirt with Ugg boots and shorts."

"Hey, back off, Tiger, I'm here, aren't I?"

"Just a few subway stops away."

Andrew snorted. "What would you know about the subway? You only take taxis or limos. And I won't be here for long if you keep me stuck in the city for another weekend. Fair crack of the whip." Andrew grinned. "Come on, let's get a hire car and go walkabout."

"Rental car, Andrew. You've got to learn to speak American if you're going to live here. And I'm ready anytime."

The last of the snow had melted from the fields north of the city, but the April trees looked brittle and gray. We stopped to admire a trim white farmhouse. I closed my eyes for a moment, tried to picture it as ours, driving up on weekends, settling in by a cozy fire with hot cider, home. In the nearby pasture a few hapless bovines ankle-deep in muck listlessly gnawed a hay bale.

"It's interesting that they do round bales here," said Andrew.

I eyed him, thinking about my friends having brunch at Sarabeth's or EJ's, perusing the *Times,* latte in hand. Surely I must be the only person I knew discussing hay bales on a Sunday morning. "As compared to what?"

"We do square back home. Easier to cart and stack in the sheds. Round bales only make sense if you cut your own hay for your own cattle. These paddocks look funny, though."

I stared at him. "Funny? Funny how?"

"No sheep. We'd need to have sheep."

Now I was slack-jawed. As any woman knows, deciphering man-speak is like breaking the Enigma code. But he'd definitely just used first person plural. Wasn't that cryptic sentence a hopeful sign? Could "We'd need to have sheep" be Australian for "I want to marry you"?

When in doubt, say nothing. Or, failing that, say nothing revealing. I ventured, "I remember my first trip to visit your folks and how surprised I was by how they cut the grass. Just move the sheep! Pretty good trick." I remembered, too, with the shutters open onto the veranda, how the sound of a flock munching was oddly restful, peaceful. *Baa, baa, black sheep. Sleep, baby, sleep, the stars are the sheep. That sheep may safely graze.* Try coming up with similarly comforting lullabies about cows.

At dinner that night, back in the city, I found I was still thinking. Thinking about what Andrew was thinking. Trying to break the Enigma code. I proceeded in an artful, time-honored manner—seeking to learn what I wanted to know about us by discussing a friend and her boyfriend who were having trouble.

"So, Andrew, do men always mean what they say? I mean, he told her not to call. But she'd really like to. She's had second thoughts, and isn't sure he understands how ready she is to make a commitment."

Andrew scoffed. "What is it with women? Why do they always try to read stuff into what men say? We're entirely straightforward. I should write a book. *Blokes on Blokes: For Women.* It would be short."

"Gimme an example."

"Okay, here's chapter one: 'If the Guy Says Don't Call, Don't Call.' Chapter two: 'Did You Read Chapter One?' "

So there was my answer. Talking about sheep was just talking about sheep. No hidden message. I got up abruptly, headed toward the terrace.

Andrew pushed his chair back. "What's wrong now?" He managed to make three words sound exasperated and tender all at once.

"Nothing."

"Obviously. What sort of nothing?"

"Just. Sheep!" I blurted out. "I mean, do you like it here? Do you think you could live here? And for how long? We could buy a few, I suppose, but there just aren't a lot of sheep in New York!!!"

Andrew looked bewildered. "What are you rabbiting on about? Would you stop carrying on like a pork chop and tell me what's wrong?"

I began laughing in spite of myself, eyes stinging. "Carrying on like a *pork chop*? What does that even mean? I do not understand you!"

"You know. Being a dag." I laughed harder. "A duffer." He crossed the room toward me as the tears started to fall, and soon he was holding me close so it didn't matter so much when he said, "Being a bloody idiot. There, do you understand that, you muttonhead?"

He nuzzled my hair and I took a deep breath of him, warm and male. I imagined I caught a whiff of clover, clear and fresh, and there was that lingering scent you can't help but notice inside when you've spent the day out in the cold.

But Andrew wasn't done, apparently. "I obviously didn't come to New York for the sheep. I came here for you."

"And you love me?"

"Crikey, Sara, what's a bloke got to do?" He was now genuinely annoyed. "I move halfway around the world, quit my job when I'm on track to make editor one day, and instead work freelance in a great big city when I love the country life, all so we can figure out if this is what we think it is. I sure as hell wouldn't have done it if I didn't think I'd marry you." I stopped snuffling. Grabbed him and held him very, very tight, but he extricated himself enough to tip my head back and looked gravely into my eyes.

"Sara, when are you going to learn? I don't say things, I do them."

I reburied my head into that ridiculously endearing Tazzie devil T-shirt. "Well, I have a tip for bloody men. A few more words once in a while wouldn't go astray."

"And I have a tip for women. Talk less."

We settled our differences in a leisurely, thoroughly amicable manner.

IF YOU'RE FORTUNATE, and I have been, there are those rare seasons in life that feel like a perfect day on a ski slope. The air wallops your lungs in icy blasts, your ears sting, but the skis carve the snow just so and you feel supremely alive as you shoot down the mountain on an extraordinary run. Not only was my boyfriend actually living in New York, but work was exciting, too. I was the regular fill-in on *Today,* substituting for Ann Curry on the news desk. And I'd just gotten what would prove to be the most exhilarating assignment of my career. Fellow correspondent Bob McKeown and I, along with a talented team of NBC producers, camera crews, editors, and engineers, would join George Tulloch and his RMS *Titanic* expedition on a journey to the site of the most famous shipwreck in history. I would cohost the first live television show ever produced from the middle of the North Atlantic. We were going to raise the *Titanic.* Or a twenty-ton piece of it, anyway.

We left the Canadian coast on a scruffy tub called the *Petrel V,* which we nicknamed the *African Queen,* for a two-day journey to the middle of the North Atlantic. In less than twenty-four hours my carefully blow-dried hair was a mess of sticky, salt-encrusted curls and the Clinique compact showed more freckles than I'd seen in years, but I didn't care. We were close to our near-mythical destination. The *Titanic* lies some 1,000 miles due east of Boston, and about 400 miles south of the coast of Newfoundland. Our fleet included three other ships, and we motored between them on dubious dinghies nicknamed *Pop* and *Sinks.* One ship, the *Nadir,* was home to *Nautile,* one of only five subs in the world capable of diving the 12,500 feet to where the fabled ship lay. And I was about to get the chance of a lifetime.

On August 10, 1998, I climbed into the hatch of the yellow submarine to become the first network correspondent and one of only a few civilians in the world to travel two and a half miles to the bottom of the ocean. As *Nautile*'s two-man French crew nonchalantly informed me, fewer people have traveled to the bottom of the ocean than have flown in space. To this day, brawny, hulking men ask me how I did it, tell me they wouldn't, they couldn't, how the claustrophobia and the deep would have proved too much. I'm not quite sure how I managed except to say I'd been told another woman had panicked and the sub had to abort the dive. I was determined not to suffer a similar humiliation, not to let anyone suggest that claustrophobia or fear was gender-related. And while Andrew might have been worried about my assignment, he knew how much I'd wanted to make the trip and never said a thing.

But when the hatch closed and the bobbing divers checked that all was secure and signaled the okay to dive, I picked up the camera—there was no room for a cameraman—and pestered the driver and engineer with questions at an even faster clip than usual to try to forget being in a tiny cabin just seven feet in diameter, sinking to the bottom of the abyss.

Underneath her jaunty exterior, the *Nautile* was a utilitarian beauty. Her four-inch-thick hull was titanium, and this inner-space capsule was a perfect sphere—the only metal, and the only shape, capable of withstanding the staggering pressures of the ocean deep. At 12,500 feet below sea level, that pressure was 6,000 pounds per square inch, and the crew's standard party trick was to descend carrying an eight-ounce styrofoam cup in the sub's outside basket and return with a styrofoam thimble. To illustrate that another way, no human remains have ever been found at the site of *Titanic*. Any breach in the *Nautile*'s hull, even one as invisible as a pinprick, and we would simply implode, disintegrating to dust.

The dive to the ocean floor took two hours and the trip would last nearly eight hours, but the *Nautile* had no heat so I wore several layers of clothing. Even worse as far as I was concerned, there was no bathroom. It might have been years since the 1991 Gulf War and I might long since have left Virginia, but southern manners last forever. So I abstained from food and drink, and thankfully didn't have to rely on the Depends I'd secretly worn just in case.

The lack of creature comforts and the threat of sudden claustrophobia were no match for curiosity. I was thrilled by this chance to journey to Atlantis, to visit that magical kingdom of fantastic sea creatures equipped with fanciful lanterns and obscene teeth. And I felt humbled to have a chance to glimpse the ship of my imagination, that once-proud and glittering liner which had shivered, gasped, and broken, falling endlessly through those frigid seas, taking more than fifteen hundred people to their grave.

As we landed gently on the ocean floor and crabbed forward, I held my breath so hard my ears rang, and fumbled to focus, knowing that if we were to get tangled in this rusted carcass, it would become our grave, too. But my fear lifted lightly as a bride's veil when the *Titanic*'s mangled flank came into view because now all I felt was the wonder of it all, and I pressed my face against our porthole and peered through it, to the porthole of the *Titanic,* a window to the past.

The section of the ship before us was a piece of the portside hull of the first-class C deck, and the historians on our expedition had determined it to be cabin C-86, ocean home of Mr. and Mrs. Walter Douglas from Minneapolis. Walter was an heir to the Quaker Oats fortune, and he and his bride of three years, Mahala, had traveled to Europe to celebrate his retirement.

There, in that sacred swath of ocean, I almost felt I could see their shadows, and could imagine that elegant, happy couple, him holding her arm, her head resting lightly on his shoulder, as they left this very cabin for a night of dinner and dancing. I pictured the grand staircase, the parade of women in riches and rubies, velvets and brocades, the men formal and austere, before privilege and delight were wrenched apart in a night of horror and chaos, selfishness and chivalry.

As the boat began to sink, Walter had insisted Mahala take a seat in lifeboat 2, but when she begged her beloved husband to join her, he'd replied, "The only honorable thing to do is stay behind with the men." Years later, Mahala had written a poem about that terrible April night.

> *Darkness comes to her suddenly.*
> *The huge black bulk stands out in silhouette against the star-lit sky . . .*
> *Slowly, slowly, with hardly a ripple*
> *Of that velvet sea,*
> *She sinks out of sight . . .*
> *Slowly it lost its force,*
> *Thinned to a tiny wisp of sound,*
> *Then to a pitiful whisper . . .*
> *Silence.*

A silence that had lasted for eighty-six years. But now, as I watched, the crew had painstakingly attached tow ropes connected to enormous lift-bags, each filled with five thousand pounds of diesel fuel, which would soon lift that shard of the *Titanic* to the surface for the first time since 1912. And suddenly it was mission accomplished, and time to head home.

As we began our slow ascent, the driver turned off the *Nautile*'s lights so that I could witness a second glorious show. Our steady climb through myriad phosphorous sea creatures made it appear that we were in the midst of a psychedelic shower, fuchsia and lavender rain shot with gold falling all around us. And then, quite suddenly, there was the genuine golden spangle of sunshine, and we were hoisted back onto the ship. And I found it hard to believe that magical trip had been real.

JUST FOUR MONTHS later, instead of journeying 12,500 feet beneath the Atlantic, I flew thousands of miles over the Pacific, to an entirely different but equally magical scene. The sheep wandered about, bleating and muttering, thoroughly addled by the bewildering sight of humans rushing about, displaying even less sense than usual.

It was Boxing Day. Traditionally the day after Christmas in Australia is a day to eat leftovers, watch *The Test* on the tube—a five-day cricket match that's mesmerizing or mind-numbing, depending on one's perspective—or head to the beach. But it was also a long holiday pretty much everywhere, ensuring that Mom, Dad, my sister Elizabeth and her husband, John, and my sister Susan could all attend my wedding to Andrew, as well as several intrepid aunts, uncles, and friends. And while Ginger, Linda, and Fiona weren't here—either home with brand-new babies or still pregnant—my friends Liz, Andi, and Toni had made the trip, too.

One great thing about a Christmas wedding in Australia was the reliably excellent weather. You could bank on temperatures in the nineties, with only the rarest sprinkle.

"So when do you think it will stop?" Mom asked.

The rain strafed the house, driven by an angry, reckless wind.

"I don't know," Andrew's sister Christine hedged, then acknowledged, "They're saying on the news it's the storm of the century."

"Well, doesn't that just make sense," I groused under my breath. "I mean, nothing about this relationship has been typical, so why should our wedding day be?" I shivered in my dress, sleeveless so I wouldn't roast in the heat. The temperature was 45 degrees. Fahrenheit.

We peered through the streaming glass at lacy white tents where we'd eaten dinner the night before yawing to stern like storm-tossed yachts.

"It will be memorable," said my sister Susan, ever sunny, "and everyone is already having fun. Who cares if it rains?" The rain I could deal with, but the hail seemed excessive. Elizabeth, recovering from vocal surgery and unable to say much of anything, squeezed my hand and indicated her support with a smile and a bright nod.

"Andrew and Trevor have raided every place they can think of to find heaters," added Andrew's sister Kate with her youngest-sister giggle. "And we've got heaps of jumpers and blankets so everyone can rug up."

"Sara?" It was Andrew's mum calling from downstairs. "It's Ginger, calling from Africa."

"Gin!"

"Oh, I hate saying congratulations by phone. I wish I were there!"

"So do I. I felt the same way when Kimber was born. But we'll show you plenty of photos. They should be pretty interesting given that there's a tempest and it's about five degrees so only the sheep are dressed appropriately, but hey, it's happening! We're getting married!"

"They say in Namibia that rain on your wedding is good luck. So you have good luck, my friend. Kimber and Nad send their love, too."

I hung up and looked around. My family. Andrew's family. Getting along as if they'd Christmased together since we were toddlers instead of meeting a few days ago. Aussies, Americans, my friend Lizzie Sanderson in from Scotland, Toni Wren from London, Andrew's translator and his family here from Japan, and a handful of New Zealanders, all jumbled together in the rambling, comfortable farmhouse where Andrew had grown up. All here, here for us. I had good luck indeed.

Later that day, in the rosy crumbling church in a field not far from the house, with the occasional sheep bleating pitifully in the background, we said our vows. I loved the service—my dad, his voice husky with emotion, pronouncing us man and wife as Mom beamed, Andrew smiling and handsome in his tux, my sisters at my side, the security of our unshakable trio. And then there was the slow exit to be bedecked with charms and hugs from the wonderful Butcher clan and our friends. Happy memories, to be sure.

But what I remember most was the laughter. Giddy laughter as guests donned flannel blankets over spaghetti straps, chunky pullovers and farm coats over satin and silk, to brave the tent, only to abandon its elegant dampness and the hundreds of beautiful native flowers as soon as possible for a noisy, blissfully overheated night of toasting and dancing in the garage turned rumpus room. And as we took off for our honeymoon in a redneck red 1970s monstrosity called a Monaro, an Australian cross between a Camaro and a Chevelle, I knew I felt luckier than the wealthiest society gal on Park Avenue. How simple in the end, how right. The man from ten thousand miles away felt just like the boy next door.

WHEN WE RETURNED to New York after a leisurely honeymoon, Andrew and I set up house in my apartment. It felt luxurious to be together, yet I was anxious to fill our home with the sound of a child's laughter, and so far we'd had no luck. Thankfully, a *Dateline* producer and friend, Roberta Oster, was investigating a human rights travesty that would help me take my mind off myself.

"These women are going through an ordeal we can't imagine, Sara."

With all that has happened since, it seems impossible to remember a time when we didn't think of Afghanistan, when we hadn't heard of the Taliban. But back in 1999, the evils of that regime were just becoming more widely known.

The dangers of the Pakistan-Afghanistan border, however, were clear. As had been the case a few years before when I'd headed to Sudan, there was a security checklist at NBC.

At home, Andrew gave me a long, strong hug. "Be careful."

"I will."

"And don't forget your Discman."

"Thanks, Andrew."

As I packed for the flight to London, then Islamabad, I still couldn't get used to it. There would be someone here at home when I returned, someone to think about when I was there so I didn't do something inordinately foolish or downright dumb. Someone—as well as something—to rely on.

In Pakistan, Bert and I interviewed an Afghan-born American woman named Zohra Rasekh, a health researcher and author of a groundbreaking report for Physicians for Human Rights which detailed the life-threatening consequences for women of living under the Taliban regime. "They say women are sinful, women are prostitutes. If they go out and show their face in public, if they mingle with men, they are bad," Rasekh told us. With her, we visited refugee camps just a few miles from the Khyber Pass, that fabled gateway to Afghanistan.

Huddled in their tents, women and children whispered of their ordeal: being forced to quit jobs as doctors, lawyers, accountants because a bunch of troglodytes said they had to stay home; educating their daughters at home by candlelight because girls couldn't attend school; living in a land where any infraction, no matter how trivial or arbitrary, could be punished by beatings, public amputations, or even execution. "I'm so afraid, sometimes I think it's better to die than to live like this," one woman told us. And for many, the symbol of their shame and oppression was the mandatory burqa which covered them from head to toe, turning women into shapeless wraiths forced to peer at the world through the rectangular window of their powder blue prison. I thought I would weep when one woman told of how her daughter had been beaten with a metal rod by one of the Taliban's religious enforcers for not wearing the burqa, even though she was only eight years old.

And as I listened to woman after woman, story after story, something remarkable happened. I felt my guilt and regret and fear bleach in the searing Pakistani sun. With surprising clarity, I suddenly knew I couldn't have lived my life any other way. As desperately as I wanted a child, there was no way to rewrite the script which had brought me here. I hadn't been ready to be a mother at twenty-five, even thirty. Only recently had theoretical desire distilled into longing. I was ambitious, certainly. But I also realized that ambition, like claustrophobia and fear, wasn't gender-specific. I loved my life. I had wanted to learn, to test my limits, to tramp about this rugged world a bit myself. I had wanted more than I could find during my nurturing, wonderful, but sheltered childhood in Richmond. Work had honed me, made me who I was, who I was happy to be, as well as the woman Andrew loved. Those women were every bit my equal in intelligence and drive, but their opportunities were meager and their resources nonexistent. Neanderthals had sacked their nation, ravaged their homes and families, and held their futures hostage. Lucky? I was luckier than I could have dared imagine. As we boarded the plane to come home, I only hoped that in telling their story, I would remind others—as they had reminded me— how fragile freedom is, how fortunate we were.

AND WHEN I returned to New York, that glorious and unforgettable run, which had taken me through 1998 and now halfway through 1999, seemed as if it might never end.

"See it? Look how quickly the heart is beating." The doctor slid her magic wand across my belly and I saw a circle on the screen and, in its center, a pulsing bright bead of light. I almost felt as if I'd been allowed to peer through a secret window, and thought back to my glimpse of the *Titanic*. But that had been a view of the past and this felt like a porthole to the future. "Everything looks great, Sara," the doctor continued.

"Thank God."

"You're eight weeks along and you can see the heartbeat, so that means your risk of miscarriage is less than five percent. Congratulations."

All those weeks and months and years of worrying, and there had been no need. Andrew and I were going to have a baby. That night we celebrated with Martinelli's sparkling apple juice.

"Do you suppose it's a boy or a girl?" I asked.

"Better be a boy," Andrew said, deadpan. Then, seeing my stricken face, grinned. "What do I care? Here's to our baby, boy or girl."

I told no one. No one except Mom and Dad, my sisters, Linda, Lisa, Andi, Scottie, Sharon, Fiona, Toni, and a few others. And, of course, Ginger.

"Oh, Sara. How wonderful!"

"Can you believe it? We'll be moms at the same time!"

I was out of my skin with excitement. The June sunshine was more baskable than usual. The sidewalks looked especially pretty. I had never noticed how cheerful and happy everyone was here in New York. I reveled in that distinctly new-pregnancy habit of stroking my belly. Mostly in the shower, as, in spite of everyone I'd told, it still felt like a delicious secret. I couldn't feel anything yet, but I knew someone was in there. I was thirty-eight years old and I was going to be a mom, going to join that secret sisterhood in which so many of my dear friends were recent initiates. Once again I'd been able to sneak in the back door. I'd managed to get pregnant in spite of the dire predictions, those you're-too-old naysayers and worry-warts.

Two weeks later I had a second, routine scan, and couldn't wait for my next look through the porthole. As the doctor greased my stomach and began the careful, chilly circles, I propped up on my elbows, craning my neck forward, anxious for my next peek at the baby.

But suddenly I felt as though I'd slammed into a glacier, and a splinter of ice pierced my heart. Where was it?

The doctor didn't say a thing, just continued those circles with increasing speed and urgency. But the fluttering little light had sputtered out.

"It's not there," I said finally, because one of us had to say something. "Where is it?"

She put down her less-than-magic wand and her cheerful expression had been replaced by the face of a stranger, that mask of a doctor forced to deliver bad news.

"I'm sorry."

She said more than that, of course, a babble of appropriate maybes and qualifiers, let's do a high-resolution scan, et cetera et cetera, but it was all just a wash of words so I could have time to comprehend that the porthole was underwater, the waves lapping over the grave, that tender light extinguished. Ten-week-old Baby was gone.

I was shivering in my white office gown when I called Andrew.

"G'day. How'd it go?"

"Not well at all. Andrew, the baby's dead." I think now how terrible that was, delivering such a cold truth without warning, but I didn't have the grace to prepare him. I was shocked and scared and sad, and only in telling him did the terrible burden seem any smaller.

"Beg pardon?"

"The heartbeat. It's gone. And that means the baby died. Oh, Andrew."

He was quiet for a moment and only now do I picture him then, at work in the new job he'd only recently taken as vice president for News Corporation, wearing a suit and a tie instead of his Tazzie devil shirt, coworkers wandering by as he got sucker-punched by his wife. Not that he ever shamed me for the barbarity of what I'd done. Instead, when he spoke, his voice was calm and kind.

"Sara, it'll be okay." I took the tissue the doctor handed me as he continued, "We'll try again. Lots of people have miscarriages." Then, with gentle humor he added, "Look, we knew it couldn't be this easy. We'll have fun trying."

A few minutes later I hung up and I blew my nose and I put on my suit, and as I walked home all I could think was how dirty the street was, how much the city stank in June, how I hated signs like "Don't Block the Box," how the buses stank, too, how stupid everything was, most especially me, for waiting so long, for putting off the most important thing for things that were more immediate, for thinking I could fool God, fool fate, fool the calendar. I was thirty-eight, after all.

And what about Andrew? Nine years younger, a man who'd made no secret of the fact that what he wanted most in life was to get married and have children. Had I asked for too much—a fascinating job, a man to love, and children? In my greed had I lost my chance? And what about his?

The perfect run down the slope had ended. It was a mountain, after all. It was a glacier. And I had crashed.

25

GINGER (2000)

Are you ready?" Nad asked, peering through the screen of our front door in Okaukuejo. "If you want to get back to camp tonight, you'd better hurry." The thought of elephants beckoned, but I had one thing left to do.

"Just a sec. I want to get this e-mail off to Sara before we go." As I hit the send button and imagined my message flying across the world, I thought about how quickly life could change. In an instant. A car tumbles down a ravine. Someone says "I do." A soldier steps on a land mine. A baby cries, those first lusty cries, while another one's heart beats for the last time. And the instant evil takes shape, when two heavily armed boys walked into a library and changed a country forever.

The tragedy at Columbine High School had made headlines around the world, including Namibia. In the weeks following the shooting, I knew that Sara and her friend and producer, Andi Gitow, had been going back and forth to Colorado, spending time with a family who'd been tragically affected by the shooting.

Sharing heartache, putting your own in perspective by helping others deal with far greater sorrow, was one way to move beyond tragedy. Perhaps this was Sara's way. I couldn't know. For the first time since that long-ago dinner in New York during which we'd reconnected, sharing stories of old and new loves as well as our evolving dreams, I felt a distance between Sara and me. After twenty years of having lives which were entirely intertwined, despite the thousands of miles which separated us, it felt as if our braided lives had come undone and were beginning to fray.

I couldn't forget our phone call just a few weeks before.

"Hey, we just got back," Sara had laughed.

I'd instantly felt off-balance. "I didn't know you were going away."

"Yeah, it was a spur-of-the-moment trip. Andrew and I went to Paris for a long weekend with Andi. We all needed a break after Columbine, plus Andi had lived in Paris for a few years, so she gave us an insider's tour. We went to the Louvre, checked out the street markets, and I ate so much yummy food I'm going to have to diet for a year." I'd listened quietly while Sara continued, breathlessly listing the shops, the galleries, the fashions, the wonderful restaurants, filling a void with excitement, with places, with things. It was so unlike her that I knew then, without her having to say another word, that she'd lost the baby.

"It sounds wonderful, but, Sara?"

I could almost feel the intake of air across the line.

I paused, then asked as gently as possible, "Did you lose the baby?"

And then I heard the tears I couldn't see. "I wanted to call you, but I just couldn't talk about it."

Since her miscarriage, Sara was at once stronger and weaker, depending on the moment and what she chose to reveal. I could scarcely imagine her pain. I remembered when I had been pregnant with Kimber, feeling him kick and hiccup, how months of joy had crystallized at the moment of his birth. But for Sara, ten lovely weeks of anticipation had ended in shock and sorrow. And while I knew she was thrilled for Nad and me and our son, I wondered if her loss made it hard for her to witness my joy. Or perhaps she thought that by avoiding me, she could keep the shadow of grief from clouding my happiness. But I couldn't help but worry that the presence of my precious child was beginning to drive a wedge between us. After we'd shared so much over the years, it was hard not to be the one she confided in.

It was also incredibly selfish. When she needed a hug or a big, messy cry, I wasn't there. I couldn't take her out for a stiff drink or drag her out to a silly movie; we couldn't stand together and shake our fists at the heavens, ranting and raging about life, fate, and timing. Not only did I live thousands of miles away, but we'd recently left our house with its precious telephone and reliable e-mail for a remote base camp in eastern Etosha, one that didn't even have a radio telephone.

"Gin, come on." After spending the afternoon back at the research station at Okaukuejo, Nad was impatient. "Kimber is about to fall asleep. Let's go."

I typed a breezy note—*Off to camp, wish us luck*—and hit send. I didn't add that I was worried that this latest heartbreaking assignment, taking on the trust and the pain of a lovely, wounded family, would add too much to her personal grief. That instead of giving herself time to heal after her miscarriage, she was willfully making choices to prove that she hadn't been shaken to the core, that she was still tough and work was still important. I knew it wasn't the time to question my friend's motives.

The computer connection closed. Nothing. Sara must be in the air.

Turning out of the gate at Okaukuejo, taking the dusty road east, I thought about the many times Nad and I had made this drive across the park when I was pregnant. Each time we'd loaded our Land Rover with tents, electric wiring, a basin, shade netting, anything we could beg, buy, or borrow to make life at our soon-to-be-constructed camp more comfortable. Along the way, we'd talked about names for our baby, wondered if he'd sleep well, and if he'd be able to tolerate the heat. With each trip the camp had taken shape. Nad had finished digging the trenches for water pipes, attaching them to a cold-water shower in an abandoned horse stable and to a double basin—one side for washing dishes, the other for washing our baby—under a large acacia tree. Near the fence Nad and a few friends had dug a twenty-foot pit for our long-drop toilet, and then our two tents had been raised. But with camp looking increasingly like home, more questions emerged. I'd begun to feel the isolation, and had brooded over what we'd do and where we'd go if our child got sick. Then I'd put worries aside and simply longed to finally see him, wondering what on earth he'd look like. Now I glanced at the sleeping baby beside me, light brown hair, blue-green eyes, and lashes as long as a giraffe's. His arrival had answered some of our questions, but there was still so much more I longed to know about my son. It would take a lifetime, and I looked forward to every minute of it.

I reached out and stroked his chubby pink cheek. After we'd celebrated his birthday back in Virginia with my family, Kimber was now a year old. Walking and chatting in a combination of languages uniquely his own, he'd changed so much since the first time my parents had seen him. They'd flown to Namibia the week after Kimber was born. For three weeks they'd strolled, rocked, and cradled their first grandson. At sunset they'd carried him to the fence to watch elephant herds descend upon the water hole. When Dad had had to return to the U.S., Mom had stayed on, hanging out countless loads of laundry, filling the kitchen with the aroma of bacon and brownies, wiping tears from my tired face, and beaming at the sound of her grandson's first delightful coos.

Mom had always laughed that she'd been a young mother, but that her girls had made her an old grandmother. She had been half my age when her first child was born. Three more daughters followed in quick succession, including Tish, with her very special needs. With Dad on the road Monday to Friday, working hard to support us all, Mom found her joy, made her mistakes, and raised her kids largely alone. Just a kid herself.

I couldn't remember my mom—now a grandmother, a self-taught and serious antiques collector and dealer, and a wicked tennis player—ever wishing that she'd had a career first and then children, that somehow order and timing had deprived her of a more interesting life. My parents weren't kids pretending to be grown up, they'd had to grow up fast, and they'd always put their children first. Once, when we were young and Tish had been very sick, I remembered asking my mom if she wanted to get rid of all of us. It was a child's question, asked with a child's innocence and raw intuition. She had laughed and then said very seriously, "Never, ever." I'd believed her then, and when I watched her playing with my baby boy, I believed her still.

But just six weeks after Mom had arrived, we'd been back at the airport. Through tears, I'd made a promise to bring Kimber to the U.S. to meet his American family before he turned a year old. Then she was gone and I was on my own.

The next few months passed quickly. Kimber's demands to be fed at night became less frequent, and he breezed past milestone after milestone. With such a healthy, bright son, I slowly began to gain confidence in my new role as mother. Problem was, I missed my old role as wildlife film-maker.

Filmmaking had become a vital part of my life, a part I wanted to share with Kimber. I had imagined turning the Land Rover into a traveling nursery, our very own four-by-four stroller. With the camera mount on one door and the box of camera gear on the seat beside me, Kimber would have the back of the vehicle all to himself. I'd pictured bold blue, yellow, and red blocks of cloth strung across the windows for curtains, an elephant mobile hanging from the ceiling, baby books, and a quiet, restful child. I would film, read, write, all the things I'd always done while out in the bush. Kimber would grab his toes and learn his ABCs. Right. Obviously I'd pictured all of this before I ever had a laughing, crying, rolling, eating, grabbing, delightful, into-everything precious baby.

Fortunately, our move to camp helped to make my life as a working mom work. With all the comforts of home, camp was also within easy commuting distance of a dense population of elephants. But that was not all. We had something my mom had never had while raising four children— a wonderful nanny. Selinda. A sturdy woman quick to smile and equally quick to discipline, Selinda was a Heikom bushman who had been born in Etosha long before the land had been proclaimed a national park. She and her husband, Ou Jan Tsumeb, a colleague of Nad's, had raised their four children here and were helping to raise their grandchildren. Fortunately for us, Selinda had agreed to help us with Kimber.

It had been eleven years since I set out alone for Africa, embracing an adventure that had turned into a way of life. From filming headless warthogs to becoming a filmmaker with an expanding résumé, from protecting my broken heart to risking the thrill and the pain of falling in love again, I knew that my next adventure would be wonderfully different: it would be shared with my family.

Beginning a new project with elephants, exploring the mysteries of their movements and their long-distance, infrasonic communication, was in many aspects reminiscent of the old way of life we had cherished in the desert, but this project also reminded us of how far we had come. Our marriage and our child were thriving, and this time our film wasn't being shot in the vague hope that it would sell. This film, *Giants of Etosha,* was for National Geographic.

FOR THE FIRST time since we'd left the baboons, I found myself completely immersed in a wild world. While the baboons' environment had completely destroyed their society, Etosha's elephants lived in a world that allowed their caring, complex, intelligent social groups to flourish. Although Etosha had more than two thousand elephants, we primarily followed one herd, getting to know their preferred feeding grounds, the water holes they frequented, the babies born to them, and the males who shadowed them in search of a female in estrus. But most of all, we got to know Knob Nose, their matriarch.

Whether I was peering through a lens or absorbing a scene with all my senses, I learned a lot about motherhood from watching Knob Nose and her breeding herd. Bonded by females with an extended family of aunts, sisters, cousins, and an assortment of their young, their breeding herd reminded me of my own extended family back in the States. Growing up under many watchful eyes, young elephants explore their world and test themselves in a warm, secure, and protective environment. Thinking of our Elee and Kimber, I watched the little ones as they walked along game paths, casually brushing up against their mother's body. At water holes they'd play, chasing smaller animals or each other, and later, in a contest of strength, the males would push their growing bulk against one another, testing themselves and challenging one another, all within the safety of the herd.

At camp, Kimber was taking similar steps, from helping his dad stack firewood, to forming a tender bond with Selinda's bright grandson Rian, to trusting his mom to return after sunset. And, perhaps most of all, learning to trust his own instincts.

This was never truer than one afternoon when Nad, Kimber, and I had been alone at camp. In the shaded area outside our tent, Nad had cut slices from a thick slab of rye bread. I'd walked back and forth from the other tent, bringing tomatoes, tuna, mayonnaise, a few basics for lunch. Kimber had moved around us, walking between our legs, under the table, helping pick up his toys, and then suddenly, at the edge of the tent where a huge steel beam held down the canvas material, he'd stopped and stood dead still.

In the next instant Nad had gripped the knife while I'd grabbed the tent pole. Kimber, my bouncing eighteen-month-old son, remained perfectly still and focused on the ground. Gliding over his feet, slowly, until the tail touched his toes, was a long, iridescent green snake, a boomslang, one of the deadliest snakes in Africa. Kimber had felt the grip of its scales, the coolness of its body, and yet he hadn't moved a muscle. When the snake disappeared around the corner of the tent, he'd picked up a ball and started playing again.

Instinct—what an awesome power, what a truly amazing blessing. When all the adrenaline in your body begs you to run, instinct tells you it is safer to stand still. Nature or nurture, thank God Kimber had it.

My friendship with Sara began as an act of instinct, knowing innately that she was someone I could trust. Our bond and my intuition were gifts I've tapped into many times since we were twelve. And my time in the bush had definitely helped to hone my senses, keeping me alert to danger, to opportunities, and knowing instinctively when not to cross certain natural lines. As a filmmaker, I'd responded by knowing when to move in close and when to pull out quickly. I'd also known when to walk away. In Etosha, the same voice I'd heard in the Kuiseb, the one that said, *Enough is enough,* still resonated.

About a year into our study, I drove out late one afternoon. I'd given up finding the matriarch, Knob Nose, and her herd that day, and simply planned to enjoy the soothing bird sounds and the cool air while watching zebra and wildebeest trek across the plains and disappear into the bushes for the night. Suddenly the sounds of trumpeting, branches breaking, and another female elephant's huge feet pounding on the road just twenty feet away broke any semblance of peace.

I threw the Land Rover into reverse, pulling away, giving my heart a chance to steady and the elephant time to relax. Then I began inching the car forward. I knew there had to be something wrong, and there it was.

Lying on top of a mound of red earth was the elephant's baby. Surrounding his body were elephant footprints and thin trunk lines in the sand, signs that his mother had tried desperately to lift him. His trunk was still; his chest had risen and fallen for the last time. I looked for wounds, for some sign of struggle with a lion or hyena, but his body wasn't scarred, there was no blood splattered on the ground, only the sad signs of a natural, tragic death.

I looked at his mother, standing guard over her dead baby, gently touching him with her trunk while keeping a wary eye on me. Clearly these images were dramatic, but this poor elephant had been through enough drama for a lifetime. She deserved to be left alone. Another filmmaker had once told me, "If you don't capture it on film, it never happened." If only that were true. My breasts ached and I decided that no amount of footage, no matter how potentially riveting for our film, was worth putting her through more agony. I left my camera in its case and went back to camp, back to nurse Kimber.

OVER THE NEXT months I left camp early, wanting to spend more time with Knob Nose and her herd. Then one morning I couldn't find them anywhere. Fifty tons of elephant had simply disappeared. Fortunately, since Nad was an accomplished pilot, we had the option of radio-tracking the herd from the air.

Through the crackle on my headset, I heard Nad's familiar voice. "This is India Sierra Echo, taking off to the east on a low-level flight in the Namutoni area. Any traffic? India Sierra Echo." Nad went through the last-minute checks, throttled back, and quickly we were airborne. Setting out to find Knob Nose, we first flew toward camp.

"I still can't believe it's ours." We'd been living at camp for over a year, but each time I saw it from the air, it gave me a thrill. From fifty feet up, it looked chocolate-box beautiful. Two tents in a grove of trees, the tin roofs covering the long-drop and shower reflecting the midday sun. A huge pile of firewood rested against the side of the smaller tent. Against the large tent there was a sandbox, yellow dump trucks and red shovels sticking out at odd angles. A swing made from an old tire hung from the thick branch of an acacia tree. Now camp looked like home, and we were the proud owners. As Nad banked the plane, dipping its wings over camp, Selinda stepped out into the sun, holding Kimber in her strong arms, both of them waving as we flew past.

"He's fine," Nad reassured me, knowing that I sometimes struggled to find the right balance between working mother and mother working.

"I'm sure he is." I smiled. "I'm fine, too, thanks. Let's go find Knob Nose."

I plugged my headphones into the radiotelemetry tracking device and flipped a small switch back and forth, right and left, listening as the beeps grew stronger.

"Turn left." As Nad banked the plane, the sound of beeps intensified.

"There they are, right below us."

In a dense grove of terminalia trees I spotted Knob Nose, the matriarch, surrounded by her herd. Even without her radio collar, the big wart on her nose made her impossible to miss.

"Looks like they are moving toward the water hole at Cameldoorin. If we head back now, you can get them coming in." The Land Rover, packed with fresh film and camera gear, was parked at the airstrip. From there it would take me about an hour to drive to Cameldooring. I would be there long before sunset.

"That's great, but I'll be back late."

"No problem. I'll get dinner going."

"Please be careful with Kimber around the fire."

Nad shook his head and laughed. "Gin, we are always careful. Give your boy some credit, he's a bush baby."

I looked out the plane's window at the game paths streaked like veins in the earth, wondering which path the elephants would choose to enter the water hole and where I would set up my cameras, thinking of our shooting script and mentally composing the shots I wanted to capture that evening. That was when I heard a big clunk.

"What was that?" The sound seemed to echo in the pit of my stomach. "I don't know, but I'm climbing." When you're flying just twenty feet above the bush, a huge clunk, followed by "I don't know," is not good news. Climbing was the only option Nad had—the only way to put enough space between us and the ground so we could have a few extra moments to find a decent place to land. Nad pulled back on the yoke and we soared several hundred feet in just seconds.

I pictured Kimber down below playing in his sandbox, waiting for dinner and his parents to return. Eighteen months old and his closest relatives, Nad's parents, lived two thousand miles away. Nad said nothing. He didn't have to. I watched him rub his sweaty palms across his flight suit. I ran my hands through my hair and concentrated on breathing.

And then, finally, we were high enough, and I saw a stretch of wide, open dirt: the runway. "Don't worry. We can glide in from here."

When we touched down, I made a silent vow to Kimber to keep my feet on the ground. With rabid jackals, scorpions, and prowling lions, there were plenty of dangers in the bush; having one parent in the air was enough for any child.

After cutting the engine, Nad squeezed my shoulder. "You okay? You can still make it to Cameldooring before the elephants."

An image flashed through my mind: elephants drifting through a cloud of dust, moving in shadows toward camera, becoming clearer in stunning light until Knob Nose and her herd emerged. It was quickly replaced by a much more powerful image: a little boy's arms wrapped around my neck, his soft cheek resting against mine. "No, I think I'll just stay home tonight."

As I held Kimber in my arms, watching as his eyelids became heavy, his breathing deepened. I finally carried my sleeping boy to bed. It was a priceless evening, worth more than any footage I might have shot. And it was followed by special moments with the elephants that were captured on film.

In the past two years we had learned a great deal about the details of the elephants' lives: their bonds, their wisdom, and their connection to their

environment. And while we'd celebrated moments of great joy while filming them, we hadn't expected to discover how much death was a part of the
elephant's journey.

The dry season of 2000 proved particularly brutal for Etosha's young
elephants, and Knob Nose's family suffered more than most. Lurking in
the soil, anthrax, a natural part of Etosha's ecosystem and an ancient bacte-
rial disease that can be ingested by unsuspecting animals, claimed the life
of Knob Nose's older son. Several weeks later we found her standing over
the body of her last child. In less than two months, Knob Nose had lost
both of her offspring to anthrax.

Knob Nose stayed with the body of her second child, gently touching
the bones, lifting her sensitive foot and running it across the length of her
little one's body. In time other elephants joined her, caressing the bones in
an ancient, eerily familiar expression of grief. As the camera rolled, I could
almost feel the breath from her trunk released onto the bones, and in the
silence, I could almost hear them mourning. While I captured these moments on film, Nad recorded sound. I was conscious of the sound of the
tape rolling, quietly round and round, capturing the stillness.

As a mother, I felt haunted by the double loss of those intelligent, wonderful creatures. Later that month back at camp, when Knob Nose and her
herd had moved to the far eastern corner of the park, I told Nad, "I'm worried about Knob Nose."

"She'll be fine."

"What if she isn't?"

Kimber, who had been adding wood to the fire, perked up, ever alert to
changes in our moods. "Mommy, what's wrong?"

"Darlin', Knob Nose's babies were sick and they both died. It's very
sad."

"Kimber," Nad chimed in, "it is sad, but it's a natural part of life in
Etosha. Disease helps to control the numbers of animals in the park; that
way there is enough food for the other animals."

"Oh yeah, like the smoke?"

"That's right, that jackal who was prowling around here had rabies. It was very sick." A rabid jackal had stumbled into camp. Nad had shot it, and Kimber had witnessed everything. Six months later, what he remembered most clearly was the smoke coming from the end of the gun.

"But Daddy saved me." Kimber smiled and hugged his daddy's leg, his head not quite reaching Nad's knee.

Growing up in the bush, in a world without television, video games, and PlayStations, Kimber already realized that there was nothing artificial about life and death.

KIMBER WAS ALMOST two years old when Nad and I closed the zips on our tent, loaded the last of our film in a box, and for the first time all three of us flew to the U.S. to edit our elephant film. Kimber stayed with my family in Richmond, getting to know his cousin Maggie, the dogs Alice and Lucky, and Millie, our big beautiful cat. I gave Millie an extra scratch behind the ears, as she was the very cat my mom and my sisters Marsha and Dona had given me years before, when Kevin had broken off our relationship. What a long time ago that seemed, and how much I loved that cat.

Creeping out before our son woke up on Monday mornings to take the early train two hours north to Washington, D.C., we would return on Thursday evenings in time to put Kimber to bed. In between, we spent our first days in Washington on the fifth floor of National Geographic in the edit suite. Gliding down the hall, wishing everyone a good morning, was Keenan Smart, head of National Geographic's Natural History Unit. I introduced him to Nad.

"I remember you from the baboon film," a simple sentence flowing lyrically in his Scottish brogue. A look passed between the three of us—of a prior screening, a past disappointment—but a look that ended in laughter.

"Glad these people finally came to their senses," Keenan continued. "We are all looking forward to working on your film. Come on and say hi to Kathy and Anny. Great girls. You'll be in good hands."

And we were. Kathy Pasternak, our supervising producer, kept us on schedule, while Anny Lowery Meza, our editor, stayed late, never complaining, always quick with a smile and a late-night toast with Cognac. She worked her magic with the raw footage, crafting beautiful scenes infused with her warmth and intelligence. One scene in particular evolved with a poignancy we could never have expected when filming in Etosha.

When we'd arrived in the U.S., we'd sent Kurt Fristrup, a specialist in bioacoustics and animal communication at Cornell University, the sound tape we'd rolled when Knob Nose had been caressing the bones of her dead baby. Other than a whispering wind and a few birdcalls, we hadn't heard a thing. But since elephants communicate below the threshold of human hearing, we'd asked Kurt to run the tape through one of Cornell's machines capable of capturing infrasonic sounds just in case. Kindly, he'd agreed.

When the tape arrived at National Geographic, Anny blew it a kiss before putting it in the editing machine. At first the room was quiet, then there was a single voice, a bellow, deep and mournful, rising and falling. Soon it was joined by other voices, a symphony of sound, subterranean and rich with emotion. Knob Nose and her herd had lingered not at an elephant graveyard of myth, but at a very specific grave site, the place where her own baby had perished. The sounds continued, rising, falling, a single voice, then others, echoing with pain, moving Anny and me to tears. It was the first time anyone had heard these sounds for exactly what they were: the mourning of a very special elephant by a very special herd. The elephants' silent language of grief.

Just as we had been with the baboon and Bushmen films, Nad and I were blessed to have an editor who treated our footage and the elephants' story as a gift, one that she protected, nurtured, and wove with clarity and care. As we worked our way through the collaborative process of filmmaking, one I'd become more comfortable with through the years, Anny continued to work her magic.

During the fine-cut screening before a host of producers, Anny turned to me and whispered, "I love this part."

The dark edit suite came alive with images of Etosha that made me glad I'd gotten out of bed on those dark, frosty mornings: green plains full of purple and white lilies, tall lilac cosmos, and pools of deep blue water. An elephant moved into frame, leading the herd: it was Knob Nose. Behind her walked a baby, flat ears and stubby black hair on her head. After losing two babies to anthrax, Knob Nose had had another, a little girl who might prove to be the herd's next matriarch.

I smiled at Anny. Our film had a real-life happy ending.

NAD HAD ADDED such a refreshing and intelligent perspective to the edit, but eventually he had to return to Namibia to his veterinarian duties in Etosha, so while I finished the film Kimber stayed with my parents. On my last day in Washington, when we'd just completed layering in sound effects for the final "mix" of the film, Sara came down from New York to celebrate. "How's it going at the Geographic? Weren't you going to pitch them a new idea?" she asked.

"Yes, on the natural history of anthrax. Nad and I think it's a fascinating story, but they said, 'No. Who wants to hear about a disease?' "

"I think it sounds interesting, too, but maybe they do have a point. It's not anything that ever happens here. Plus it only kills animals."

"It's more complicated than that, but that's the challenge. When we figure out how to tell the story in a more captivating way, so it's not just some rotten old disease, we'll be able to make the film. Anyway, what time is your interview tomorrow?"

"I have to be at Senator McCain's office at ten A.M. I've done most of the prep work, so there's no rush tonight."

"Great." We moved around each other in the luxurious bathroom at the Ritz-Carlton, sharing lipstick, blow-dryers, and memories.

"Nothing like my bathroom in Okaukuejo."

"Speaking of Okaukuejo, I have a little something for Kimber."

She went back into the bedroom, rummaged down to the bottom of her suitcase, and returned with a beautiful Babar print, a delightful scene of a little elephant blowing on a campfire.

"Not that I'm quite sure where you'll hang it, given that you still live in a tent! I can't believe I haven't met him yet, but when I saw this in Paris I thought of him."

My dear friend who had gone to Paris to forget, at least for a weekend, about her miscarriage, had remembered my son. As I hugged her, I knew without a doubt that my feelings of being out of sync, disconnected, had passed. I no longer feared that our friendship was fraying. It was stronger than ever, and so were we.

"Thank you, Sara, it's beautiful and so is he, but you'll see him this weekend. Come on, I'm starved."

In a restaurant known for its delicious food, Sara pushed her dinner around the plate.

"Sara . . ." with a raise of my eyebrows, was all I had to say.

"I think I might be. But I don't want to get my hopes up."

The next morning Sara crept into the bathroom while I pretended to be asleep. Not for long. She ran out and jumped on the bed.

"It's positive, it's positive!"

"Let me see."

"It's in the trash can!"

"Are you crazy, get it out!"

She ran into the bathroom and ran out waving the tiny stick with its two pink lines clearly visible.

I grabbed her and hugged her and wouldn't let go. "Sara! What wonderful news! You're gonna have a baby!"

Like my little boy, I trusted my instincts. And this time I was just sure there would be another real-life happy ending, and this one would be Sara's.

26

SARA (2000–2001)

HAVE A SEAT, Sara. What's up?" asked Dick Ebersol, president of NBC Sports, gesturing to one of the comfortable sofas in an immense office that smelled not so faintly of cigar smoke.

It had been just a couple of weeks since I'd seen Ginger in Washington. The story I'd shot there would air during NBC's coverage of the 2000 Summer Olympics and I was due to leave for Sydney in a couple of months.

"I think you know how excited I am about this assignment," I began, "especially covering the Games in my husband's country, but there's a complication."

Dick raised an eyebrow, waited for me to continue.

Much as I liked Dick, I'd agonized about this encounter. I hated letting people down, not doing what I'd promised, putting anyone in a bind. But most of all, the guiding principle which had gotten me to the network had been Put Work First. And I always had. Until that minute.

His twinkling blue eyes said, *I think I can guess,* but all he said was, "Yes?"

In the end I just blurted out, "I'm pregnant." My present and future in two and a half words.

His grin widened. "Congratulations. That's great news!" The proud father of four, Dick proceeded to tell me how his wife, former *Kate & Allie* star Susan St. James, had been a pioneer when it came to bringing babies to the set as she'd juggled being a mom with her acting career. As I left, he gave me a smile and said, "You're doing the right thing to stay home."

He'd understood. I was off the hook. As I stumbled out of Dick's office, I was knocked off-balance by a wave of relief so enormous I was stunned to discover that it was followed by a hidden riptide of loss. I'd just volunteered to watch the Games on television instead of being on television to report them. I'd miss the sweaty drama of front-row access to gymnastics, swimming, track and field, not to mention the diverting sideshows and controversy that invariably erupted. And of course there was the prospect of real news. I'd covered the Atlanta Games in 1996, raced to Olympic Park just minutes after a bomb had exploded, covered the chaos as terror supplanted celebration. Homegrown or imported, kooks and crazies with a cause would always be lurking, hoping to hijack the Games.

To turn down a significant assignment felt not just odd, it felt wrong. I hardly knew how to say no, and doing so felt like trying to flex an unfamiliar set of muscles. My baby wasn't even born yet and I found myself confronting the dilemmas of motherhood, the need to "juggle" and "prioritize." I couldn't help but think about male colleagues for whom having a baby had no impact on career trajectory. Most had wives who stayed home with the children, and even those who had working partners generally delegated child care arrangements to the mom. In my current situation I realized I had no choice, as my wise and caring obstetrician, Dr. Kessler, had unequivocally nixed this trip. While I dutifully put the needs of this new, growing person ahead of my own, I still experienced occasional selfish twinges. Imagining Baby as a smiling, cooing, and distinctly separate being felt entirely theoretical.

I was thirty-nine years old, this was my third pregnancy, and it was still early in the first trimester. I knew better than to stroke my belly this time, knew better than to indulge in show or even tell. Our families knew, and Ginger of course, having been there when that sliver of plastic glowed with twin pink lines. Somehow, having her there to confirm the news made me feel as if perhaps this third time would charm up a baby. Or maybe it was the fact that for the first time I felt queasy. I craved shakes made with tofu, strawberries, and bananas. I couldn't stand the smell of meat or vegetables cooking, so every night Andrew ordered delivery while I ate peanut butter and jelly sandwiches. When I craved ginger I baked Christmas cookies in

July, glaring when my husband complained that while the air might smell good, it was now 97 degrees inside. Then a Proustian longing for crepes prompted me to scour the city for the perfect pan. Andrew watched with by-now-silent amusement, having learned that virtually anything he ventured to say was wrong. For starters, how dare he feel so confident that everything would be fine, after all we'd been through? I'd felt no flutterings, no hint of the "quickening" I'd read about, and I wasn't ready to believe.

The weeks passed slowly. Given my history and age, I'd switched to a high-risk ob-gyn practice in New York. These days I braced myself before every look through the porthole, but week after week, the flickering lighthouse held steady. And soon it seemed as if a fog had lifted and I could see more. There was the head, the abdomen, budding arms and legs, fingers and toes, as the baby rocked gently inside its underwater cradle. And finally it was time for amnio.

While Ginger's doctor had only performed a handful of procedures, my practice performed several hundred a year. My procedure went smoothly. But the wait was another matter. Ginger had spent those long days of uncertainty thinking about her sister Tish. And now I couldn't help but think of Tish, too. As an older mom—three years older than Ginger had been when she delivered Kimber—I'd been encouraged to see a genetics counselor who'd matter-of-factly informed me of our baby's risk of Down's as well as far more catastrophic chromosomal missteps. I knew how Tish's severe health problems had plagued her, causing anguish and uncertainty for her and the rest of the family.

But I also knew that so much of life was unpredictable, no matter what tests were available. After all, Tish's first sign of trouble only came when she was four years old. I knew far too well that traumatic, devastating events could happen to anyone, at any time. And I'd also seen families, including the Mauneys, make their way through such heartache with courage and grace. What's more, I knew how gentle and compassionate Ginger was. My friend who had been unable to film her beloved baboons in their distress. My friend who had been the first to offer to fly to New York when my first marriage had ended. My friend who felt more at home with a pride of lions than with the proud Masters of the Universe who strutted through

New York. My friend who rarely complained. After all, what was there to whine about when you compared your life with that of a beloved younger sister who suffered seizures so frequent and severe that they limited her choices and often robbed her of control.

Ginger's secret fear, the one she'd confided so many years before, had been that she and Tish could have traded places. Tish might have been Gin. She might have been Tish. It was a fear that made her feel guilty and ashamed. But I believed that very fear had forged her. And I couldn't help but believe that witnessing a sister whose life was necessarily narrow had driven Ginger to expand her own horizons, to have the courage to gamble, to reinvent herself. Ginger knew she was fortunate. It was a gift she dare not waste. But what I didn't think Ginger knew was that in a way she'd incorporated a part of her sister into herself. Ginger was worried that in choosing Africa, she'd run away from Tish. I felt that in choosing Africa, Ginger was living her life, a great big dream of a life, for both of them.

I realized I hadn't said any of this to Ginger. It had only just become clear to me. I needed to tell her that having her as a friend actually had reduced my worries about having a child with medical woes. It had by no means erased those fears, and I prayed nightly for a healthy baby. More than anything else, I just wanted our baby to survive. I wanted this test to tell me there was nothing so catastrophically wrong that our baby would die before it could be born. I just wasn't sure I could make it if another child growing inside me were to wither away.

Being forced to wait always makes me want to escape, to catch a plane. Fortunately, by then the doctors had determined that my pregnancy was far enough along that such a choice was safe, so I headed to Tampa, Florida. It was the early autumn of 2000, and the presidential election was just weeks away. NBC had gathered a focus group there to watch the debate between Texas Governor George W. Bush and Vice President Al Gore. Afterward I'd interview the Floridians to see what they'd thought. As I pawed through my wardrobe searching for the largest jacket, only to discover I still couldn't button the button, I realized my pregnancy must be a secret in name only. I chose a skirt with an elastic waist, wore a don't-ask-me smile, and said nothing.

When the plane landed, I couldn't stand it any longer. It was just after nine in the morning. I stood in the lobby of the hotel and used my cell phone to dial the doctor's office.

When I got off the phone, my hands were shaking. I punched in the numbers for Andrew.

"G'day. How was the flight? Are you feeling okay? Or am I not allowed to ask that, either?"

"Today you can ask anything you want. *Anything,* Andrew, because I am great! The amnio is back and everything is fine!"

I do not remember what my husband said, because, after all, the news was exactly what he'd predicted. I thought of the little flicker inside me, which I could now think of as a baby. Our baby. So much happiness feeding on that slender wick of wonder, that flaming beacon of life. I had no idea what my future would be like. I just knew that now I felt like I was living it.

FOR ME, THERE were two pregnancies—before and after amnio. With my status secure, I reveled in everything. The baby had started kicking, all right, kicking so hard we nicknamed it Thumper.

"You're carrying high. That means a boy."

"You're carrying forward! Definitely a boy."

Secretly I agreed. Suddenly I could eat anything and wanted to eat everything. Work was busy and diverting and flying never bothered me. I always made a point of walking around the metal detector at security, opting for a pat-down to avoid needless X-rays. Baby first.

When I wasn't on the road I generally filled in on *Today,* enjoying the opportunity to catch up with all of my pals there, both on- and offscreen. And on that fateful election night of November 7, 2000, I anchored the coverage for one of NBC's sister networks, CNBC. A few weeks later, shortly before the Supreme Court designated George W. Bush president-in-waiting, I escaped with Andrew for a Roman holiday. When I returned, my friend Soledad O'Brien, the *Weekend Today* anchor, lent me her fabulous maternity clothes, including leather pants which I wore to my baby shower, so I could get through the long, snowy winter in style.

But as I moved into the third trimester, I realized that while I'd accepted that I was going to have a baby, I knew nothing about being a mother. Fortunately, I lived in New York, a city in which it's not uncommon to tackle motherhood in your thirties, forties, or even fifties rather than your twenties, and I had plenty of friends who could offer recent advice.

"Get a baby nurse," advised Sharon, unofficial spokesperson for the group. Years after we'd compared notes on our disastrous dating lives, she'd married a wonderful man named Steve Seltzer. Nine months and one week later, they'd had daughter Samantha, soon followed by son Jake.

"What's a baby nurse?"

"*What's a baby nurse??? A baby nurse is indispensable.* She stays at your house overnight, feeds Baby when he wakes up, and gets him on a schedule."

I listened politely but had already crossed this tip off my list. I was accustomed to getting up at 4 A.M. when I read the news on *Today*. I'd anchored an overnight newscast. I was accustomed to surviving on little sleep. I called Ginger.

"So, Gin, I figure that while I'm home on maternity leave, I'll have loads of free time when Thumper is napping, right?"

"I don't really remember any." She sounded doubtful. "Come to think of it, I can't remember much of anything during the first six months. Nad used to call Kimber 'Abu Nidal'—the little terrorist who had taken us hostage for life."

That sounded ominous and uncharacteristically melodramatic. Perhaps sensing my distress, Ginger tossed in a comforting disclaimer. "But look, maybe your baby will be different."

I cheered up. Ginger lived in Africa, after all, where her only available role models were elephants. I lived in New York, and while pachyderms were scarce, books and classes were widely available. I read Dr. Sears. Penelope Leach. *The Girlfriends' Guide to Pregnancy.* And, of course, the bible,

What to Expect. I signed up for any class with baby in the title, from "Infant CPR" to a jazzy little number called "How to Diaper an Infant." The nurse who taught the class looked at every one of us with mild alarm. Clearly we were in for it if we couldn't even figure out how to Velcro a Pampers.

And then there were the childbirth classes.

Andrew was dubious.

"Why Bradley? Didn't the quack recommend Lamaze?"

"It's similar, but Bradley focuses on going through childbirth without drugs. I want to do this by myself so I have the genuine birth experience, and that means I won't get an epidural."

Andrew looked incredulous. "Why not?"

"What do you mean why not?"

"Pretty simple question. As you know, I'm no fan of drugs, but why not take medicine if it reduces pain?"

I gave an exasperated sigh. "Be*cause* it's unnatural. It interferes with my authentic experience and it means Thumper gets drugs that slow him down when he's born. Women have been having babies without drugs for a gazillion years and doing just fine. It's just all the movies, the Hollywood hype, trying to convince us it's going to hurt a lot."

"Sara, let me give you the egg flip on this. It's gonna hurt."

"Well, I'm strong. Besides, I'm also taking pregnancy yoga, like LP did. I'm learning breathing techniques."

Andrew's mouth clamped down at the corner as it does when he's stifling a laugh.

"But didn't Ginger say—"

I cut him a look.

"Have it your way." He shrugged.

My mom was more blunt. "That sounds ridiculous. You *hate* pain."

OUR BABY WAS due on March 6. The day came. The day went. *Dateline* executive producer Neal Shapiro sensibly insisted I stop coming to work. No babies born at the office, thank you.

As a natural childbirth devotee, I didn't worry about the delay. Babies had their own schedule. Dr. Kessler was tolerant, to a point, but demanded I be induced if the baby hadn't arrived in two weeks. "Much as you are clearly enjoying this pregnancy, Sara," he told me, "you *are* going to have the baby."

On the night of March 19, I was typing an e-mail to Mom and Dad when I felt a light squeeze in my abdomen.

"Andrew! Grab the watch, let's time my contractions!"

I followed the Bradley instructions to get into a warm bath to ease the pain. A few minutes later I jumped up again, dripping.

"We have got to get to the hospital. This baby is going to be born any minute!"

"Sara, your contractions are only twenty seconds long and they're twelve minutes apart. According to those classes you made me take, it's still very early."

"Arrgh!" I screamed. "The classes are wrong. This hurts!"

"Okay, okay, settle down. That's why they call it labor. Let's call Dr. Kessler and tell him we're on our way."

My apartment was only half a mile from the hospital. The doorman flagged a taxi for us, wished me luck. I bit down on a scream.

The taxi driver took one look at me and hit the gas. Unfortunately, he also hit a pothole. I moaned and grabbed Andrew.

"Ouch! Take it easy," said my husband, extracting my fingernails from his arm.

When we arrived at the hospital, I wondered if I would be five centimeters dilated, or all the way to ten. Dr. Kessler shook his head compassionately. "Zero."

How could such a thing be possible? I held on for a few drug-free hours, but by 5 A.M. had had enough. "You know, there's no crime in it, Sara," Dr. Kessler comforted me.

Andrew said nothing. Not one thing, for which I will always be grateful. I'd flunked Bradley but I no longer cared. After the epidural, I was actually enjoying my birth experience. And before I knew it, the long months of waiting compressed into a few frantic minutes of pushing, followed by a strong, welcome cry.

It was shortly before noon on the first day of spring, March 20, 2001.

"It's a girl!" Dr. Kessler said.

"Hello, Sophie James Butcher," I said, laughing and crying as I looked into her large, serious eyes. Our gorgeous, glorious baby. "Now get a cuddle from your dad."

I watched as Andrew cradled our little treasure, still dressed only in her birthday suit, before he carried her off to be weighed, pricked, and swaddled. She was perfect. I was forty years old and I'd just become a mom. I knew one moment of being utterly, perfectly happy.

"THERE ARE EATERS and there are sleepers. You got an eater," pronounced Nurse Nancy at the pediatrician's office, squeezing one of Sophie's juicy thighs. My baby had just had another excellent checkup. She was sailing over milestones. First smile. First clap. Rolling over. Nearly five months old, she loved her toys, loved to be held, seemed to take everything in with her wide hazel eyes. The only problem was, she never shut them, waking every two hours to nurse. I stumbled and blinked outside. I had trouble dialing the phone. I wept when someone left the freezer door open and I had to pour out the stored breast milk. I snapped at anyone who suggested I was tired. But in a few months, I was going back to work.

"Let the baby cry it out," one friend suggested.

"I can't."

"Ferberize her," said another.

"You and Andrew will figure out what is best, and Sophie will be okay," said Andi, whose credentials as a psychologist as well as producer made me feel better.

It was so difficult to get Sophie to sleep that we sometimes let her sleep all night in her car seat. "What's with her neck?" asked my pal Lynne.

"It's just a little crooked. It's okay."

Lynne cocked her head in an unflattering imitation. "Have you asked the doctor if it's okay?"

Sophie moved to a crib. But while her neck straightened out, her sleeping patterns didn't.

I called Ginger. "Why didn't you tell me how hard it was?" I wailed.

"I did," she reminded me gently. "Abu Nidal, remember?"

I remembered.

"But I'm sure she's also wonderful."

"Oh, Gin, she's fantastic. I take her to the park, and she loves the grass, the swings. She is everything to me."

I stopped, keenly aware of how trite such tributes sounded. But they were heartfelt. I had no words to express the size of my feelings for our little girl, the wonder of being a parent after so long. There was life before Sophie. And there was life after. I realized there was much I needed to figure out, about how I was going to be Sophie's mom and work, too. But I couldn't think until I'd had some sleep. Ginger understood.

"Look, it'll work out. You're going over to Australia in a couple of weeks to take Sophie to meet Andrew's family, right? When you come back, your nanny will start and you'll still have a little time before you go back to NBC. Aren't you lucky that *Dateline* gives such long maternity leave."

But life didn't quite work out that way. Because Andrew, Sophie, and I returned to New York on September 9, 2001.

27

GINGER (2001)

I STEPPED OUTSIDE THE dark editing suite into the crisp sunshine. After a cold night, the last vestige of an African winter, it was a beautifully clear, breezy day. Standing against a bare wall to catch the sun, I warmed my hands, then punched our home phone number into a borrowed cell phone, hoping to reach Nad and Kimber.

The phone rang and rang. No reply. They must be out in the park, I thought. While I'd been away in Windhoek for the past few weeks working on the edit of our latest film, *The Chase,* about game capture in Namibia, Nad was home in Etosha doing double duty at work and with Kimber.

After a few more minutes of soaking in the sun, I walked back into the edit suite, opening the door and letting pale light cast a shadow across the computer screen. Josef Nyberg, a bright, talented Swedish film editor, looked up and asked, "How's Nad?"

"Don't know. There was no answer. I'll try again later."

"Come and take a look at this sequence."

I sat down beside Josef, who had stopped cutting film and started drumming his pencil to the soulful African rhythms of Erykah Badu. Rapid shots of giraffe, eland, black rhinos, ropes, trucks, helicopters, and men set to a background of vibrant music filled the edit suite. The pace was quick, the atmosphere fun. Just then, the door to the suite abruptly slid open.

"A plane just hit the Twin Towers in New York!" The man breathlessly speaking was someone I'd passed in the halls at the editing studio, nodded to, but didn't know.

"What?" I was completely disoriented. Music, airplanes, rhinos, buildings. "What are you talking about?"

"I heard it on the radio just now, on my way back to the office. I don't know anything more." Then he was off, running down the hall.

"No, that is crazy." Josef shook his head. "I'm sure he misunderstood." Josef turned back to the editing machine.

For a few moments I thumbed through index cards, trying to concentrate on the right order of shots for the scene we were about to cut. But I couldn't concentrate on anything. I kept thinking of a plane, the Twin Towers. New York. Sara and her family. No. It wasn't possible. But still.

"Josef, I'll be back in a sec. I'm just going to go check the Internet."

I walked into the office next door and logged on to CNN.com. The connection was slow, too slow. When Sara was nervous her toes curled, but I'd always run my hands through my hair over and over again. Waiting for the connection to work, I felt like I was pulling my hair out of my head. Then, slowly, in bits and bytes, an image began to appear. Light gray blocks at the bottom of the screen, blue to the left, and a mass of black, white, and dark gray in the middle. A building. The sky. An explosion. I fell back into a chair and tried logging on to other web pages, but the screen was frozen on the image of a plane hitting one of the Twin Towers.

I felt a hand on my shoulder. "Ginger, come on. It's impossible to get any work done. Let's go back to the house." It was Paul van Schalkwyk, our dear friend whose offices we were using and who, with his gracious wife, Rieth, and lively young teenagers, Henri and Nina, had opened up their home to Josef and me while we worked on the film. "Rieth and I were there a couple of years ago." He shook his head, thinking back, and continued, "We had drinks at the top. It was the best bar in the world."

"Oh, Paul. This isn't happening." I turned to face him and then nearly turned away at the sight of pain and concern on his face.

"Have you heard from Sara?" he asked gently, and then I remembered that Paul and Rieth had stayed in Sara's apartment a few years earlier when she'd been in Australia. They'd gotten to know her not only through my stories, but through the photographs on the piano, the art on her walls, and by feeding her big cat, Jagger.

"No," I replied, involuntarily rubbing my arms as they were suddenly, inexplicably freezing cold. "I haven't heard a thing."

I walked in a daze back to the edit suite to get my keys. Josef was standing by the door, my pocketbook in hand. He hugged me and led me down the hall. Now he too knew it was true. That a plane had hit one of the towers that defined the Manhattan skyline, a symbol of power, of beauty, and of a country I loved. But it was so much more than that.

Those towers were full of people, chief executives, secretaries and clerks, cleaners, accountants and lawyers. No longer defined by their jobs, they were simply husbands who had kissed their wives good-bye that morning, mothers who had dropped their children off at day care with a hug, sons, daughters, friends, all with families who loved them and who were now desperately, horribly scared.

WE SAT IN stunned silence in Paul's den watching as horrific images ran across the screen. CNN, BBC, Sky News, it was the only story. Josef rubbed my shoulders, Paul tried to smile. My Swedish editor, my Namibian friend, a mini United Nations, and we all knew the world would never be the same.

A phone rang in the background. "Ginger"—Paul spoke quietly into the phone before passing it to me—"it's for you. It's Nad."

In a half whisper, half shock of disbelief, the first thing he said was "Can you believe it?"

"No, it's impossible. But how are you? How's Kimber? And how did you find out?" We didn't have satellite television, so we only got the news once a day at 8 P.M., Namibian time, and it was only three o'clock.

"We were just walking home from the Institute and Piet called to us to come quickly to his house. He had the TV on, and even though they kept showing those horrible images over and over, none of us could believe what we were seeing."

"Did Kimber watch the news?" I asked. "Does he understand?" I thought of my son, just three years old, such a light, joyful child, of him and his father walking hand in hand down the road at Okaukuejo. Zebras braying in the background, the warm sun on their faces. Then I thought of explosions and chaos, the thousands of innocent people trapped in airplanes and skyscrapers with no way out. In a wave of sadness that threatened to engulf me, I thought of Maggie and Zan, my dear niece and nephew in the States, of sweet Sophie, and especially of Kimber, wondering, like parents everywhere, what kind of a world our children would inherit.

"Kimber seems to think it's a movie," Nad said, breaking my thoughts, "but then when he really listens, there's such urgency in the newsreaders' voices that he gets confused. He's also worried about you. He's afraid you might be there."

I just wanted to hold him, but all I could do was reassure him over the phone. "Let me talk to him, please."

Nad pulled away from the phone. I heard a toy drop and the patter of feet getting louder before the sweetest little voice said, "Hi, Mommy."

"Hi, my lovebug. Are you having fun with Daddy?"

"Yeah. This morning we went to see a big truck that had flipped right over."

"That's exciting. Maybe you can show me when I get home. Remember, just three more sleeps and I'll be there."

"Goody!"

"I love you, darlin'."

"Okay, bye, Mommy." The receiver hit the ground and he was gone.

Nad picked it up, stopping the clanging, and said under his breath, "Don't worry, he's fine, but what about Sara? Have you heard anything from her and Andrew and Sophie?"

"I'm not sure where they are. I can't get through to an international line. But I'll let you know as soon as I reach them."

I hung up the phone, praying that they hadn't been in the wrong place at the wrong time.

A few minutes later I picked up the phone again. "Paul, do you mind if I try one more time?"

On TV, the towers were beginning to crumble.

"You must."

* * *

"Sara?"

"Oh, Gin. It's you."

"Are you okay? Andrew, Sophie, are they okay?"

"We only just got back from Australia. It feels like a jet-lagged nightmare, but it's not. It's true."

"So you weren't anywhere near downtown?"

"No, thank God. Sophie and I were at home and Andrew's office is in midtown. All we hear is the noise, the sirens, the jets. And . . . wait a minute?" I heard a door slide open. "I'm going outside on the terrace. I don't want Sophie to hear me."

The background noise on the phone changed. I heard wind, horns, sirens, the same noises Sara was hearing.

"Oh, Gin. I looked out the window and thought I must be mistaken, but I'm not. It's ash, white ash, floating across the city. Her voice broke and then she continued, "It's falling onto our terrace. Oh God. It's everywhere."

I pictured Sara's terrace on the eighteenth floor with its long view down Third Avenue. It had been the scene of so much laughter and so many latenight confessions, and now Sara was standing there outside, alone in a mist of ash.

"Gin, what are you guys hearing over there? Do you know about the plane hitting the Pentagon?"

"We've heard that horrible news and sketchy information about a plane crash in Pennsylvania."

"There is so much speculation, and so much fear, Gin. I can't begin to tell you."

But I knew if only from afar that a city that pulsed with life had been hushed by tragedy. A country that I loved had been savagely attacked and I wanted to be there, to hold the ones I loved, and to share the fear and the pain and the anger.

"Sara, please be careful."

"I will, but I must go. I need to call work."

"Give Soph a big hug for me, and Sara, we love you all so much."

"We love you, too, Gin."

After I hung up the phone I said a silent prayer for Sara and her family, for my family, and every other family affected by the events of that tragic day. I shivered again, a wave of pain hitting my core, and I wondered if there would be more attacks, and if the madness that started that day at 8:46 A.M. in America would ever truly be over.

28

SARA (2001)

MY BREASTS ACHED. I glanced down quickly to make sure I wasn't leaking, as that would qualify as a disaster. I was sitting at the *Nightly News* desk, wired up with microphone and IFB, ready to anchor any special reports. It was late September 2001 and that had been my assignment since returning to work on September 12. These days, urgent bulletins seemed to occur with alarming frequency.

"Can I get up for thirty minutes?" I asked.

"Sure. Brokaw just got in, so we're covered. We'll see you later."

I headed back to my office, where our nanny, Sherry Daisy, was playing with Sophie on the carpeted floor. Originally from Trinidad, Sherry managed to be both relaxed and thoroughly capable, with a quick laugh and loving personality our daughter adored. I also admired Sherry's serenity, which she attributed to her deep faith. Sherry had been bringing Sophie to the office for a few days to ease the transition for me and my baby, as I'd come back to work earlier than I'd expected. Of course I'd also taken the opportunity to parade my first child shamelessly through the halls of *Dateline, Today,* and *Nightly News,* introducing her to friends and colleagues.

Sophie looked up and blew me a raspberry. "Thank goodness you brought her in," said Mary Casalino, assistant to the correspondents. "She cheers everybody up."

Sherry stepped out of my office and I closed the door and settled back on the sofa, relieved to nurse. Outside, the spires of St. Patrick's Cathedral pricked the bright blue sky as bagpipes wailed. I usually loved the fierce, ragged music. It reminded me of my last trip to Scotland, where I'd hooked up with dear pals and their families, including Fiona, whom I'd met in Charlotte, and Lizzie, who'd flown to Australia for my wedding. But now the pipes sounded melancholy, forlorn. Another funeral for another fire-fighter. I pulled Sophie to me tightly and she drew back in puzzled alarm. I forced myself to relax both my body and my expression and she settled back to work.

I'd witnessed a great deal of heartache and misery in my professional career and had never grown accustomed to it. But the disasters I'd covered had taken place in another town, another state, another country. Terror had been something I could escape. Not this time.

While we'd been incredibly fortunate, New York was a city in mourning, Manhattan an island of anxiety. You could smell fear in the putrid, smoky air. Hear it in the sound of circling fighter jets. See it on the faces of rifle-toting cops manning bridges and tunnels. Feel it in the way your abdomen twisted when you walked past fading, tattered posters of those beloved men and women who'd never come home, past makeshift shrines of candles and teddy bears, past firehouses draped in bunting.

As a new mother, I realized I felt both intensely protective and excruciatingly vulnerable, keenly aware that, for the first time in my life, I was responsible not just for myself, but for our baby. Suddenly, living on the eighteenth floor seemed too close to the sky. How would I carry her down so many flights of stairs in an emergency? And if I made it to the street, how would I make it off the island? After 9/11 we'd watched those vital exits slam shut, leaving millions of us under lockdown. Pitching dangerously between extreme emotions, I'd felt as if I might capsize, and had been grateful to return to work, where covering the travails of others was an instant reminder that my small, wonderful family was only one of so many cast adrift in a violent, bewildering storm.

Sophie sat up. I buttoned my blouse, put on my jacket, and opened the blinds to let the incongruously cheerful sunshine stream in. I gave my bright-eyed girl a parting hug and kiss. I knew it was time to end her visits to the office, much as I enjoyed them. While having her close by made me feel that she was safer, I also knew she needed a rhythm and routine I couldn't give her at the office. "Thanks for bringing her in, Sherry. I'll see you both this evening."

ON OCTOBER 12, I was alone in my office when the phone rang. "Get down to the studio. Now."

I walked as rapidly as I dared toward the studio elevator, knowing that to run would only leave me sounding breathless and out of control. As I got off the elevator, I saw my friend Andi running toward me with a panicked expression. "Sara! There's anthrax in the building!"

I stopped and shook my head as if to clear my ears. It almost felt as though she were speaking underwater, the words thick and muffled as they echoed in my mind. "What are you talking about?"

"Here! There's anthrax right here, on this floor!"

It had been just over a week since Secretary of Health and Human Services Tommy Thompson had stunned the nation, reporting that a Florida photo editor had contracted anthrax. Sixty-three-year-old Robert Stevens had died the next day. Testing by the Centers for Disease Control revealed anthrax spores in his workplace and the chilling fact that several other people had been exposed. Someone, somewhere, had turned anthrax into a lethal weapon and was sending spores through the mail, leaving the entire country on edge less than a month after 9/11. My *Dateline* producer friend Roberta Oster Sachs, now married and a mom, had confessed she'd begun taking Cipro just in case. "It's the only antibiotic that's strong enough. But the supply is limited. They'll run out of it if there's a major attack."

"But that's not going to happen," I'd insisted. All the same, Andrew and I made sure Sophie was nowhere near when we opened our mail. I couldn't help but think back to the film Ginger had proposed, and how foolish it seemed now to think of anthrax only as an African scourge. It was happening here. How wrong I'd been.

Suddenly the whispers were everywhere, and then someone handed me the NBC News press release which I would read on the air. An anthrax-tainted letter had been sent to Tom Brokaw and been opened by his assistant, who had contracted anthrax on her skin and was being treated with antibiotics. I felt a wave of nausea. I knew Tom's assistant, Erin O'Connor. She was a lovely woman and also the mother of a toddler, and I hoped she'd be okay. Meanwhile it seemed the entire third floor—including the studio where I was about to do the special report—was considered contaminated, and uncertainty and anxiety permeated the air, invisible but toxic. Mary Kahler, a makeup artist, had tears in her eyes as she thrust a thin paper mask into my hand. "You take it, Sara. You're a mom."

I shook my head, incredibly touched, and hugged her. "No, Mary! Thanks, you keep it. Though I'm afraid these don't do much. Listen, let's try not to worry yet."

But as I turned toward the phone, there was no way I could take my own advice. My fear was boiling over and I had just moments before I went on the air. I punched in my husband's work number, and when he answered, the words tumbled out in a barely comprehensible jumble.

"Andrew, I'm about to anchor a special report because Tom just rushed out to Mayor Giuliani's press conference because—there's anthrax here at NBC."

"Sara, slow down." The calm voice of the man I loved and trusted cut through the chaos. I tried to rein myself in. "I'm not worried about me, Andrew, it's Sophie! Oh God, I've taken our baby all over these halls. We even visited Tom in his office, near where Erin opened the letter, and I've got to go now and can you call—"

"I'll handle it," Andrew interrupted, his even voice cracking for the first time before it steadied again as he said, "I'll call Dr. Lancry, and Dr. Davies, and I'll find out what we do."

"I love you."

"You too. It'll be okay."

And then it was time to be on air. In my ear I heard the voice of Specials producer Beth O'Connell from the control room, addressing me by the nickname she'd used since I'd first met her at the *Today* show nearly ten years before. "Young Sara. Breathe. Just breathe. Okay? We'll get someone back here to check on Sophie, too."

I nodded. It all felt surreal. At NBC we covered news, we weren't part of it. But I knew my husband was doing everything that could be done for our daughter at that moment, and I had to do my job. I found my voice and pressed down, down, down until I hit a surprising well of calm as the pounding music ended and a deep voice announced, "This is an NBC News Special Report. Here's Sara James."

And so began a report that hardly seemed real to me, a report that began, "We have learned that there has been another case of anthrax, this one a cutaneous one, here at NBC."

WITHIN A FEW hours, both the FBI and the Centers for Disease Control had set up a command center at 30 Rockefeller Plaza. Everyone in the affected area was given a nasal swab and advised to do exactly what I had questioned my friend for doing—take Cipro. It was the only known antidote to anthrax.

"But what about my daughter?" I asked after explaining our situation, because I knew she was too young to take the powerful drug. "And what about our nanny?"

The sympathetic CDC agent spoke in a measured voice. "Your nanny needs to take Cipro, just like you. And your daughter—she can take another antibiotic that is milder."

"But that won't work, will it?" I pressed.

"Let's not worry about that yet. She may not even have been exposed. And by the way, you'll have to stop nursing. Cipro penetrates breast milk."

I turned away so that he wouldn't see that I was on the verge of weeping. I had planned to nurse Sophie until she was a year old. He put his hand on my arm. "Look. You're not the only one. There are women here who are pregnant. They've got tough choices, too."

The tears froze. How selfish I'd been. *Please, God,* I prayed. *Just let Sophie be okay.*

The next morning was Saturday, but when the phone rang at 9 A.M. it was an investigator from the CDC asking if Sophie had started her antibiotics. I said yes.

"Good. Very good. And how is she?"

"She's fine." I paused. "She has a rash under her arm and a mild cough," I confessed, "but I'm sure it's just a cold."

I heard his sharp intake of breath. "I am advising you to take Sophie to your pediatrician. Now. We won't get the nasal swabs back for a few days. Let's not take any chances."

I felt as if someone else were getting in the taxi, handing money to the driver, unbuckling a car seat, walking into the office. I was tapped out on fear, momentarily numb and ominously calm. Andrew had contacted experts on his own who'd told him that anthrax wasn't even a footnote in the medical books. Sophie's pediatrician, Karen Lancry, was intelligent and compassionate. "Don't worry, this is just a precaution," she said as she donned gloves. But her eyes gave her away. After examining the rash, she'd said, "She looks just fine. But under the circumstances I think we should send her to a specialist. Just in case."

More gloves, masks, poking and prodding. More tests and "We'll wait for the results."

Andrew and I were sick of waiting for answers. What's more, we knew one person who might be able to help. And that person was married to my best friend.

"Gin?" As I rushed headlong into a breathless explanation, she stopped me.

"Sara, Nad's actually treated someone with anthrax."

"*What?* A person? I thought that in Africa just elephants got it!"

"It's rare, but sometimes people pick it up, and it happened once here in the park."

"He probably knows more about it than anyone in the U.S."

"Hang on, I'll get him."

Just hearing Nad's deep voice made me feel better. I told him about Sophie's symptoms. The cough. The rash.

He listened patiently. Then asked one question.

"You say rash. Is there any one spot?"

"No, I don't think so."

"It would be large. It might look almost black."

"No."

He paused. Then, through the swampy overseas line, his voice came through with strength and clarity. "Look, what you're describing, it's not anthrax."

"You're sure?"

"Ya. One hundred percent, Sara. One hundred percent."

My face telegraphed the news to Andrew across the room and his shoulders sagged with relief.

WITHIN DAYS THE anthrax threat had spread, striking ABC, CBS, the *New York Post,* New York Governor George Pataki's office, Capitol Hill, the White House mailroom, with postal workers especially vulnerable. Striking closest to home for us—the baby of an *ABC World News Tonight* producer, just a month older than Sophie, contracted cutaneous anthrax, probably after coming in contact with spoors while crawling on the carpet in the newsroom. Thankfully, the baby recovered, as did our NBC colleague Erin. In all, twenty-two people would be infected by anthrax, and five would die, when the attacks—which began one week after 9/11—ended as inexplicably as they'd begun.

On the day that all of us tested at NBC got the welcome "all clear," Andrew brought home a rainbow bouquet and pulled out the camera. We took a picture with our beaming, contented daughter, oblivious to the drama that had swirled around her, and sent it by computer to family and friends around the world. He captioned it "Safe Soph."

IN THE MORNINGS that followed I'd say good-bye to Sophie and walk to work. I needed the exercise. But I also couldn't stand to take the subway because going underground meant losing contact, and the world could see-saw in an instant. In the evenings I tried not to cry when Sophie pushed the bottle away and attempted to nurse. She was perfectly healthy. She'd make the transition.

But I was less certain of my own transition. I was struggling, unwilling to admit how anxious and uncertain I felt. And what would it be like when my current assignment of handling special reports ended and I was back on the road, back to the life of a full-time correspondent? It was too much to contemplate.

A FEW DAYS later Ginger called. "Are you ready for this? Suddenly National Geographic wants our anthrax film."

"Congratulations, Gin. I'm so glad to hear you've got another project, even if I can't stand the word anthrax. But, anyway, it's certainly topical."

"Exactly. Actually, they want to broaden the story, talk about weaponized anthrax as well as anthrax in the wild."

"That makes sense."

"I agree. But I'm worried about how they want to do it."

"What do you mean?"

She paused. "Because they want to include your story."

"Us? You're kidding."

"No, I'm not. They want to talk about what happened to you and Andrew with Sophie."

Now it was my turn to pause. And then the irony hit me. "You know, Ginger, our lives are pretty strange. I do a story on you for *Dateline*. Now you're going to do one on me. And for National Geographic, for crying out loud."

"Sara, in all seriousness, I just don't want to be a vulture, swooping in on—"

"You could never be a vulture," I interrupted. "And remember, we're fine. I'm glad they want to do your film. Look, as long as Andrew and NBC say yes, I'm fine. Besides, you'll get to meet Sophie, and I'll get to see Kimber!"

"Finally!" She laughed, and I laughed, too.

SEVERAL MONTHS LATER Ginger was standing in front of me, waving a finished copy of the film. "Want to see yourself on TV?"

"I'm not sure. I wasn't crazy about being interviewed instead of asking the questions."

"I know what you mean. But remember, you'll also be watching Miss Soph's television debut. And I'll get a chance to play with your girl," she continued, holding out her arms for Sophie, who cheerfully abandoned ship.

"What a bright spark she is." Ginger smiled.

"I always wonder what she's thinking. I can't wait to get down to Virginia to get my hands on Kimber. What a love he is, and so bright."

Ginger grinned. "Hybrid vigor. Just ask Nad."

"What on earth are you talking about?"

Gin settled back on the sofa with Sophie squirming playfully on her lap. "I made the mistake of telling my husband how gorgeous and smart Kimber was. You know, just normal mom bragging. Anyway, he says, 'Well, we're from two different continents, completely different genetic stock. That's what's called hybrid vigor.' "

"God love your husband. The mystery and romance of children, hmm?"

"That's what you get when you marry a scientist, I suppose. They keep you thinking."

"Speaking of thinking . . ." I paused. "These attacks, everything . . ."

Gin nodded, encouraging me.

"Gin, I never imagined I'd feel this way, but working full-time isn't working out for me right now. It just doesn't fit. I love *Dateline* and *Today* and Specials, but I feel like I never see Sophie."

Gin smiled in understanding. "For me it's different. I'm here for a couple of months, working flat out, but then we're back in the bush and I have loads of time with Kimber, and I love that, too."

"Exactly! That's what I want."

"But will they let you? Do people go part-time at the network?"

"Not a lot. But a couple of correspondents at *Dateline* did a job share, so maybe there's a precedent. Anyway, I just know that I have to try."

Ginger paused. "Sara, you know as well as I do that tailoring life means making sacrifices, especially when you have a child. I know mine have been worth it. I bet you'll find the same."

"I hope so. I just know my stomach hurts when I think about scaling back. But it hurts more when I try not to."

"Then that's your answer."

But as I turned out the lights that night and went to bed, I wondered. Knowing that I needed to make a change didn't mean knowing what would happen when I did. Could I handle the aftershocks? Would I disappear? Who was I without the tagline NBC News? I'd gone from cub local reporter to married local anchor to divorced network correspondent to married correspondent to working mom. Evolutions personal and professional. Maybe as a woman, change just went with the territory. But if my dilemma was nothing new, it was still a dilemma. Ginger had re-created her life post-motherhood. Could I?

29

GINGER (2003–2004)

"Nad, do you want to take this box? It's full of wires and switches."

"No, we might still need it here. Remember, we aren't leaving camp for good. We'll move back and forth between here and Okaukuejo. It's just, now that the elephant project is finished, I need to spend more time at the Institute."

I looked around camp. Though the cupboards were half empty and our stash of firewood wouldn't last a week, it still felt like home. At least the tents were still standing, always a good sign.

"Kimber, come here, darlin'. What toys do you want to take with you?"

Sitting on his black "motorcycle," Kimber pushed himself over to where I was squatting in front of his toy chest.

"Umm"—he reached inside, scattering toys—"I'll just take a few of these blocks, and maybe this ball, and I'll leave the rest for Rian."

My son was born with a generous spirit, and we'd done our best to hone it, following many wonderful examples set by family and friends. But at that moment I thought of Kristy and her dear daughter Emma, who was just seven months older than Kimber. Kristy knew firsthand of the great need even in her affluent Lookout Mountain, Tennessee, community and worked against the prevailing sense of "more is more." Over the past five years she'd spent a lot of time at the Children's Hospital with her daughter as the doctors deciphered the degree and depth of Emma's illness. In the waiting room, Kristy had seen many parents struggle to carry growing children who were unable to walk into the clinic. Not satisfied to sit back and watch, Kristy went door-to-door collecting strollers for these families. Even at forty-three, I was still learning from my friends.

"That's nice, my boy." I ruffled Kimber's hair, pulled him close, and whispered in his ear, "I am so proud of you."

He pulled back and looked at me very seriously. "When are we going? I want to play with Rocky before bedtime."

Rocky was Kimber's new best friend at Okaukuejo, so at least Kimber was excited to return to our house. "Don't worry, we'll leave soon."

My feelings about returning to Okaukuejo were more mixed than my son's. At camp, even a trip to the long-drop toilet could turn into an adventure, with a black rhino grazing against the fence or a snake slithering past your feet. I relished that wonderful mixture of comfort and suspense, elephants and lions, cold showers and hot fires, a place charged with peace and anticipation; it imparted the essence of the bush, the same dichotomy that had drawn me to Africa more than a decade before. I couldn't believe that I'd been in Namibia thirteen years, but picking through the detritus of camp—a copy of Nad's thesis on the baboons, a duiker skin with colorful beads woven in circles that was a treasured gift from Old Old/Gui, one of the Bushmen healers, and my most recent filming notes documenting Knob Nose's life through our lenses—I felt exceptionally blessed. It was also a good reminder that if I hadn't embraced change back then, these moments would have remained dreams, and in time those dreams, unfulfilled, could have become tainted, bitter what-ifs and if-onlys. Now I couldn't imagine my life without them.

Sometimes it takes startling events to make us realize that we only get one shot at creating the life we want. Since September 11, I'd thought of the many women and men who never got the chance to embrace another day. A year had passed since those tragic events, a year of reflection for many. For Sara there had been an abrupt end to her maternity leave and a sudden return to working full-time. Since then she'd been juggling deadlines and diapers, steeped in adrenaline and guilt. Now she longed to cut back, to work part-time.

Yet as hard as it might have been for Sara to see other correspondents taking on stories she longed to tell, filling seats behind news desks where she once felt at home, *home* was where she needed to be. Not all of the time, but, hopefully, if she could work it out with the brass at NBC, part-time. To have cut Sara completely off from work would be akin to removing a vital organ, it was so much a part of her life. But Sophie was nearly a year old. In the past twelve months she'd learned to sit, crawl, spit, chew, coo, scribble, walk, talk, and learned to love those around her with boundless affection. I felt like I'd closed my eyes and Kimber was one year old. When I'd opened them again, he was nearly four. While you're agonizing over choices, time can disappear, and you don't get it back. Sara's desire to spend more time with Sophie was the right choice for her, though sometimes the right choice is the most difficult choice of all.

By comparison, the change I was facing was easy. Okaukuejo was 120 miles away from camp, still in Etosha, still spectacular, and it still provided me with the opportunity to do the work I loved. I looked at Kimber, happily throwing his toys in the car, ready to go. Clearly change was all in the attitude.

THE VIEW FROM our home in Okaukuejo wasn't bad at all. I placed my computer on a desk in front of a large window where I could watch zebra move in single file down to the water hole, spy brilliantly colored birds swooping in for a quick drink, and listen to the sound of Rocky's and Kimber's sweet young voices as they played in the backyard.

From this vantage point, I heard them charging into the house. The door slammed and Kimber called out, "Mommy, Mommy! Rocky and I found a little baby bird in the yard." He threw his arms around my neck and then added tenderly, "But, Mommy, it is so sad. The bird is dead."

"I'm so sorry, darlin'. Do you know what happened to it?"

"I think I saw some little tiny genet tracks around or maybe the owl got it, but can we bury it?"

"Of course."

"God won't be mad?"

"No, my darlin'. God will be very glad."

The serious look on his face evaporated. He smiled and called to Rocky as he ran back outside.

The two boys huddled together, and then they both pointed to the far end of the yard, grabbed shovels, and ran to a spot under their treehouse and started digging.

Pushing shovels into the ground and tossing dirt over their heads, an activity that was usually accompanied by laughter, today took on a somber quality. I peered through the window as they gently lowered the baby bird down into the hole they'd dug. Scooping up handfuls of dirt, they let it sift through their fingers down into the hole. Scoop after scoop until the hole was full. Then they patted the ground down so that it was hard, and I heard Kimber say, "This is so the jackals can't dig it up."

Rocky shook his head solemnly. "Come, Kimber, let's get the flowers."

Barefoot, the boys ran to collect yellow and red blossoms from the succulent flowers growing near our house. I saw them under the window, their heads touching, their hands moving together, and a gentle song coming from Rocky's lips. "Amen, amen," he sang over and over. Rocky, a child of Africa, a child who knew the rituals of death, and my son's best friend.

Moments like this made the move back to Okaukuejo worth it. First thing in the morning, Kimber would stumble down the hall in his pajamas, eyes half closed, and crawl into my lap. His first slurred words were always "When can I go get Rocky?" Quickly changing into his "daytimes"—shorts and a T-shirt—Kimber would jump onto his bike for the short ride to Rocky's house. The two boys would come racing back to our house for breakfast, and then they'd be off to the water hole. From the water hole, I'd see them coming down the road, having swapped bikes, returning with "the morning report"—their detailed, out-of-breath description of how many animals they'd seen that morning. It reminded me of my first African news bulletins, from Jen and Des Bartlett at the Skeleton Coast, when I'd learned how to read the news printed in the sand. Kimber and Rocky's version was far less serious. Usually their report ran, "at least a thousand springbok, twenty-two zebra and one having a *huge* pooh right in front of us, then five wildebeest, and one big elephant having a *fart* at the water hole," followed by a fit of giggles.

Whether they began the day riding their bikes, playing in the mud, stripping off all their clothes, and running around the yard screaming "naked rain dance, naked rain dance," Rocky and Kimber usually ended the day crashed on the sofa, watching a video, arms and legs intertwined. Their friendship had a natural, physical closeness true of many friendships. In women you still see these outward expressions of intimacy even when we are adults. Like Sara and me, women walk arm in arm, wipe tears from each other's faces, hug unashamedly, touch each other for reassurance and warmth. Men tend to slap each other on the bottom or punch each other on the arm, gestures of affection but also of distance. I wondered how my son would remember these precious moments with Rocky, how they would shape the man he would become.

When we'd left Okaukuejo for camp, Kimber had been a needy baby. Now that we were back, he was a growing boy, busy exploring and making far fewer demands on my time. Though Selinda was no longer with us, Absalom Kalakoma, our gardener, adored Kimber and the feeling was mutual. With Absalom outside and Rocky a steady playmate, the time was liberating for both Kimber and me. I worked on project proposals, filmed ostriches for the BBC. I was also helping friends at AfriCat, a cheetah welfare and research organization at Okonjima, a stunning lodge south of Etosha, develop an idea for a television series based upon their fantastic work. Over the past ten years AfriCat's small, dedicated team had helped to rescue and rehabilitate more than six hundred of Namibia's big cats. It was time for their annual cheetah medical check weekend. Kissing Nad and Kimber good-bye, I packed my cameras and left for Okonjima. Turned out I wouldn't be there long.

It was Friday evening, quiet after an intense day of immobilizing, vaccinating, weighing, dipping, and releasing twenty cheetahs. Relaxing in the office while the cats slept off the anesthesia outside, I picked up the phone and called home.

"Nad, hi." I stretched out my legs and sighed. "It's been a great but tiring day. How are things there? How's Kimber?"

"He's got a bit of a fever, but I don't think it's anything to worry about."

"Give him my love, tell him I miss him and I'll see him on Monday."

"Fine. Have a good time."

That night at dinner I joined a Japanese television crew who were making a documentary on AfriCat hosted by a former Formula One race car driver. The next day at 7 A.M., I was called to the phone.

"Gin, get home now," Nad said firmly. "Kimber is really sick."

I threw my cameras in the Land Rover, said a hasty good-bye, and starting driving. Nad had told me nothing more, no details, just get home now, before he hung up the phone. I had two hundred miles in front of me to imagine all kinds of horrors. Sick. What kind of sick? Had he been bitten by a snake, a scorpion, a rabid jackal? Were diseases suddenly jumping from animals to humans? Every sort of mad thought took on dreadful proportions as the miles ticked by. But then I thought about Nad, a skilled veterinarian, a well-trained medic, and a father who loved his son intensely. I thought about Kimber, my tough, resilient boy, so thin and so strong. I even smiled when I pictured him patting a wild cheetah on the head, one that had jumped into our Land Rover when we'd been filming years before. I'm convinced that if Kimber had panicked, the cat would have torn him in two. Instead he had laughed. Six months old and laughing in a cheetah's face. Whatever was wrong, Kimber would be all right, I thought, a mantra repeated over and over again.

Two hours later I pulled up at our house. Before I could cut the engine, Nad ran outside onto the lawn. He had Kimber in his arms.

"Let's go."

I climbed into the backseat and Nad laid Kimber's head on my lap. "Here, use this." He handed me a cool wet cloth and ran back inside for a suitcase he'd already packed.

Kimber was hot, cold, shaking, sweating. His eyes rolled in the back of his head, he couldn't focus on anything, and he had no idea I was there.

"Kimber, it's Mommy. I'm home, honey, and everything will be all right." Words I'd used all too often over the years, with baboons, a baby rhino, our young elephant, and now my own little boy. Words meant to reassure him as much as me.

Our nearest doctor was based in Outjo, a small town one hundred miles away. Late on a Saturday morning, Dr. Kesslau was waiting in his office when we got there.

"Come in, come in." He gestured. "Lay him down on the table."

I stood beside Kimber, stroking his arm, while Nad observed the doctor.

Dr. Kesslau checked Kimber's temperature, his eyes, and his skin. "I can do a blood test," he told us, "but I see hundreds of these cases a year, and I can tell you without waiting for the results that your son has malaria."

It took a moment to sink in. One doctor in one small town sees hundreds of cases of malaria a year. Multiply that by all the doctors, nurses, and clinics in all the small towns in Africa, then add those suffering who never make it to a doctor, and you get chilling figures. Malaria, a parasitic blood disease transmitted by the bite of a tiny female mosquito, kills over a million people a year in Africa; that's about three thousand people dying each day, and children under the age of five are among the most vulnerable. Kimber was four years old.

Dr. Kesslau shook the thermometer. "His temperature is 105. When did he start with this fever?"

"Yesterday afternoon." Nad looked up from Kimber and added in a strangled voice, "It wasn't too bad, but it got worse in the night."

"You caught it early. That's good. The sooner we start him on chloroquine the better. So do we test him first or do you want to start the treatment?"

"We treat him. Now," Nad and I said in unison.

For the next week, twice a day, we had to give Kimber one chloroquine tablet. At first he was so sick he didn't resist, but by the third day he cried when we gave him the bitter pill and immediately vomited. For the next few days we tried grinding the tablet and disguising its sour taste in mashed banana, chocolate, or yogurt. Nothing worked. He spat it out. We tried dissolving it in water and shooting it through a syringe down his throat, then his throat constricted and it oozed down the sides of his mouth. If we were lucky, we got a total of one tablet in him a day, half the recommended dose. To complete the course and effectively kill the malaria parasite, Kimber still needed to take the drug for two more days. Two days when I'd be on my own with him.

"Gin, I'm supposed to leave tomorrow for Angola," Nad reminded me. "Are you sure you'll be okay with Kimber? I'll change my plans if you're worried."

"No, there are lots of people counting on you flying that park survey, you go ahead. We'll be fine."

The next morning I managed to get Kimber to take half a chloroquine tablet. That evening was a different story.

Kimber sat on the edge of the kitchen counter, tears running down his face. "Mommy, please, I don't want it. It's awful."

"Kimber, *do not spit this out!* This is the third time I've tried to get you to take this and I am sick and tired of it!"

I turned to the refrigerator to see if there was anything else I could use to possibly disguise the flavor, and when I turned around he was gone.

"Kimber? Kimber, get back in here! Now!"

Nothing, not a sound.

I ran into the bedroom and flung open the closets. Nothing. I ran through the living room into his playroom and called again. Nothing.

I ran outside into the dusk. "Kimber, darlin', where are you?" My voice was urgent but gentler now. It was met with silence.

I looked across the street and saw lights on in our neighbor's house. I'd thought that they were away, and then thought maybe Kimber had gone there. I threw open their front door and was met by stares. "Hi, come in," laughed Jan.

"Jan, Kimber's gone. I was trying to get him to take his medicine and he disappeared."

"Sion, Tristian," she called her sons, "get on your bikes and see if you can find Kimber."

The sun had set. It was dark; I heard jackals calling. I felt a chill run down my spine, and across my mind flashed images I had filmed of jackals ripping apart a springbok lamb. God, where was Kimber? I dashed back across the street, and when I stepped into our quiet living room, relief flooded over me. My tiny boy was huddled under a table in the corner, knees drawn to his chest and his arms wrapped protectively around his legs, whimpering. He looked up at me with his big hazel eyes and pleaded, "Mommy, please, I don't want it."

I crawled under the table with him and held him tight. "Don't worry, darlin'. You don't have to have it. I'll put you on a drip before I go through this again."

BORN WILD. IT was an apt title for our next filming project that would feature Kimber. In a series of phone calls between Kathy Pasternak, a supervising producer who'd become a friend after we'd worked on our elephant and anthrax films together, and me, we learned that National Geographic planned to make a film that would explore the survival strategies animals employ for raising babies in the wild. They wanted us to be their "human example."

As anyone who has ever worked freelance would understand, when a project comes to you unsolicited, it's a milestone. For once a film is made without the agony of mailing proposals that are thrown into the trash, of placing endless phone calls which are never returned, and, worse, when you finally do get someone on the line, of hearing "Sorry, but no." On this rare occasion a contract would be signed and paychecks would arrive without drama. Amazing.

Being asked to be involved in this project was a sign of recognition and acceptance for Nad and me. But *Born Wild* was that and more. In the past Nad and I had largely operated alone and were seen as individuals, even when we were working together. He was the veterinarian, the scientist, or the pilot. I was the filmmaker. Now, with Kimber, we were a complete team, a family who together had a history and that history, though brief, could help to tell a story.

Saying yes to the project gave us a chance to work with our old friend Paul van Schalkwyk, a filmmaker with an unerring eye for a beautiful shot. We'd worked together on the Bushmen film, sat together in warm silence as the embers of many campfires turned to ash, and shared that tragic day in front of the television when the world changed on September 11. Now we'd get a chance to share this much happier experience.

Filming at our favorite haunts gave us an opportunity to relive many special moments we'd had in the bush. I compared my labor pains with those of a springbok (twenty hours versus twenty minutes), the length of my pregnancy with an elephant's (nine months versus twenty-two months), and reminisced about the kidnappings in our baboon troop, tragic behavior that had taken on a painfully different dimension for me since I'd had a child.

When we saw the first cut of the film, there was one special, unexpected gift that Pam Caragol, the producer, and Geoff Luck, the editor, had tucked into the film for us. Across the screen rolled images of Kimber— at four months old in his stroller holding a roll of film, toddling up to the camera in another shot, his long blond locks glowing in backlight; climbing onto my lap, running to meet his father at camp, sharing a swing with Rocky and a battle of bashing sticks with his father. Our son, growing up in front of the camera. Four, almost five years in the bush captured in twenty brief, delicious seconds. I played this scene over and over, and each time it gave me great joy but also a strange sensation of finality, that a chapter was coming to a close.

Back when I became pregnant with Kimber, we knew our time in Etosha was finite. Our son would experience the wonder of having elephants in the backyard, of flying with his father across the plains, of being oblivious to the fact that his best friend was a different color, a different race from him. Etosha had everything for Kimber except a school. When Kimber turned six, if we stayed in the park, our only option was to send him to boarding school. For us, that wasn't an option. I couldn't imagine sending Kimber away from home at such a young age. I wouldn't do it, even though it meant that after fifteen years of living in wild, wonderful places, to stay together we'd have to leave the bush.

But I wasn't ready for that, not yet. First Kimber and I were going home, back to Virginia.

30

SARA (2003–2004)

Sophie was snuggled into her bed. We'd read *Bilby Moon, Go, Dog. Go!* and *The Gruffalo.* We'd sung "Twinkle, Twinkle." Had hugs, kisses, pats. Even at two and a half, Sophie still fought sleep, and getting her settled down was a forty-five-minute proposition. Now there was just one more thing to do. With stuffed animals Cutie the Cat tucked under one arm and Sophie the Dog under another, Sophie closed her eyes and thanked God for Nana, Pa, Granne, and Opa before adding an impromptu postscript of her own. "And dear God, please give me a baby sister. Amen."

I sat very quietly, hoping she couldn't see my face in the dark. Was this simply her own wonderful wish? Or had she guessed? Perhaps I'd been unable to hide first my elation, then the crashing wave of desolation as the old pattern of miscarriage following miscarriage had repeated itself. I was struggling to make peace with the notion that perhaps Andrew and I were only meant to be the parents of one child. Thank God we had Sophie. How dare we be greedy? And yet, stubbornly, silently, I couldn't help but echo my daughter's prayer. *Please, God, let us have one more.*

THE NEXT MORNING there was no need for an alarm clock.

"Cock-a-doodle-doo!"

Since being introduced to the chickens at a neighbor's house near our home in the country, Sophie had a new way of greeting the morning. I smiled even before I opened my eyes, then wandered around the corner to get her.

"Boo!"

"Hi, Mommy. You don't have your work clothes on yet."

"Not yet. Today I'm staying home with you."

Sophie nodded as a princess might. So I should.

As I picked her up and carried her into the kitchen, enjoying the fact that I could still carry my big girl, I drew the drapes to get a glimpse of the city below. I glanced at the television set but didn't switch it on. I knew someone else was filling in on the *Today* show news desk, and sometimes it felt easier not to watch. Besides, today was my day off with my girl.

At forty-two years old, I'd gotten exactly what I'd asked for—a part-time deal. I reported a set number of stories annually for *Dateline,* which meant I traveled far less than I once had. I could write from home. And no one looked askance when I didn't volunteer for dangerous assignments like Kabul or Baghdad. While I understood and respected my colleagues, male and female, who'd made a different choice, I'd been to my share of war zones, tempted fate more than once. As a mom, I considered my most important assignment to be loving our daughter for as many years as possible, hopefully until she'd grown up. There were no guarantees, of course. In recent years, colon cancer had claimed Katie's husband, Jay Monahan, father of their two little girls, and a sailboating accident had killed my *Dateline* colleague producer Bruce Hagan, who also had a young daughter. And then had come 9/11. But I didn't want to increase my odds by taking unnecessary chances. I loved the fact that I could still call Mom and Dad for advice, and I knew how much Mom still missed her mother, even though Grannykins had lived to be ninety-six.

While I was clear that I wanted to work part-time and appreciative that former *Dateline* executive producer and current NBC News president Neal Shapiro had agreed, change and adaptation rarely come without discomfort. I'd signed a new contract for less than half my old salary. I wasn't called on to anchor as frequently. And I missed the adrenaline rush of covering a breaking news story which might last for days on end. But I knew I couldn't have it both ways, and the prospect of being on the road virtually every week, having to croon "Twinkle, Twinkle" through a cell phone and missing my cheerful rooster, was unbearable. I had waited a long time to be a mother.

"You're lucky, Sara," said former *Today* show executive producer Jeff Zucker. He and his wife, Caryn Nathanson Zucker, had three children. Jeff had battled back from colon cancer to continue his meteoric rise at work, and was now president of NBC entertainment as well as being in charge of the network's news and cable operations.

I was lucky, too. I knew it. The chance to work part-time was rare for anyone at the network. And I could afford the financial sacrifice because Andrew was doing well. But I also realized I was in the same spot as every mom I knew, whether she worked in an office or exclusively at home. Like Ginger, I'd realized it simply wasn't possible to do everything. While men with children advanced in careers as they always had, women with children made choices as best they could. And I'd made mine. Slowly, the stabs of longing for my former life became less frequent, less intense. And I realized that in choosing to change my life, perhaps I'd also saved it.

"TAX*IIIIII*! " SOPHIE, ALL two feet nine inches of her, could hail a cab with the best of them.

"Don't step off the curb, sweetie. Those cars are fast."

"Don't worry, Mommy, I'm *very* fast. Fast like a dog."

"Well, dogs stay out of traffic, too," Andrew added. "Hold on to your suitcase, sweetie."

One of the advantages of being part-time was taking a vacation of more than two weeks during the holidays. After years of working virtually every Thanksgiving, Easter, and New Year's Day, I relished our family's upcoming trip to spend Christmas, 2003, with Andrew's family in Muckleford.

WHEN MOST PEOPLE think of Australia, they picture the outback with its mysterious, gigantic red rock, Uluru, so sacred to the Aborigines. Or maybe they think of the Great Barrier Reef with its brilliant fish and ominous great whites. But the southern state of Victoria is entirely different. It's as if someone grafted a Tudor rose onto a eucalypt—a hardy English bloom thriving in the Antipodes. On the drive to Andrew's parents' farm from Melbourne, I caught glimpses of sedate men and women playing lawn bowls dressed in their pristine whites. From Daylesford to Maldon, Bendigo to Castlemaine, Victoria is famous for its quaint Victorian and Edwardian homes, as well as for charming shops which sell spotless linens, right next to local pubs serving up VB—Victoria Bitter.

"Andrew! Sara! Look how Sophie's grown!" marveled Andrew's mum as she and his beaming dad embraced us. For Andrew, getting home meant not just seeing his family, but a dash to the local cricket ground with his brother Trevor. I found the game incomprehensible, and was always amused by the break for tea—watching sweaty men quaff a steaming beverage from a white china cup under a blistering sun. And I still found it odd to celebrate Christmas during the summer. But I loved Australia, and felt at home in rural Victoria. I couldn't wait to see what Sophie thought of the kangaroos that munched complacently near Andrew's parents' farm. Of the magpies, galahs, and kookaburras. Of the cows and all those sheep. I wondered what she'd notice first.

"Mommy!" she exclaimed. "Nana and Pa have a *dog*. And a *cat*."

I looked at Andrew. He shook his head and I did, too. Sophie had been lobbying for a pet since she'd been able to talk, which had been shortly after she'd been born.

And then we heard children's voices. The thrill of this trip for me was that Sophie would get a chance to know her wonderful Australian relatives, including a new crop of cousins. There was Lloyd, Trevor and Helen's son, with his bright smile. Just a few months younger than Sophie, he looked like her brother. And in the pram was the newest member of the family, Annaliese, born just a few weeks earlier to Katie and her husband, Andrew. Annaliese's arrival was especially welcome and poignant. Katie and Andrew had lost their first daughter, June, to a catastrophically premature birth when Katie had been diagnosed with a rare blood disorder and other complications during her pregnancy. Katie's life had also been in grave danger. To see this cooing infant in her healthy mother's arms was an unbelievable delight. And Andrew's older sister Chrissie was there, too, with squeezes for everyone, especially Soph.

Wearing her Blundstone boots with a T-shirt and shorts, Sophie helped Lloyd decorate the Christmas tree. Our little girl. Half American, half Australian. At home in both countries, loved by both families.

WEEKS LATER BACK in the U.S., I was still finding it difficult to recover from our trip. The jet lag obviously hit harder as you got a bit older. Worse yet, my cycle had gotten completely thrown by the travel. To rule out the obvious, I took a pregnancy test but was in no mood to celebrate when it turned positive. "Sure," I scoffed at the little pink lines, then heaved the stick in the trash. Sure enough, the feelings waned and two subsequent pregnancy tests were negative. This baby, too, had stopped before it really started. Doctors called it a "chemical" pregnancy, an antiseptic medical term for a condition in which hope raises its tender head, only to have it lopped off a few days later.

But clearly something was wrong with me, so I called the doctor's office and was told to come in for a few blood tests. The timing was cruel. It was my forty-third birthday. I left the doctor's office and immediately headed to Richmond, where I'd be delivering a speech the next day. Thankfully, I'd be staying with Mom and Dad, as I felt worse than ever.

"Mom," I moaned, "do you think you could make me a peanut butter and jelly sandwich?"

Her eyebrows shot up. "Are you—?"

I shook my head. "Not a chance. Just a bug."

"You never know. You're the same age Grannykins was when she had your Uncle Tony," Mom smiled.

"Actually, skip the sandwich. I just want to go to bed."

When I called the doctor's office for the blood test result the following morning, the nurse was using her extra calm voice. "Are you ready for a surprise?"

"Good or bad?"

"You're pregnant. Very pregnant, from the numbers, probably six to eight weeks. You'd better come in as soon as you get back from your trip."

I put down the phone. I counted to ten. I counted to ten again. And then I screamed. *"MOM!!!!!!!!!!"* Then I picked up the phone to call Andrew.

ANDREW WAS AS excited as I was. My symptoms were exactly the same as they had been with Sophie, which I regarded as a positive sign. But given my history, not to mention the weird phenomenon of the conflicting pregnancy tests, caution was the only sensible option.

"Told you we'd get two," Andrew said complacently.

I called Ginger. "That's fantastic! I have a good feeling about this, Sara."

"I hope so. I'm still scared about amnio." The statistics, which had been sobering at forty, were now gloomy. Compared with a thirty-two-year-old woman's 1-in-725 chance of having a baby born with Down syndrome, my chance was 1 in 53. And the risk of other genetic abnormalities increased as well.

But this time the wait for results was shared. My youngest sister, Susan, had gotten married to her grad school sweetheart, Danny, and they were expecting their first child. Susan and I spoke endlessly about our pregnancies, and were indulged by our middle sister, Elizabeth. Both babies were due in late September, and when both amnios were normal, we finally relaxed.

I felt well but was busier than ever. Sophie was a bright, inquisitive, delightful three-year-old. Andrew and I were busy apartment hunting, as we'd decided our current home was too small for two children. And I was trying to finish my work assignments, including an hour-long segment with producer Geraldine Moriba-Meadows called the "Dateline Bridal Diet Challenge." As the brides' waistlines trimmed down, mine expanded, and I couldn't wait to go on maternity leave. One day I arrived to narrate a script and the producer looked at my flushed face with alarm. "You should go home, Sara. You look beat."

There never seemed to be time to sleep.

But in May, six months pregnant and feeling both enormous and exhausted, I was about to get a break. Ginger and Kimber were on their way over for a lengthy summer vacation. Sophie and I would meet them at her parents' new home in Virginia, and Andrew would join us for the weekend. I couldn't wait to pack.

31

GINGER (2004)

SARA, YOU AND Sophie can have this room. Is that okay with you, Soph?"

Sophie climbed onto the high four-poster bed, kicked up her heels, and looked around the bedroom in my parents' new home. An early American pie safe in one corner, a maple chest of drawers, an old quilt at the end of the bed, a houseful of antiques I remembered from our home in Richmond, but the outside of their new house had beautiful views across the water near the Chesapeake Bay. It was a restful, personal place, and I'd immediately felt at home.

"This is great," chimed Sophie, "but where is Kimber sleeping?"

"Next door with me."

"Good, that's wonderful! Kimber, Kimber! Where's Kimber?"

"He's outside."

"Me too. I'm going to find him right now!"

"Okay, but be careful going down the steps." Sara shook her head. "Watch out, Kimber."

Sara's beautiful little girl was a bundle of energy, all motion all the time. At three years old, she had a vocabulary that rivaled many adults', bright eyes, and an infectious smile.

"She's got a thing for older men," I laughed.

"She doesn't get that from her mother."

We could hear Sophie chatting away as she walked down the steps. I wasn't sure if she was talking to my parents, our cat Millie, or herself. It didn't seem to matter. As she told us, "I only talk when I have something important to say. And I have a lot of important things to say."

When her voice faded, I turned to Sara and laughed. "I can't stand it any longer."

"What?" Sara looked at me quizzically.

"You're *fat*!"

"Gin, that's not fair."

"I've been wanting to get you back all these years since I was pregnant with Kimber. I still can't believe that I never saw you pregnant with Sophie. And you sent me one—yes, *one*—picture of you taken in glorious profile at a baby shower, but that was it."

"Not the prettiest picture, I'm sure."

"No, I love seeing you fat."

"Gin!"

"I mean pregnant."

"It feels wonderful, most of the time. But then again, nothing fits! I hate *all* my clothes."

"Mom's got a pretty skirt that would look great—"

"Gin, are you out of your mind? Your mom is a tennis player. Nothing she wears will fit me now!"

"It has an elastic waist! Come try it on."

"She's gonna kill you."

Later that day my sister Dona and her husband, John, plus their two children, my beautiful niece and nephew Maggie and Zan, came down from Richmond for the weekend. As always, Dona's arms were laden with homemade cookies, bottles of freshly squeezed orange juice, and a sinfully delicious shrimp dip. Of the four girls in my family, Dona was our family's keeper, the one who lovingly helped Mom look after elderly relatives, the one who could fix any problem with an embrace, the one who held us all together.

Later that day, taking any excuse to flee the city, Andrew joined us at the river for a few days. Together we cooked, we laughed, we fished, we ate too much, we woke up late, lounging around in our pajamas, we read the newspaper at the breakfast table, we played cards, we talked politics and sports, we patted Sara's belly and talked about babies. We were a family, by love and by choice. Andrew slipped into the mix as easily now as he had nine years before when we first met him at my wedding, and the weekend passed all too quickly.

On Sunday morning, after saying a sad good-bye to Dona and her family, we took Kimber and Sophie to the docks in Urbanna to see the boats bringing in the season's first soft-shell crabs. Two sisters, who were also Virginia's first women licensed crabbers, were hoisting buckets of crabs off the boats and tossing their catch into shallow tanks. These two women had been working together on the water for sixty years. I looked at Sara, who was guiding Sophie around the crab tanks. We were both forty-four years old. We'd been friends for thirty-two years, and I could easily imagine at least thirty more years of friendship, with her family and mine all mixed up in one wonderful bundle.

"Sophie, come look at this one," Kimber called out. "He's missing a pincer."

Sophie ran to his side. "Be careful, Kimber. They bite!"

Sara and I smiled at each other. Andrew shook his head.

Back at my parents', we stayed outside with the kids. It was hot and sticky and the mosquitoes dove and bit, but Sophie and Kimber were undaunted. They poked for crabs in the brook, swam in the gentle breakers off a sandy island, and then hopped in a battery-powered Jeep, Kimber at the wheel. As they drove off through a pine glade without a backward glance, I put my arm around Sara's shoulder.

"Riding off into the sunset," I laughed. "Wouldn't it be great if they wound up together?"

"Can't you just see it?" Sara grinned.

Andrew scoffed. "Give it a rest, will you? Don't you know Nad and I will be the ones choosing their husband and wife." He smiled, because he knew we never would. It was too good a plan.

Later we joined my mom and dad at the kitchen table. From there we could see Kimber and Sophie playing outside in the sand. I unrolled a long sheet of paper on the farm table.

"These are the house plans. It's hard to tell on paper, but it will flow

down the hill with the natural slope of the mountains to the east of Windhoek, so there are three separate levels and beautiful views from every
room."

"Gin, it is hard to picture you living in a real house in a real town,"
laughed Sara.

"I'm not sure I can see it either, Sara." After fourteen years and as much
as she loved Nad, my mother was still coming to terms with my choice to
stay in Namibia. Kimber's arrival had added to her contradictory feelings,
making it harder for her because she desperately missed seeing him grow
up, and yet easier because he was clearly so happy.

"If Kimber needs to go to school, there are plenty of good schools right
here. I know that Christchurch School loves to have boys from other countries. Kimber could stay with us and Ginger and Nad could stay in the
bush."

"Mom's got it all figured out." I smiled at Sara. "Maybe one day, Mom,
but not now. St. Paul's is just a few miles from our house site, and it's a good
school, too. Nad can fly out of Windhoek and I'll find something to do."

Mom put her glasses back on and focused on our house plans, ignoring
the fact that she'd lost this round, but, not, as far as she was concerned, the
fight. Never. "Well, how many bedrooms do you have?"

"Three. The master, Kimber's, and a guest room, which means everyone must come visit."

"So you'll need at least three beds. Let's go and see what we can find. At
least your move will help us clear out the garage."

Dad, a patient, devoted grandfather adored by Kimber, Maggie, Zan,
and now little Sophie, drew his eyes away from the kids playing outside in the
sand and started to stand up. With four daughters and a wife passionate
about antiques, moving furniture had become one of his fortes. I patted him
on the back. "Don't worry, Dad, there's a nice golf course in Windhoek."

Sara darted past us, practically singing, "I love a Mauney move!"

Sara and Andrew's country home was full of treasures gleaned from
the antiques my parents had sold when they moved to the river. A linen
press from my old bedroom was now in theirs. A long, elegant dining room

table where Civil War generals had once gathered went from my parents' dining room to Sara's. Whenever I knew she was having guests in the country, I loved picturing Sara, Andrew, and their friends sharing special occasions around that table just as my family had.

"I've already got my eye on a few things. Come on, this should be fun!"

But the fun never lasted long enough. We'd enjoyed fleeting visits with Beth, Danny, my godson Trent, and his lovely sister Elisa. Tish had spent a few weekends with us, lavishing candy and attention on her niece and two nephews, whom she so truly adored and who adored her, too. Then Mom, Kimber, and I had driven to Tennessee to see Kristy, Gordon, and Gordy, and to finally meet Emma and the latest addition to the Davenport clan, a crackerjack just like her mother named Carter. We also spent a wonderful few days with my sister Marsha and her boyfriend John in Nashville, antiquing, dining out, and cruising Music Row. I thought back to when we were children, when I had tried so hard to peer into Marsha's dark eyes to where her dreams lay. Now I knew. After years of changing so many children's lives for the better as a special education teacher, Marsha was finally pursuing her dream, writing and singing country music. Sitting in her stylish living room, we tapped our feet to the beat while she strummed her guitar and sang her most recent songs for us. Her lyrics touched a core, resounding with feelings for Granddaddy and his love of the land, and of our love for each other. Then, all too quickly, we were gone, on the road again, heading back to the river.

It didn't matter if I had one week, two months, or six months at home, in the end there was never enough time to see everyone, go everywhere, and do everything I wanted to do. Work had been a relatively short part of this trip home. Before *Born Wild* aired on Mother's Day, Sara had met me at National Geographic in Washington, D.C., for a public screening. We packed a great deal of fun into one night in D.C. and now with this trip to the river, it seemed like Sara, Sophie, and Andrew had only just arrived and they were packing up to leave. But before that, Sara and I had promised to take Kimber and Sophie for ice cream.

Once we'd buckled the kids into their car seats, Sara and I climbed in the front for the fifteen-mile drive into Kilmarnock.

I looked at Sara's expanding tummy. "Is this ice cream treat for the kids or you?"

Before Sara could speak, Sophie chimed in, "My mommy *loves* ice cream. She eats it *every* day." And she didn't stop. For the next fifteen miles, Sophie gave us a running commentary on the buildings we passed, the games she normally played to pass the time in the car, what she wanted to eat for dinner, what she planned to tell her father when they drove back to New York later that day. Every vibrant thought that popped into her mind popped out of her little rosebud mouth.

Sara smiled. "Forget about Andrew and Nad. Those two seem to be getting along so well. Maybe there's hope yet. We really could end up related by marriage."

I looked in the rearview mirror. Kimber had his fingers in his ears, shaking his head. My bush boy and her big-city girl.

"I'm not sure, Sara. I'd love it, but right now I'm just glad they're friends."

Sara squeezed my hand. "There's nothing better."

32

SARA (2004)

WHEN I LOOK back to the late summer and early fall of 2004, time feels both elongated and compressed, recollections alternately intensely singular and dizzyingly blurred. At times it almost felt as if I'd fallen asleep to awaken with neither peripheral vision nor perspective, trying to chart a course with only a ripped fragment from a map I didn't recognize.

And yet, I'd felt so clear and confident when Andrew, Sophie, and I moved into our new apartment on a 93-degree day in late July. I look around, wishing Ginger could see the place now, as it had been under renovation when she'd helped me apartment-hunt just a few months before. But even through the dust and debris, she'd been able to tell that it would be spacious and full of light, and had adored the wide terrace. I imagined planting orange trees and jasmine, the scent wafting through the bedroom. Sophie had other ideas. "Mommy, this is big enough for my trike!"

I was so excited to finally move that, despite Andrew's admonition not to lift anything, I picked up a heavy box and promptly bumped my enormous stomach. I kept forgetting that I was seven months pregnant, not to mention forty-three years old. Panicked, I scheduled an ultrasound for the next day. But everything was okay—our baby still frolicking like a manatee in its watery world. I envied the baby. I had boxes to unpack. Baby items to wash and buy. Sophie's room to organize. Not to mention my work at *Dateline*.

I had recently met Wendy Kopp, the founder of Teach for America, an organization that places top college graduates in the nation's worst public schools for a two-year teaching commitment. Impressed by further research on Kopp and the extraordinary corps she'd created, I'd written a brief proposal, or "pitch," for a possible story. I'd suggested we follow one teacher during her first year in the classroom—a story of drama in its own right, but also a prism through which we could examine public education in America. *Dateline*'s senior producers and executive producer agreed, and I was scheduled to fly to Atlanta to interview the young teacher we'd selected on the weekend of August 7. I wasn't worried. Sophie had been two weeks late, so by my reckoning, the baby wouldn't arrive until early October.

But my sensible obstetrician was unimpressed. "You can't know when any baby is going to be born, Sara," Dr. Kessler told me. "If anything happens, you'll be giving birth in Atlanta."

So instead I spent that weekend relaxing in the country with Andrew and Sophie. It was a decision for which I would thank God hundreds of times in the weeks that followed, because on Monday morning, August 9, I discovered to my horror that I was leaking. Except I couldn't be. It was impossible. Our baby wasn't due for another two months.

Andrew and I rushed to the hospital, where Dr. Kessler's partner met us. "As you guessed, your waters have broken, so we'll start an antibiotic drip to prevent your baby from getting an infection," Dr. Edersheim explained, and her kind, competent manner acted as a tonic. "We'll hope to keep you here on bedrest for the next few weeks. But when the membranes rupture, usually a mom will deliver in the next twenty-four to forty-eight hours."

I swallowed hard. "How big is our baby?"

She paused. "Probably about four pounds."

I closed my eyes, which were suddenly leaking, too. To think what I had almost done.

Andrew patted my arm. "Everything is going to be okay."

But the baby wasn't born that night, or the next, or the next.

"Do you feel any contractions?" a nurse asked, tightening the blood pressure cuff.

Instead I felt bizarrely fine, as if nothing had happened. "Nope. Not one."

"Good. And your temperature is normal, so no infection. Keep it up! If we can keep you here a month, your baby will be a good size."

After several days of being allowed out of bed only to use the bathroom, I earned a daily two-minute shower, and found to my surprise that I was settling in. I was at a first-rate hospital and I trusted my doctors. Andrew brought my computer, a stack of movies, and, best of all, Sophie. The first night her lip quivered. "Daddy will sing 'Twinkle,' Soph." She gave a watery nod, but for once said nothing. But before long she'd met the entire floor and made her own rounds, checking up on her favorite nurses and patients as well as "Dr. Kess-a-ler" before finally coming to my room to fiddle with the levers on my bed and draw pictures to decorate the stark walls.

Sophie and Andrew got me through the evenings. Friends and family got me through the days. "Here's your decaf latte and a turkey sandwich," offered Andi. "I've got *chocolate,*" said Lisa. Sharon brought a lovely baby bag; Amy, a purse and magazines. "Nothing heavy," she grinned. And Roberta pulled open the curtains overlooking the East River and assessed, "This plant will make your room look *much* better." Ginger telephoned, Mom and Dad visited. My sisters Elizabeth and Susan called every day. But it still seemed there were endless hours to fill and I was restless and bored. For me, that usually meant one thing.

"This is the NBC operator. Atlanta, are you on the line?"

"We are."

"We're here, too." I heard *Dateline* producer Izhar Harpaz and senior producer Ellen Mason chime in.

I propped two pillows under my arm, trying to get comfortable.

"Ms. James? Are you ready for the conference call?"

"Yes, I am."

School started in Atlanta in just a few days and we needed to iron out the final details with the local school board for our story on Teach for America. I refused to fast-forward to the end of September, when I'd need to leave our tiny newborn for a couple of days to fly to Georgia to interview the teacher and her students. I adored this story and somehow, someway, planned to complete it.

* * *

BY THE END of August, I'd been in the hospital for nearly a month and was thirty-six weeks pregnant. While our baby was still one month shy of full term, Dr. Kessler and his colleagues decided it was time to induce labor, because the baby's risk of contracting an infection now outweighed the risk of being born premature. Andrew and I agreed. I couldn't wait to meet our child. So early one morning, I was hooked to an IV of contraction-inducing Pitocin for what everyone assumed would be a quick labor. After all, this was my second child and the amniotic sac had been broken for a month.

But hour after hour, the contractions continued, as the obstetric team carefully added more Pitocin. By midnight there was talk of a C-section but the operating rooms were full. Andrew and I anxiously watched the fetal stress monitor, but our baby seemed perfectly tranquil. Finally, after twenty-four hours, at 6 A.M. on August 28, Jacqueline Elizabeth made her debut.

Andrew and I looked into the sweet face of our newborn. Just under six pounds, she seemed tiny compared with her three-and-a-half-year-old sister, yet we knew she was a healthy size. Relief and delight mingled on my husband's face, emotions I knew were mirrored on mine. "Hello, little treasure," Andrew said. "She's perfect, just like Sophie." And she was. Indeed Jacqueline was doing so well she was allowed to come straight to my room. As I held our tiny daughter, leaning forward to breathe in the newness of her, I felt a bright, bracing happiness as if I'd tapped a deep, clear spring. I'd had a child at forty-three, just like my Grannykins. Our family felt complete.

The celebration lasted less than twenty-four hours. The next morning Jacqueline seemed listless and refused to breast-feed.

"She's a little yellow. Probably jaundice," one nurse suggested.

The pediatric team wasn't convinced. "Even though you were on anti-biotics, it's possible Jacqueline contracted an infection. We'd like to do a spinal tap to know for sure."

Andrew and I looked at each other. A needle plunged into our baby's spine. My friend Julie and her son had been in New York a few years before when Tarl had contracted meningitis. Thankfully, he'd made a complete recovery. But I knew from that experience how painful a spinal tap was. So when doctors returned with news that our newborn hadn't cried, I didn't know whether to weep from joy or fear.

While the test showed no signs of infection, Jacqueline still wouldn't nurse. I willed myself to be calm. Lots of infants got jaundice. Kimber had had it. But I felt slashes of anxiety: stealthy, unpredictable, sharp as lightning cleaving a darkening sky.

Exhausted, that night I fell into a deep sleep interrupted by a careful knock. The light from the hall outlined an indistinct shape in scrubs, one hand holding a mask.

"I'm sorry to disturb you, especially at four in the morning. Look, everything is okay, but we've moved Jacqueline to the NICU—the neonatal intensive care unit."

I sat up on the bed, held on to my knees for support, rocked like a baby. My mouth wouldn't work properly. My tongue felt swollen. "Why is she in the NICU??" I managed.

"She was a little blue."

"She's not breathing?"

"Please don't worry," responded the doctor. "She's fine now. But in the NICU, all babies are hooked to monitors and we have far more nurses. We'll just keep her for observation."

For observation. Such a safe, innocuous term. Little could I know the next four days would be the most harrowing of my life.

The following morning I stumbled as I gathered together my belongings to check out of the hospital. Maternity clothes, Sophie's artwork, the plant from my window. But inside the tiny infant carrier, no baby. I wept all the way home. "She'll be home soon," Andrew consoled me. A few hours later the telephone rang. "Could you come back to the NICU? Jacqueline is okay, but we believe she's had a seizure."

A SEIZURE. THE word struck like another slash of lightning. I simply could not believe it. This could not be happening. I had a sudden, terrifying

image of Jacqueline's mind shorting, arcing out of control. I pictured wildfires like those I'd covered in California, the hills orange and crackling. My
feverish mind clattered, jumped tracks, and now the image was of hurricane winds ripping down electrical poles in a crash of sparks, all this fury
unleashed in my baby's brain. How much did it hurt, the jolt from those
mangled lines, everything burning, melting?

I knew too much. Too much from Ginger. Too much about dear Tish.
Her sister. Now our baby. And Jacqueline was only three days old.

We took a taxi to the hospital and I hobbled into the hospital clutching
Andrew's arm, struggling to walk after a month in bed and an arduous
labor. Jacqueline didn't open her eyes. A feeding tube had been threaded
through her nose. One arm was splinted and her tiny hands were salted
with pricks from IVs and blood tests. Her head was wrapped in gauze, a
tiny cap with a whale spout of wires.

"We've put her on phenobarbital, to suppress any seizures, and that machine is an EEG. It will map her brain waves," a nurse explained, guiding
us toward a machine where a series of lines moved up and down to the
unseen conductor in Jacqueline's mind. It was like trying to decipher a score
if you couldn't read music. The paper had already pooled on the floor, reminding me of the old wire service machines, the day's news distilled to be
ripped and read. "And tonight we'll do an MRI," the nurse continued, "to
see if there are any . . . structural issues."

I'd been afraid before. Afraid for my own life in remote, hostile situations. And during 9/11 and especially anthrax, terrified for Sophie. I'd en-
dured hours, even days of fear that suffused everything, where you counted a
minute by the pulse thumping in your neck. But no matter how dire the situation I'd always been able to spot the crack of light that led to the escape
route. I'd never felt fear like this, fear that I would never escape fear. This
was a sickening tumble through mile after mile of a briny Atlantic that had
no bottom, trapped in a tiny titanium sphere and sinking, endlessly sinking.

I called Gin.

"Oh, Sara. How I wish I were there."

"Not as much as I do."

Ginger was calm, although I knew she must be thinking about Tish, too, about all that she'd seen, about all that she'd told me. But when she spoke, what she said was "Sara, she's a fighter."

In spite of myself, I was surprised. "I don't know, Gin. She's so small. Less than six pounds!"

"Maybe, but she's your little girl, Sara. She's a fighter. You'll see." But I felt like I was in a free fall, trying to hide my fear from three-year-old Sophie, clutching desperately to Andrew, unable to rescue anyone, even myself.

OVER THE NEXT few days we learned a lot about what Jacqueline did not have. The MRI scan of her brain was normal. A second spinal tap also showed no sign of infection. Yet Jacqueline appeared lifeless, as if bewitched, as if the pricks in her arm had come from a spinning wheel and our girl was an infant Sleeping Beauty lying in a glass casket instead of a plastic isolette. Around her, the White Coats flapped and fluttered, chattered and conferred. Perhaps her near-comatose state was a result of the medicine. They reduced the pheno. Jacqueline seized again. They shook their heads, tried another drug, Dilantin, even though they warned us that it might thicken her gums, cause hair to sprout all over her body, coarsen her lovely features. More wicked, wicked spells.

Our daughter had been in intensive care for a week, but she remained an enigma. Did she have some catastrophic disease? Were the seizures connected to my ruptured membranes or to a lengthy labor? I prayed not. Even with their expensive equipment and state-of-the-art tests, the brilliant doctors were flummoxed.

I try not to remember those days. They return unbidden, in fragments, pieces of a quilt. A memory here stitched to a recollection there, a shred of conversation connected to an image, scraps of color, broken threads, often out of order, a pattern I knew wouldn't become clear for months.

I called Linda, who'd left life at the network to spend more time with her son, Ryan. "Listen, I'm picturing you here at Goose Rocks Beach this summer. Jacqueline healthy. Sophie and Ryan running around. Can you hold on to that?"

I tried. In mid-September, Sophie started nursery school. I'd looked forward to this day. I hadn't imagined dashing over from the hospital. And as we met the other parents, Andrew was forced to speak for both of us as I withdrew, afraid of dissolving. Sophie knew something was wrong, even drew pictures of her family without her baby sister. I was glad she'd have three hours a day away from the electrical current of fear and uncertainty. Wearing a pink-and-blue-striped dress and a hesitant expression, she gave us a wave. Then she squared her shoulders, smiled up at her teachers, and never looked back.

BUT SLEEPING BEAUTY slumbered on. The first week became the second. At the hospital, while I took the day shift, Andrew would come home from work, have dinner with Sophie, then head to the hospital, where he would remain until the early hours of the morning. The sight of him gently holding our fairy-tale daughter in her Medusa cap of wires made me want to weep. Yet holding her was all we could do.

It was more than Andrew and I could handle alone, and our families rallied, forming a rotating crisis support team. Mom reorganized her busy schedule of piano students and Dad brought his research material for the paper he was writing on theologian Paul Tillich. Their presence was a comfort to us, and Sophie. "You make the best chicken, Granne! And I even ate my carrots," raved our big girl. And Mom patted Andrew's arm and told him softly, "It's hard to be the strong, silent one." Dad, the professor, offered analogies. "Think of Jacqueline as a diamond and the medicine as a chisel. You're going to chip away the rock to reveal her true facets, the brilliance of your girl."

My sister Elizabeth took time off from her job in development at Saint Mary's College of California to fly east. A talented singer and music professor, she'd had to start a whole new career after sustaining a vocal injury. My sister's misfortune had made her stronger. Her hugs were filled with love and loyalty, and she immediately set to work spoiling her nieces. And my sister Susan, herself due in just a few weeks, called daily, and sent us Psalm 91: ". . . He will cover you with his feathers, and under his wings you will find refuge."

When my family could stay no longer, Andrew's mother flew across from Australia for an entire month, leaving her husband's side for the first time in their thirty-eight-year marriage. By day Nana laughed and played games with Sophie and visited Jacqueline. "Ah, look at her," Nana said, her large blue eyes welling with tears when she saw her silent, slumbering granddaughter for the first time. But it was a rare moment, for she was resolutely upbeat. Only in the evenings, after preparing an enormous feast, would Andrew's mother's face show the strain, and she'd knit her sorrows into lovely sweaters for her granddaughters. The rest of the Butcher clan called frequently, and we spoke to Andrew's sister Chrissie every day. A skilled nurse who'd worked with premature infants and in an NICU, Chrissie could translate all we were hearing in the hospital. One night she had a question.

"Have they tried pyridoxine?"

"Peer-a-what?" Andrew replied.

"It's actually a vitamin, B_6. But in Australia, we also use it for seizures in newborns."

The New York doctors were polite but somewhat skeptical. Nevertheless, Jacqueline had been asleep and on a feeding tube in intensive care for nearly two weeks. Whether humoring us or running out of options, they gave our daughter the vitamin in addition to her Dilantin. Several hours later a nurse at the NICU telephoned.

"Come down, right away!" she exclaimed. "Jacqueline opened her eyes. And she's crying!"

After endless days of silence, what a sweet sweet sound it was.

TWO AND A half weeks after she was born, Jacqueline was finally well enough for us to take her home. We tucked her pretty pink and white frock into her car seat, took pictures of her and Sophie with the beaming nurses. I finally felt ready to open the baby gifts I'd shoved out of sight, including a soft, fawn-colored blanket hand-stitched with a pink giraffe from Ginger, Nad, and Kimber. Now both girls had a touch of Africa in their rooms, for they'd already given Sophie a beautiful karakul rug bordered with elephants, rhinos, and giraffes. Every eight hours we administered our daughter's two medicines, a small price for having her home with us.

But a few days later the telephone rang. Jacqueline's doctors had decided she no longer needed Dilantin, with its potentially serious side effects for newborns.

"You want us to stop cold turkey?" I asked, anxious to know if I'd heard correctly.

"Yes." The doctor explained that our daughter was already on such a low dose that the medicine couldn't be working. It seemed too good to be true.

In the middle of the night, barely twenty-four hours later, Jacqueline made a strange distressing cry. Was this a seizure? We'd never seen one. Forty-five minutes later we had no doubt. This time Jacqueline screamed as if someone had stabbed her through the skull with a stiletto. And then she began to jerk, short, terrible twitches, once again under an evil spell, her arms and legs moving rhythmically.

"Andrew, she's not breathing!"

"Hang on, she is, yes, yes she is, yes she is! Hold on there, sweetie," he crooned, cradling our tiny girl as she gasped for air, her pale skin turning a frightening muddy color. And finally the seizure ended and her eyes closed and her labored breathing returned to normal. We scooped her up in a cocoon of blankets and dashed downstairs to the taxi, the fastest route to the emergency room. She had been home three days.

OVER THE NEXT twenty-four hours in the hospital, Andrew and I would witness our newborn have five more seizures, each precipitated by a shattering scream. The sight of her jabbed and stuck and clapped with an oxygen mask as she struggled to breathe caused my milk to dry up in a day.

"Please give her Dilantin," I begged. "She doesn't respond well to pheno."

The emergency room team gave her pheno, the first choice for newborns with seizures.

Hours later she seized again. More screams, more oxygen. I knew I must look crazy, judging by the increasingly calm expressions of everyone around me. "It's okay, Mom, don't worry. We've got another med. We'll figure out mg's per kg's—the right dose for your girl," the doctors tried to reassure me. "And we've also hooked her up to video monitors. Maybe we can diagnose her condition from the appearance of her seizures."

I slumped at the thought of someone, somewhere, casually watching this tape, slurping coffee and scribbling notes while watching my daughter seize. She wasn't a cipher, wasn't a code to be broken. She was a baby, our baby girl.

Andrew stroked my hand. I didn't recognize myself. The wild-eyed face in the mirror. My shaky hands. The biting sound of my voice. I felt like I must be losing my mind. I called Gin again.

"How did your mom do it?"

"I don't know, Sara. She had four kids and one endless search to find the right doctors for Tish. But she managed and so will you. Look, Sara, didn't you say doctors told you Jacqueline's MRI was normal?"

"Yes. And she's had two."

I could hear her sigh. "Sara, that is great news. That's not the case with Tish. I wish it were. Once they figure out the medicine for Jacqueline everything will be all right. I just wish I could be there! Do you want Mom to come up?"

I felt tears well up again. We had been friends so long that Gin's family now felt like an extension of my own.

"We'll be okay."

IT WAS SEPTEMBER 21, 2004. Jacqueline's due date. Instead she was three and a half weeks old and still in the NICU. The new medicine hadn't worked, and she'd had seizure after seizure. I felt as if I were living a *Dateline* story. And I hated it. I'd always considered myself a reporter by nature

as well as training, instinctively curious. But now I was stripped of everything save the desire to see our little girl get better. After more than 20
years as a reporter, suddenly I didn't care about chasing stories. Let someone else fly to Atlanta, report on Teach for America. What an idiot I'd
been, sitting in my hospital bed, thinking such a thing were possible. I'd
lost my balance, and with it my inquisitiveness. I realized I no longer cared
what disease or disorder Jacqueline had. I just wanted her to get better.

Yet even as part of me rejected work, I discovered that all those years of
training were impossible to ignore. I couldn't erase the knowledge of how
to ask questions, how to analyze. I was neither dismissive of White Coats
nor cowed by them. I was Jacqueline's advocate, her ally, her mom. No one
knew Jacqueline better than Andrew and I, no one loved her more. Slowly
I realized that to be the mother of a sick child meant being a reporter. It
certainly felt better to walk into the intensive care unit armed with notepad
and pen than to sit by her bed and weep. And while I knew that Jacqueline's case was rare and difficult, and while I was a mom, not a neurologist,
the time I'd spent at her bedside had given me confidence in my observa-
tions. Andrew and I were convinced our daughter needed to be placed back
on the combination of medicines which had allowed her to come home in
the first place. The doctors reached the same conclusion, and slowly began
the gradual, challenging process of weaning her from one medicine while
starting another.

All through those bleak days, family and friends rallied to support us.
Andrew's sister and my NBC colleagues scoured medical journals and
trawled the Net, searching for any condition similar to Jacqueline's. They
sat by us at the hospital. And they reached out to us at home.

"Sara," said Andrew's mom, "what's this?"

"Bob and Suzanne Wright," read the tag on the Moses basket overflow-
ing with food, baby clothes, blankets, and bibs. The chairman and CEO of
NBC Universal and his wife. Next to it was a giant box of food from Agata
& Valentina, courtesy of Bridget, Linda's college roommate and now my
friend, too. "This is just the beginning," she warned cheerfully. "You'll get
Elena's tomorrow." Twice a week for months the boxes arrived, each with a

card listing friends from *Nightly News,* from Specials, from the front office, and, of course, from *Dateline.*

On a quiet weekend near the end of September, I suggested Andrew take his mom and Sophie to the country. They needed a break and Ellen, my friend from *Dateline,* would join me at the hospital. Jacqueline hadn't had a seizure in several days and seemed to be improving. She still wore her cap of wires, but at least she was now in a crib. As Ellen and I chatted quietly, a neurologist scanned Jacqueline's EEG report, appearing increasingly agitated.

"What is it?" I asked, alarmed.

He shook his head. "I cannot begin to tell you how concerned I am about your daughter's brain."

It seemed as if the floor were suddenly undulating, even sinking. I put a hand on the metal bar of Jacqueline's crib to steady myself. "Excuse me?"

He gestured to the EEG reading. "I cannot sugarcoat this."

"But she's getting better!" I argued. "She's opening her eyes, looking around—"

He shook his head impatiently. "I am sorry, but look, I must tell you. The electrical activity in your daughter's brain is a mess. A mess. This is not about bedside manner. This is about telling you the truth, getting you prepared."

Frightened as I was, I fought to remain calm. I did not believe him. I would not. I could not.

"But her MRI was clear!"

He shook his head. "This is not a normal brain. This is a brain with problems."

"So what are you telling me? What does that mean for the future? Her development?"

He shook his head again. His only answer was to open his hands, the answer unknowable. But the expression on his face made me shiver.

I felt vanquished. I looked over at my friend. Ellen's face had crumpled, too. Tears coursed down her face. She had a daughter, too. Lovely Natalie. She understood.

I called Andrew. "We'll be home in two hours," he said, then paused. "Look, things have a way of working out." But for once his voice sounded hollow, flat. And I realized how much I wanted to throw my arms around him, realized how much the husband who loved and supported me needed support himself. But to do that, I needed to pull myself together.

I called Ginger. "I don't know what to think, what to believe. It sounds like the doctor's saying Jacqueline could be like Kristy's daughter Emma," I finished.

"Sara, I'm still not sure I believe that. But you must call Kristy."

When I did, Ginger's old friend, a friend who'd become my friend, too, called back immediately. "Sara how can I help?"

I paused. "Just one thing, really. I just want you to tell me that I'm going to get through this."

To my surprise, she didn't hesitate. "Of course you will."

"You promise?"

"I promise."

I drew a shaky breath. I believed her. And to believe her restored my belief in myself. The free fall was over and I'd landed on firm ground. Suddenly I heard the sound of cheering in the background. "Kristy, where *are* you?"

She chuckled. "Well, I'm actually at the starting line for a half marathon but figured I had time to call you first."

I began laughing, and laughing felt good. "You are too much. I can't believe how together you are."

"Look, Sara, it's not that we don't have problems. Emma can't walk. She can't talk. We don't know how much she understands. And yes, she has seizures. I'd be the first to tell you, sometimes it's scary. But Gordy and Carter are great with her. We all love her. And we're happy."

I hung up the phone and I realized with relief that I didn't feel crazy anymore. Sad, yes. Angry and confused. But not crazy. I could go on, I knew it. I could be strong, as my husband was strong, could support him as he, more than anyone else, supported me. And the person who had helped me get there was the friend of a friend.

I had been lucky in life, I knew. Blessed to have loving parents and sisters I'd always known I could count on. And blessed to have extraordinary friends. Friends I'd known most of my life. Friends I'd met along the way. And those whom I barely knew, but who'd been willing to help in a crisis, simply because they were friends of a friend.

ON OCTOBER 1, my sister Susan became a mom. "His name is Sebastian," she told us, euphoric if exhausted.

"Oh, Susan, that's fantastic!" I said, thrilled for Danny and her, and for the chance to be Sebastian's aunt. And a few days later, on October 5, there was another reason for excitement. Six weeks after her birth, Jacqueline was again coming home from the hospital. This time our departure was muted. We had oxygen tanks, CPR instructions, additional details about administering her medicine every three hours. But we also had experience. We'd learned to prune expectations, to hold fast to hope. It was dangerous to look too far ahead. But then again, it was far more dangerous not to be grateful, to miss out on the chance to savor one extraordinary day. Please, God, let tomorrow be the same.

33

GINGER (2005–2006)

IT WAS THE eighteenth of February 2005. Back in Richmond, Mom said it was unseasonably warm, that a dense ceiling of clouds had trapped the heat but kept the sunlight out. And Sara had called to say that in New York they'd woken up to a blanket of thick snow and temperatures near freezing. But in Windhoek, it was 95 degrees, a light breeze was blowing in over the mountains, and the sky was indigo blue and clear. It was the perfect day for moving.

"Gin, where do you want this?"

I looked up. Nad was coming down the stairs from our garage carrying a hand-carved cherry headboard supported by thick turned legs.

"That's Kimber's bed. It goes in his room." I smiled, thinking how my son's bed had once belonged to my great-cousin Charlotte. Since I'd been four years old, whenever I visited Charlotte and her parents, my Great-Aunt Oral and Uncle Charlie, on the farm where first Mom and then my sisters and I had spent much of our childhood, I'd slept on that bed. Aunt Oral had tucked me in at night, kissed my cheek. I'd felt the wisps of her long gray hair fall from her bun and brush across my face, caught the clean smell of Ivory soap on her skin. I'd felt so safe, so loved. Soon Kimber would climb into that bed and I'd tuck him in, kiss his cheek, generation to generation, the roots spreading wider and deeper.

I wandered from room to room. End tables that had been wedding presents to my grandparents from my Great-Aunt Ise were now in our guest room. The twin beds Dona and Tish had shared as children, the ones we'd turned into trampolines, jumping back and forth for hours and driving Mom crazy, were in that room, too. A pie safe from my mother's prized collection stood in the kitchen. For a decade, my dear friend Beth and her family had lovingly cared for my dining room table, and now it was in our home. In an old flat-back cupboard, a wedding present from my parents to Nad and me almost ten years ago, I arranged Oral's silver, Lottie's sugar and creamer, Ceil's china, treasures from my wonderful great-aunts, who had never traveled farther from their homes in Virginia than to Maine. China, silver, crystal, wood, linens—every piece I unwrapped told a story, a part of my family's history, transplanted to Africa to begin a new chapter on an ancient continent.

Added to the memories of flash floods and baboon chatter, of moving Sara out of New Jersey and then, years later, into the country with Andrew, of elephants' trumpets and my baby becoming a boy, of my sisters and me together as kids, as adults, and as dear friends, and I wondered where this new chapter would lead. It was tempting to look forward; to attempt to peer into the future and by force of will try to make things happen. But fifteen years in the bush had taught me to be more patient. In a world controlled by devilish winds and the often empty promise of rain, by stalking predators and vulnerable prey, I'd learned not only to question but also to observe, to let details emerge and to acknowledge that there are some things I'd simply never understand, including why Tish was sick, rather than me. Whether it's a matter of fate, of grace, or the luck of the draw, some things you simply must accept. These are the random blessings we are given. What we do with them is up to us. I had finally learned to accept mine, to silence the voices of guilt and doubt, and to stop questioning why.

It was a lesson Sara was learning, too. She'd had to step back from a world of breaking news and live reports, of sound bites and instant answers. Jacqueline's illness had taught her to wait, to watch, and to never, ever give up hope.

In my early twenties, I'd thought I had life figured out. That if I wished for something hard enough, it would happen. I'd expected to marry my old boyfriend, Kevin, settle in his adoptive state of Texas, and live happily ever after. A life that was easy, comfortable, and secure. Yet now it was a life I could barely picture, of a girl who would have become a completely differ-ent woman.

Since those heady days at Wimbledon, I'd stumbled, fallen, and literally eaten dirt in my quest to discover the person I wanted to be. At times I fought hard against the changes, clinging to a perception of the woman I had once thought I would become, wanting the adventure without the risks, the safety without the fight. When I'd been down to my last dollar and my last idea, the image of the boy next door shadowed me, curling his finger as if to say, *Come, there is an easier way out.*

But for me, there wasn't. Twenty years later, I'd learned that the chal-lenges you face shape your life. How odd that I couldn't see this when I was at home, surrounded by examples from every generation in my family. In-stead I'd had to run halfway around the world to find my own version of the yellow brick road to Oz, to figure it out. But it was a path I needed to explore. Full of detours, dangerous curves, and lucky breaks, the journey taught me many things.

From embracing a home without walls in the desert to moving into our new home in Windhoek, I'd learned that conventional and unconventional lives can be married. That neither had the exclusive right to love or adven-ture. It was up to me to combine them, no matter where I was. The chance had been there when I lived in Manhattan, but I wasn't strong enough to take it. I'd needed to be pushed, to learn the language of baboons, to feel the power of a Bushman dance so potent that it heals, and to find a love so strong that it leaves an elephant powerless. And I needed my son, Kimber, who in his own backyard fought fires, buried baby birds, saved rhinos, and defeated the Evil Zurg, to teach me that adventures are great, but that real joy is found in the heart.

In time, I realized that my parents' constant love and support and the grounding I had from my childhood in Richmond—plus treasured friend-ships that have sustained me ever since—had given me the security to later buck and kick, reinvent and change. Yet it had taken the unconditional ac-ceptance of baboons and elephants to make me realize that sometimes you don't have to change at all.

Without Nad's constant, quiet commitment, I might never have known how healing and liberating it could be to trust the right man with your heart. And I'd learned how great a heart could grow from the love of one precious boy. Now, without betraying my roots or my soul, I knew that home was a state of mind larger and more wonderful than just one place. Part of me was American and part was African, and Kimber embodied this.

As I watched Kimber dart up and down the stairs, happily lugging furniture and moving boxes, my heart swelled. As much as I longed to hold his dimpled cheek close to mine for as long as possible, I knew that one day he'd set out on his own, following his own path and creating his own destiny. I could only hope that I'd be as brave and as generous in letting him go as my parents had been with me.

I stopped unpacking boxes of china and followed the laughter into Kimber's new bedroom. "Ginger, we need your help!" Our beautiful friend Rieth, who had generously opened her home to us when the building of ours wasn't complete, was standing in the middle of the room with three rugs in her arms.

"Which do you want to use in here?"

"That one." I pointed to the multicolored karakul wool rug in her left hand. "The one Sara gave us."

Rieth propped the others against the wall while I unrolled Sara's rug. Like our friendship, the textures were dense, the colors true, the pattern intriguing, even after all these years. In lilting English infused with her native Afrikaans, Rieth pronounced, "It's perfect." And it was. And in that moment, that rug became a sort of talisman, a perfect blend of old and new friends, those friends who link our past, our present, and our future.

One more thing I'd learned along the way was that I couldn't imagine my life or my future without my friends, a sisterhood that included my sisters, Marsha, Tish, and Dona, and sisters I'd chosen, like Beth, Stacy, and Kristy, and especially Sara, who helped shape and who'd shared so much of my journey. It seemed she had always been there. From young girls sharing secrets in the dark to adult women revealing, chasing, and changing our dreams. The threads of friendship we cast as children had grown into a deep, sustaining bond.

Many times when I've looked in the mirror, I've seen Sara looking back, daring me to dig deeper, to aim higher, to let go and risk failure. Because she believed in me, and I believed so strongly in her, I summoned the courage to take chances, and to run headlong after my dreams. Her vision of me helped to inspire the person I am, and it will remain, inspiring the person I hope to become.

When almost everyone else thought I was mad, Sara still believed in me. I paused as an irony hit me. I knew there'd been people who thought Sara had lost herself when she arrived on the set of network television. But I'd known exactly who she was. Though wiser and wounded by heartache, softened by the love of her husband and two dear children, and chiseled by the incredible stories of those intrepid, endearing, and occasionally awful men and women whose tales she has shared through the years, she was still at her core the same thoughtful, bright girl I had been drawn to in middle school. The woman looking back in the mirror had the same sprinkling of tawny freckles, but her green eyes now were flecked with knowing and compassion. I'd recognize her anywhere.

I cannot imagine my life without Sara. Our friendship centered me when I was lost, rallied me when I was defeated, and comforted me when I felt empty and alone. Along the way, the image in the mirror of two women gazing at each other seemed to fuse, until sometimes it seems we each reflect what is best in the other. And the masses of beautiful, tangled threads that bind us have become essential to my life, and to where it will lead.

June 2006

"Nice shot, Kimber." Kimber's tennis coach, my friend Elizma Nortje, clapped her hand against her racquet. Kimber threw his arms up in the air, a real little champion. Forget Wimbledon, this was true happiness.

We had been living in Windhoek for just over a year. In the mornings

I'd sit at my computer, alternately typing and gazing out the window at the purple mountains surrounding the city. Just after noon, I'd pick Kimber up from school. I'd help him with his homework, do my share of car pools, enjoy spending time with other mothers, and four times a week I'd take Kimber to cricket and tennis lessons.

I sat on the bench on the sidelines, surrounded by little kids running on and off the court. Elizma was wonderful with them all, a positive, loving force in such a competitive world. About five years before, I'd been introduced to her when she'd visited Etosha for a weekend.

"Nice to meet you." I'd smiled, and her radiant smile beamed back.

"Oh, you won't remember but we've met before."

I shook my head. "I'm sorry. I don't recall. When was it?"

"A long time ago. You were with Kevin at an exhibition tennis match. I was a ball girl, and . . ." She giggled.

"And . . ."

"Well, I have your autograph."

I laughed, and it felt wonderful. "*No!* Burn it!"

THE EVOLUTION CONTINUES. From globe-trotting girlfriend, to wildlife filmmaker, to car-pooling tennis mom, the progression feels right. I know it's only a matter of time before life will change again. I'll adapt into another version of the woman I was meant to be, and at heart, I know the next change will likely take us back to the bush, to the place where Nad and I fell in love, the place where I imagine we'll grow old. But for now, I plan to enjoy these days, every single one of them.

On the court, I heard Kimber cheer. Elizma turned and smiled. "He's really good, Gin. I think we'll be seeing a lot more of you guys at the courts."

It was my turn to smile. I wondered if Sophie or Jacqueline would learn to play tennis. Kimber, mixed doubles, mothers-in-law?

I had to call Sara.

34

SARA (2005–2006)

Mommy, look! i'm riding next to Ryan!"

Our four-year-old was bright as a sparkler at the prospect of test-driving her new bike with training wheels in her first-ever parade, and was glued to the side of my old friend Linda's seven-year-old son Ryan. It was the Fourth of July in Goose Rocks Beach, Maine, and any kid on wheels could participate, including Jacqueline and cousin Sebastian, who sat side by side in their strollers, wide-eyed at the red, white, and blue commotion. My sister Susan grinned and hugged me. "Isn't it fantastic?" she whispered.

I found it hard to believe the entire James gang was here—Susan, Danny, and Sebastian up from North Carolina, my sister Elizabeth and John all the way from California, Mom and Dad from Virginia, as well as our tribe of four, all gathered at Linda's beach home to celebrate the nation's birthday, and my mom's. A few days before, Granne had turned seventy. First there was a photo shoot of the entire family frolicking on the beach, a present from Linda and David, who had turned their love of storytelling and images into a thriving documentary wedding photography business. Next had come an elaborate feast. But perhaps Mom's favorite gift of all had been the "card shower" organized by my sisters. Dozens of dear friends, students, colleagues, and relatives had written, including Mom's four close-knit brothers and sisters. Letter after letter had praised my mother's talents as a teacher and musician, and her loving, even nature.

Beaming, my father looked on. While he'd retired from the University of Richmond, Dad stayed busy writing scholarly papers and books, as well as playing trumpet in a Dixieland jazz band, and relished his new role as babysitting Opa. I watched Dad reach for Mom's hand, gently touch her ring. I thought back to how, as a twenty-two-year-old, I'd been angry, sure that Mom had been cheated out of a more lucrative and perhaps more highly respected career. "But I'm happy, Sal," she'd replied. And as I'd watched her open those cards, witnessed her overwhelmed expression as she'd gazed at her husband and children and their husbands and the three grandchildren, I felt only grateful that she'd chosen the path she had, a choice I understood so much better now.

And then I felt a small, sharp pang as I realized something else. As a mother, I had learned that the impulse to protect a child from danger and suffering is hardwired. With breathtaking clarity, I now understood how difficult it must have been for my parents to watch me willingly put myself in harm's way. And yet they had never forced me to choose between their love and support and the life and career which I adored. I hoped I would have the same courage and confidence in our girls when they embarked on odysseys of their own, hoped I would give them the same gift of that harbor called home.

"Mommy!" Sophie brought me back to the present. "The parade is about to start!"

"I see, honey. Granne, can you push Jacqui's stroller in closer so I can get a picture of all of you? Linda, slide in. You're family, too."

But I don't need a picture to remember what happened later that afternoon.

"Look at her, Sara. She loves it," Linda whispered.

Jacqueline sat on the sand, letting the grains trickle through her fingers. Then she shoved a handful in her mouth. Our little girl not only was out of the NICU, but sitting on the beach at Goose Rocks. Linda's prediction from ten months before had come true.

* * *

AS THE MONTHS passed, Jacqueline continued to get stronger. When it came to milestones, she had her own timetable. She rolled over at six months. By her first birthday, she could sit unassisted. Two months after that, she began to crawl.

"Look, Mommy!" crowed Jacqueline's physical therapist, Alyssa Dominianni, just before Christmas. "Look who's climbing the stairs."

Enrolled in a federal program called Early Intervention, Jacqueline received many hours of physical, occupational, and speech therapy each week. She was making steady, wonderful progress.

Since she'd come home from the hospital the second time, Jacqueline hadn't had a single seizure. "Sometimes babies just grow out of them," Andrew's sister Chrissie explained. "We'll just have to wait and see." It was incredibly comforting to have an NICU nurse in the family. What's more, the medicine we'd initially given her every eight hours now only had to be administered twice a day, and we were decreasing the dose as well. I tried not to let myself get too excited. I'd learned not to look too far down the track.

With Jacqueline thriving, slowly, carefully, I eased back into my part-time schedule at *Dateline*. It felt right. I was a mom. I was a reporter. Somewhere along the way the two had fused, and I was just me, Sara. It felt good to work on projects with a beginning, a middle, and an end, to think about the drama in someone else's life instead of focusing on my own. And it felt good to work in a field I'd always loved with people who were dearer to me than ever before. But I had no doubt what came first.

"Dr. DeVivo, do you think Jacqueline will get those awful side effects from the medicine we were warned about: extra hair, thick gums—"

"No," he responded. "Her dose is low, and getting lower all the time." Gentle and wise, Dr. Darryl DeVivo was the director emeritus of pediatric neurology at Columbia University Medical Center. He'd been recommended by Wendy Belzberg, a new friend I'd met through my pal and Linda's college roommate Bridget. Wendy had given us a wealth of practical information and astonishing personal support as we'd navigated the world of infant seizures.

"Will we ever know why she had them?" I asked Dr. DeVivo.

"Probably not. It may have been genetic, but don't fret. There are some thirty thousand genes that make up the human genome, and it's estimated that half of them play a critical role in the developing brain. A person can have a small genetic error and function normally. Besides, I think she looks great."

We did, too.

IT WAS JANUARY of 2006. I was just back from France, my first overseas trip for *Dateline* since Jacqueline's birth.

"We have a surprise for you, Mommy," said Sophie. "It's—"

"Shh, Soph, it's a secret!" said Andrew, smiling. Then he gave his nodding permission for her to tell.

"Jacqueline's off her medicine!"

It was fantastic news, especially coming on the heels of our baby's recent EEG, which had been excellent. Despite that early assessment by one of the neurologists back in the hospital, our daughter's brain was not a mess. And the best thing of all was—you didn't need an EEG to know it.

A MONTH LATER, as a frosting of February snow on the ground outside made our country house seem even warmer and more cheerful, Sophie and I went through the closets looking for ski gear. I pulled out a bright red NBC Sports jacket.

"Mom, what's that?"

"It's what I wore when I was covering the Winter Olympics four years ago. You were there. I brought you and Sherry with me for the month."

"Why aren't you going to the Olympics this year?"

"I only work part-time, Soph, remember? That way I can spend more time with you and Jacqueline. We'll have our own Winter Games up at Catamount. What do you think?"

"I'm glad. I like you home."

I liked home, too. More than I'd ever imagined as a young woman, restless and roaming, certain that excitement was a destination, and one that required a passport. Yes, I had missed the Olympics. But I'd witnessed a couple of gold medal events of my own. Andrew had been taking Sophie to a gentle ski slope near us, where she'd been practicing on the "magic carpet." The week before, I'd watched my four-year-old ski down a green slope unassisted.

And I'd just witnessed another extraordinary sight, this one in our own living room. Our seventeen-month-old daughter had giggled, and taken her first proud steps, all on her own.

Step by step, Jacqueline was making progress, sometimes following in the path of big sister Sophie, often forging her own way. We loved her irrepressible chuckle. The way she adored peekaboo and blew endless raspberries. "You know what?" Andrew confessed. "I even like to hear her cry. And I don't mind her little temper tantrums. Shows a bit of spirit. I'm going to find it hard to ever discipline her after having watched her in that hospital for so long."

Now Jacqueline was playing with Sophie, and I caught a glimpse of the three of us in the mirror. I realized I had many hopes for our daughters. I prayed that they would be healthy and happy. I hoped they'd appreciate having a sister as much as I adored and counted on mine. I hoped that they would be fortunate when it came to love and work. I hoped each would recognize what a unique gift she was, how much she could offer. I hoped they would know when to be bold in seeking their dreams—and when holding fast was the braver, truer course. I hoped they would have children of their own one day, and that it wouldn't take them quite as long as it had taken me. And I hoped that they would also meet wonderful friends along the way—friends who made them laugh and who wiped away their tears, who cherished and occasionally scolded them, friends who reminded them to be happy for all they had, but especially for all they were, friends who would become like sisters.

Many years before, I'd left home in search of adventure only to discover it could be found at home, as well as on the road. I'd been bent on reinvention only to discover that, whatever the earrings, the scarves, or the hairstyle, the freckled face in the mirror was still my own. I'd been certain that real life involved risk, a view I still held. But sometimes you dare to travel to the bottom of the sea, and sometimes you dare to give up something you love for something you love so much more.

I touched the Olympics patch on the jacket. I loved my job as much as ever, but I no longer felt like my last name was NBC News. All those years on the road had taught me so much. But being Sophie and Jacqueline's mom had taught me so much more. I'd learned to savor perfect moments instead of holding out for a perfect life. I'd learned to beware of those who predict the future. I'd learned that hope, wild and strong, can crack through a moonscape of despair, and that you must dare to let it take root. I'd learned that a career that makes you rich is no substitute for a rich life. I'd learned that sometimes love deserves a second chance. And sometimes separating the alluring from the essential takes a second look. When I'd met Andrew, I'd been drawn by his wit and banter, his confidence and success. But in a husband, those weren't the qualities I ranked first. Instead it had been his kindness and dependability, old-fashioned, undervalued virtues, which had been tested during the anthrax crisis with Sophie, and again during all those nights by Jacqueline's bedside. The same qualities I found in friends like Ginger. And finally, I'd learned that no matter how much you learn, when it comes to the most important lessons, you almost always need the occasional refresher course.

Just a few days before, Sophie had told me, "Mom, one of my friends has gone off the turnpike of loving me."

"Then, Sophie," I'd said, instantly scooping her up, "that's not a real friend. Not like Gin. Or LP. Or any of Mommy's other friends."

She looked at me. "Ryan," she told me, "Ryan is a real friend. He's one hundred percent."

"Exactly."

As I put down the jacket, I thought of Ginger and our improbable friendship. We were from the same town. The same background. She had three great sisters, I had two. We'd both married men with passports and accents. We were both moms later in life. But she lived in the African desert. I lived in New York City. She worked behind a camera. I worked in front of one. She documented animal drama, I covered human sagas. Our lives were totally opposite. But at heart we were so much the same.

Perhaps that was why we'd learned so much from each other. From her, I'd learned to trust my instincts. She'd learned to trust her intelligence. I'd learned to narrow my focus. She'd learned to widen her circle. And we'd both learned that sometimes you have to blaze your own trail. And sometimes you have to let others help you along.

I had been blessed with many extraordinary friends. But in some ways, because Ginger was my alter ego, she could also be my truest self. The woman who'd lived big dreams for me when I'd lost faith in my own. The woman who'd celebrated when I'd dared to dream again. She was the woman I'd often wanted to be. Except if I'd been her, she couldn't have been my friend.

To think we'd met so many years before, in the same town. But she'd gone left, and I'd gone right. A decision that could have ended our friendship had instead given each of us an eyewitness account of the road not taken. And in the end, while she lived on one continent and I lived on another, we'd wound up in the same place.

It was time to make a call.

"Listen to this, Gin!"

"Ba-ba," giggled Jacqueline.

"She said bye-bye! That's wonderful! And what was that other sound?"

"She just kissed the phone. She must know her Auntie Gin is coming over and she's excited."

"Well, I am, too. I can't wait to see those girls, especially since you *never send me pictures*! The last ones I have are from when you saw Dona and Mom."

"I know, I know. I will. But there is one thing you need to see in person. Jacqueline is walking!"

I could hear the shout of joy all the way from Namibia.

ACKNOWLEDGMENTS

SOME PEOPLE SAY writing a book is a bit like having a baby. If so, this book was an elephant calf, as it had a two-year gestation. That it was born at all is a tribute to the unflinching support of many people, beginning with Nad Brain and Andrew Butcher. Smart, thoughtful, and always amusing, our husbands not only believed in the idea of this book, but were brave enough to allow their lives, as well as ours, to be put into print. Had it not been for Nad's eternal optimism, Andrew's savvy edits, and the willingness of them both to fly solo with the kids when we were tethered to our desks, this book might have been an essay. We love you both, madly.

This book is dedicated to our children, but we would like to acknowledge them here, too, for all they put up with and all they did to pull us through. Thanks to Kimber for spirited games of cricket that drove through the toughest writer's block and for tossing wildly wonderful title ideas into the air. Thanks to Sophie for cheerfully keeping us company as we labored over the final draft by writing her own book, complete with illustrations. And thanks to Jacqueline for those joyful dance sessions, and for reminding everyone that it is always important to giggle. We hope that when all of you are grown up, this book will be a window into the hearts and minds of your moms, a journal about the journey that took us from the children we were to the mothers of children we adore.

We owe a big thanks to our agent, Elyse Cheney, who had the vision to imagine an actual book with chapters and a cover when presented with a one-page proposal. Your astute advice was invaluable as we churned through draft after draft until we finally had a finished manuscript.

We are indebted to our editor, Jennifer Pooley, and the entire team at

William Morrow, who shared our conviction that one memoir could be written by two authors. Jen, your patience when life's emergencies shelved our project for months was a godsend. Furthermore, your gentle guidance and endless enthusiasm liberated us to explore the contours and detours of our story.

Special thanks must go to our parents, Don and Dale Mauney and Rob and Anne James. We believe our quest to live full, adventurous lives is in part a reflection of your continuing passion to grow, learn, and evolve. Yet you also had the wisdom to know that in order for us to fly, we needed a safe place to land. It is impossible to thank you enough for this grounding and to say how very much we love you.

And that brings us to our wonderful troop of sisters. You are women to treasure, and we do. We also are inspired by you: by Marsha's soulful writing and bold reinvention of her life; by Tish's bravery and tenacity in spinning happiness out of hardship; by Dona's sense of comfort and her boundless capacity to give, including the gift of her wonderful children, Maggie and Zan; by Elizabeth's perseverance and faith, which helped her to recover her lovely voice and to blaze a new career path; by Susan's deep well of optimism, restorative during days of emotional drought, and by her delight in all children, especially her darling Sebastian. Quite simply, we adore all of you. If we were not family, we would seek you out as friends, for you are both to us in equal measure.

While this is a book about our friendship, it is also a book about friends and friendship in general. We could not imagine our journey without all of you. While many of our dear friends are mentioned by name, others are not, but you know who you are. We love and thank you all.

We also would like to thank the men, women, and children who spoke to us, often at times of extreme duress, for their breathtaking eloquence and courage. And we thank, too, those creatures who shared their tales not with words, but by granting us acceptance. All of their stories have inspired us, taught us, and changed us.

Finally, any memoir is a record of events, which, by definition, is personal. In an attempt to be fair and accurate, we cross-checked our memories both with each other and with others in an attempt to clarify and amplify our individual impressions, as well as to ensure the integrity of this memoir overall. In the end, of course, this is our story. We have told it, to the best of our ability, and as we remember, and have worked hard to be accurate, honest, and true.

The Best of Friends
Discussion Questions

1. Sara and Ginger trace the beginnings of their friendship back to a slumber party when Ginger shared a deeply personal secret with Sara. Why do you think Ginger felt she could share her secret with Sara? In your experience, how do secrets bind friendships, or have you had an experience where a secret destroyed a friendship?

2. In the first several chapters, Sara and Ginger are leading completely different lives and, from the outside looking in, each perceives the other's life to be very different from the reality. Why do you think they were drawn together again? Have you ever picked up the phone and contacted a long-lost friend? If so, what was the call like? Did it reestablish your friendship or reinforce the reasons why you had drifted apart?

3. Do you agree with Sara's statement: "Friends were a collection of spices, with this person or that adding just the right flavor to any occasion"? Is your friendship cupboard full of the basics or do you have more exotic friendship mixtures? What qualities do you consider essential in a friend?

4. In recent studies, friendship has been identified as a factor contributing to better health. Laughter, strong physiological medicine, was

described by Ginger as one of the keys to her and Sara's friendship. How do you think friendship contributes to the quality of your life?

5. Given Ginger's heartache and search for reinvention, do you think she was running away from reality or running towards a new life when she returned to Africa on her own? Have you experienced the need to reinvent your life, and, if so, when? Do you think this comes with age or only after particularly trying times, such as divorce?

6. When her first marriage ends and later when she longs to have children, Sara reflects on the cost of ambition, wondering if her career objectives may have come at the cost of her personal dreams. How do you balance the desire for a fulfilling personal and professional life? Do you think women today want too much—an exciting career, a great marriage, and wonderful children? Can we have it all?

7. One reader described the book as having two different parts—one before children and one after. Do you agree? How does this describe the choices that women make before and after they have children?

8. In her final chapter, Ginger writes, "Along the way, the image in the mirror of two women gazing at each other seemed to fuse, until sometimes it seems we each reflect what is best in the other." Do you think we choose friends whose qualities reflect the best in us or friends whose qualities we would most like to reflect? Do you see versions of yourself reflected in your friends? And, if so, how?

9. Throughout their friendship, both Sara and Ginger acknowledge the fact that as old friends there was so much they understood about each other that could remain unspoken. Knowing each other as kids, they were keenly aware of the paths and challenges it took to achieve what they had as adults. In describing the depth and longevity of her friendship with Ginger, Sara writes, "And in the end, while she lived on one continent and I lived on another, we'd wound up in the same

place." Do you think this feeling—of having a similar grounding and background—is unique to old friends? And, if old friends bring unspoken understanding, what do new friends offer us? Do you think it is important to have both? Why or why not?

10. What is it like as an adult to be or have a best friend? How is it different from your childhood version of a best friend?